TANTRA

Its Mystic and Scientific Basis

By the same author

❄ Buddhist Tantra: A Philosophical Reflection and Religious Investigation

---

About the Author

Professor Lalan Prasad Singh spent about two decades as a mendicant in search of truth and salvation. During this period he went through the rigours of Tantra Sādhanā. He came to a conclusion that Tantra is neither a lifeless ritual nor a religious dogma. It is an intuitional science which rids the practitioner from the snares of false subjectivity and takes him to the state of spiritual sublimity and divine effulgence. After going through test and turmoil of life of mendicant he returned back to active academic life. In January 1996 he retired as a Professor of Philosophy from Magadh University, Bodh Gaya and in February of the same year be became Senior Fellow of Indian Council of Philosophical Research, Government of India. In 2000 A.D. Professor Singh was awarded Fellowship of Indian Institute of Advance Studies, Shimla. He bacame a Visiting Research Professor in 2004 at the Catholic University of America, Washington D.C. He was also awarded Indo-French Cultural Fellowship in 1994. During his sojourn at Paris, he delivered series of lectures on Tantra at the Department of Philosophy, Soubourn University IV. Paris (France). He also addressed the students and staff members of Department of Philosophy of Nihon and Toyo University, Tokyo in 2006. He presented many papers at the National and International Seminars and Symposia such as World Philosophical Congress 1975, International Congress of Orientalists, Mexico City 1976, First Sanskrit Symposia, Mexico City, World Sanskrit Congress, Lieden, Holland. Prof. Singh is a distinguished Professor of Philosophy and a Social Activist. Currently he is a Visiting Fellow at Department of Boddhist Studies, University of Delhi.

TANTRA
Its Mystic and Scientific Basis

Lalan Prasad Singh
M.A., D. Litt.

CONCEPT PUBLISHING COMPANY PVT. LTD.
NEW DELHI-110059

ISBN-13-978-81-8069-640-4 **ISBN-10-81-8069-640-5**

First Published 1976
Revised Edition 2010

Published and Printed by

Since 1974

Concept Publishing Company Pvt. Ltd.
Regd. Office:
A/15-16, Commercial Block, Mohan Garden
New Delhi-110059 (India)
Phones : 25351460, 25351794, *Fax* : 091-11-25357109
Email : publishing@conceptpub.com,
Website: www.conceptpub.com

Editorial Office:
H-13, Bali Nagar, New Delhi-110 015, India.

Cataloging in Publication Data--*Courtesy:* D.K. Agencies (P) Ltd. <docinfo@dkagencies.com>

Singh, Lalan Prasad, 1936-
Tantra, its mystic and scientific basis / Lalan Prasad Singh. -- Rev. ed.
p. cm.
Includes bibliographical references (p.).
Includes index.
ISBN 13: 9788180696404
ISBN 10: 8180696405

1. Tantrism. I. Title.

DDC 294.5514 22

To the Sweet Memory of
My
Mother and Father

DR. KARAN SINGH
MEMBER OF PARLIAMENT
(RAJYA SABHA)
CHAIRMAN
COMMITTEE ON ETHICS

Office : 127, Parliament House Annexe,
New Delhi-110001
Ph. : 2303-4254, 2379-4326
Fax : 2301-2009
E-mail : karansi@sansad.nic.in

Foreword

Philosophy in India has never been considered a purely theoretical exercise. The very word Darśana implies seeing or experiencing. Ultimately, all philosophy in India has been judged by the yardstick of spiritual realization rather than in terms of neat intellectual syllogisms or a barren rationalism. The entire thrust of philosophical and mystical literature in India has been towards providing the seeker after truth with a direct, intuitive and definitive contact with the Reality that pervades all existence. As Śaṁkara says, not all the rules of grammar and prosody will help one to cross the dark barrier of death, nor all the fasts and pilgrimages in the world ensure that overwhelming contact with the Divine from which, as the Ṛgveda has it, words fall back along with the mind, unable to comprehend.

The Indian tradition has a vast treasure of spiritual literature based upon the practice and realization of countless generations of sages and seers stretching back unbroken over many millennia to the very dawn of our civilization. In this great heritage, the Tantra tradition represents a particularly brilliant and evocative strand. Based as it is upon psycho-physical endeavour aimed at expanding human consciousness so that it can comprehend vibrant realms hitherto entirely beyond its ambit, the Tantra represents a powerful and impressive corpus of knowledge to which not sufficient attention has been paid by students of Indian philosophy. Despite the pioneering work done by Sir John Woodroffe, the whole science of Tantra remains a subject of general ignorance or, at best, misconception.

In the present age when theoretical philosophy is rapidly losing such appeal as it had over the minds of men, Tantra represents a vigorous and virile approach to suprarational experience which should evoke widespread interest in India and abroad. Based as it is upon the twin Śiva-Śakti concept, the union of which alone can bring about spiritual transformation, the Tantra lays special emphasis upon a system of carefully disciplined and deeply meaningful practice directed towards arousing the 'Kuṇḍalinī', the mysterious 'serpent power', which represents and symbolizes the dynamic aspect of cosmic becoming. Whether one practices Tantra or not, a knowledge of its principles and application is essential for a full understanding of the rich and varied Indian spiritual tradition.

Lalan Prasad Singh has presented an impressive analysis of the Tantra and has explained both its mystical as well as its scientific basis. It is a useful addition to the literature on this fascinating and many-splendoured science.

New Delhi
1.10.2008

(Karan Singh)

Preface to the Second Edition

In quest of identity and destiny man discovered philosophy and religion. In search of realization of philosophical truth and religious *summum bunum* of life Lord Śiva expounded scientific and mystic tradition known as Tantra. Tantra forms the esoteric basis of all religion and provides sound philosophical foundation of spirituality. This book presents an indepth analysis and reflection of the root concepts of Tantra such as *Kuṇḍalinī, Mantra* and *Yantra.* Tantra provides an esoteric and physiological significance of *Pañcamakāra Sādhanā.* Tantra believes that poison that kills a man when scientifically cultured by physician it becomes the elixir of life. Sex when sublimated, it opens the door for salvation. Tantra is a happy and harmonious blending of enjoyment *(Bhoga)* and salvation *(Yoga).* It is neither a dogma nor lifeless rituals. It is an intuitional science. The Canonical literature of Tantra is written in Twilight language (Sandhyā Bhāṣā). Its apparent meaning is quite different from the real meaning. Only those who get initiated by a proper Guru in Tantra Sādhanā understands the mystic significance of different symbols and esoteric practices. This book provides a deeper insight into the scientific and mystic significance of *Kuṇḍalinī, Mantra* and *Yantra* which are the main constituents of Tantra. This book presents a scholarly analysis and evaluation of Tantra and explains both its mystic and scientific basis.

I feel great pleasure in presenting the second edition of my book before the reader in general and world of academia in particular. I would like to express my sincere thanks and deep gratitude to Dr. Karan Singh for writing the foreword of my book. Dr. Karan Singh needs no introduction. He is a larger than life size statesman, thinker and a poet. He has become a legend in his life time. I would like to put on record my love and gratitude to my wife Ahilya without her loving care I would not have achieved anything in my life. She left me alone when I needed her most. My son-in-law Prabhat left a permanent scar on my life by making a sudden and untimely pilgrimage to heavenly abode. My children Manju, Arvind, Amitabh, Ashutosh, Varsa and Anand Vijay have filled my life with their love and affection. My grand-children Janu, Shanu, Kishu and Rakshu are the greatest source of my happiness without their love my life would have become insipid and meaningless. My children and grand-children have become whole of my being and existence. I put on record my sincere thanks to my friend, philosopher and guide Mr. U.P. Singh. I express my sincere thanks and deep gratitude to my best friends and well wishers Shri K.M. Singh, Member National Disaster Management Authority; Dr. Vidya

Nand Singh, Founder and First Chairman, First Liberty Bank, Washington D.C.; Philonthropists Shri Adyanand Singh and his wife Mrs. Pratima Singh of U.S.A. for their constant help and co-operation in my life. My thanks are due to Shri S.K. Singh, I.P.S. I.G, C.R.P.F. and Shri Kumar Sanjay, I.R.S. Income Tax Commissioner. My thank is due to Mr. Sanjeev Kant Soni, Vice Chairman, Bank of America, and his loving wife Shalu for their constant help and loving care. I express my gratitude and thanks to the authority of National Museum, New Delhi, specially Shri R.R.S. Chauhan, Dr. Sanjib Kumar Singh, Shri J.C. Grover, Shri S.M. Pathak, and Shri J.E. Dawson for their invaluable help by providing some rare photoprints for this book. I want to express my gratitude and homage to Late Naurang Rai, the Founder of Concept Publishing Company and his wife Late Smt. Kamla Devi. Naurang Rai was a man of great commitment and dynamism. He lived his life on his own terms. I am thankful to Shri Ashok Kumar Mittal, the able and the visionary son of Naurang Rai, for undertaking the Publication of Second Edition of this book.

2nd October, 2008 **Lalan Prasad Singh**
New Delhi

Preface to the First Edition

Tantra, till today, is regarded as a system of black magic. Perhaps, therefore, it still remains a neglected branch of study. That Tantra has a rich spiritual heritage and a developed form of cultural history, and is rich in literature and sublime in philosophy has remained a fact only. It has not received the attention it deserves. The large stock of its literature is still in manuscript form. But thanks to Sir John Woodroffe for his enormous endeavour to show that the Tantric cult and culture are neither magic nor an immoral practice. The *Sādhanā* of *Pañcamakāra* (Five M's) has created many misgivings about Tantra which is full of symbolism. Further the esoteric and deeper meaning of the mystic symbolism of Tantra cannot be understood without one's initiation into its science. To a layman *mantra* is a nonsensical syllable and the Five M's are morbid forms of a sexo-yogic process. But, for the initiates, *mantra* is full of mystic power and the Five M's are esoteric symbols of Sādhanā which brings liberation from the fetters of the world. Tantra Sādhanā cuts asunder the trammels of Māyā and gives occult power taking man to the higher realm of mystic experience.

Tantra is known as Āgama Śāstra. The Śivādvaita School of Tantra philosophy is a unique contribution of India to the speculative metaphysics. In Tantra, Advaita means the eternal coexistence of Śiva and Śakti which constitute the Absolute of Tantra philosophy. Śiva is transcendental and Śakti the immanent aspect of the Absolute.

The *Kuṇḍalinī*, *Mantra* and *Yantra* are the three mystic principles of Tantra Sādhanā. Reality is open only to mystic experience. The incomprehensible certainty of the Absolute cannot be explained by any grammar of metaphysics. The mystic experience of Tantra Sādhanā is vivid, direct and integral. In the intuitive experience, the yogi feels the impact of Reality.

The mystery of the Absolute cannot be rationally determined. It is beyond the scope of logical concepts. The Vedas give only the negative account of the Reality. According to them the Supreme Reality is 'not this, not this'. He is non-being. He is nothing, that is, the Vedas simply affirm that the Reality cannot be realized through the various categories of reason. But Tantra is an intuitional science for the realization of God. The mystic and the scientific basis of Tantra are variations of the central theme that the Divinity is to be realized with the awakening of the *Kuṇḍalinī*. This awakening of the *Kuṇḍalinī* is a mystic process of divinization. It leads one to the path of inner spiritual transformation. The rousing of the *Kuṇḍalinī* brings about an inner transformation in the physical, vital and psychic forces. The conversion of mechanical energy into psychic force is called *Upavidyā* and the practice of this force for physical gain is called *Avidyā* Sādhanā. The transformation of psychic energy into spiritual force or bliss is called Vidyā Tantra.

Tantra Sādhanā leads to higher and spiritual levels of perfection, and yogi continues till he achieves the supreme end of life, becomes one with Parama Śiva. This is called Parā-Samvit.

Tantra Sādhanā, in fact, is meant for the attainment of the fourfold objective, of life *viz. Artha* (wealth), *Kāma* (mundane possessions), *Dharma* (virtue) and *Mokṣa* (salvation). It is not, as is ordinarily misunderstood, devoted to salvation alone. Human life is multidimensional. And the Sādhanā which does not fulfil these four objectives of life, which follow one another in one's spiritual progress and perfection, remains a futile pursuit.

The material science does not give any holistic view of the Reality. Its method is analytic. It explains the phenomenal world in mathematical forms and physical concepts. These forms and concepts are mere abstractions. The approach to Reality through science remains only partial. Physics, which employed mechanical models of the universe to explain the fundamental principles of the Cosmos has now changed its course and theme because the models have failed. Of late physicists have taken shelter in concepts and ideas, and agreed with Newton in the view that things 'certainly are not mechanical' entities. To Tantra Sādhanā, both philosophy and science are bound up with mysticism. Tantra combines science and spirituality, fact and ideal. Philosophy in India is not mere speculation but a way of life. Mysticism is a philosophy of oneness. It is based on the rule of identity in life.

The mysticism of Tantra denotes a state of consciousness which is characterized by a complete cessation of sensations, ideas, concepts and subject-object relationship. Through Tantra Sādhanā, the mind reaches the pure state of Consciousness and Bliss. The Sādhaka attains the state of equal-mindedness which finally leads to salvation. Tantra leads to the integrated elevation and evolution of human personality. Tantra is mysticism as it takes man to the realization of Param Śiva which is beyond the dualism of subject and object. The awakening of the *Kuṇḍalinī*, incantation of *Mantra* and use of *Yantra* (mystic diagram) are mystical in import.

Tantra and the Veda are the two streams of Indian culture and civilization. Tantra is ancient and indigenous to India. It is a cult whereas the Veda is a creed. But all their apparent contradictions and conflicts have long been resolved and both assimilated into the organism of Hindu culture. Tantra is Agama and the Veda Nigama. Tantra deals with *tattva* and *mantra*, the former a cosmic principle and the latter a mystic sound.

The account of Tantra philosophy has mainly been drawn from *Śiva Sūtra, Tantraloka, Svachanda Tantra, Mālinī Vijoyottara Tantra, Pratibhijñā-hṛdayam, Kāmika Āgama, Śiva - Dṛṣṭi* and other works of Kashmir Śaivism. My interpretation of the Tantra cult is based on *Śāradā Tilakam, Ṣaṭcakra Nirūpaṇa* (*Serpent Power*), *Mahānirvāṇa Tantra, Kulārṇava Tantra, Tirupurā Rahasya, Saundaryalaharī,* etc. I have also made use of *Hevajra Tantra, Sādhana Mālā* and *Guhya Samāj Tantra* as the base books in dealing with the Buddhist Tantra. I have derived considerable help from the works of many authors, especially Sir John Woodroffe, Dr. Gopinath Kaviraj, Dr. P.C. Bagchi, Swami Pratyagātmānanda and Dr. Benoytosh Bhattacharya and am deeply indebted to all of them.

This book has grown out of the thesis submitted to Ranchi University for the award of D.Litt. degree. The preparation of the thesis would not indeed have been possible without the benevolent help of many individuals and I am thankful to them. I am specially deeply indebted to Dr. R.S. Srivastava, Professor and Head of the Department of Philosophy, Ranchi University, who took great interest in the present work and offered precious help to me in all possible ways.

I acknowledge my deep gratitude to Dr. Karan Singh, Union Minister of Tourism and Civil Aviation and a scholar of repute, for writing a Foreword for this book.

I also record my sincere thanks to Dr. G.C. Pande, Vice-Chancellor, Rajasthan University, Jaipur, and Dr. Frederick Spiegelberg, Director, Asian Studies, Stanford University, U.S.A., for recommending the thesis for the award of D.Litt. degree. I am also grateful to Prof. S.C. Dube, Director, Indian Institute of Advanced Study, Simla, for awarding me Guest Fellowship which gave me a rare opportunity to revise the present work there. I must also express my thanks to my friends, Mrs. Indu Jain, Sri K.C. Sharma, Advocate, Sri Maniram Gupta, Sri B.P. Sinha and Sri Hari Kishore Singh, M.P., for their encouragement and kind help in the publication of this book. I am also indebted to Prof. H.G. Singh for his kind help and inspiration. Sincere thanks are also due to my brother, Devendra, my nephew, Bageshwari, both of whom helped me in many ways, and Late Sri Suraj Narayan Singh, a close relation, whose help and inspiration were quite invaluable in completing this research project. Lastly, I am thankful to my friend, Sri G.R. Hingorani, of *The Statesman*, New Delhi, for his editorial assistance and some valuable suggestions.

Rashtrapati Nivas
Simla.
Vijaya Daśami
October 25, 1974

Lalan Prasad Singh

Contents

List of Illustrations

1 Background of Tantra

The word Tantra has been used in many senses in Sanskrit. It connotes a system and refers to some śāstra. Śaṅkarācārya uses the word Vaināiśika Tantra for Kṣaṇabhaṅgavāda of the Buddhist system.[1] The philosophical systems of Kapila and Gautam are also known as Kapila Tantra or Ṣaṣṭī Tantra and Gautam Tantra. Vācaspati Miśra, one of the greatest scholars of philosophy, has been honoured with the title Sarvatantra-svatantra (versed in all the śāstras). The well-known Tāntric commentator Bhāskararāya has termed the Mīmāṁsā School of Philosophy as Jaiminī Tantra.[2] In the Tantrādhikārinirṇaya of Bhaṭṭoji, the words Pūrva Tantra and Uttara Tantra refer to the Mīmāṁsā and Vedānta Schools of Philosophy, respectively. Śaṅkara also calls Sāṅkhya a Tantra as he looks upon it as an esoteric branch of spiritual knowledge. Sāṅkhya Kārikā itself uses the word Tantra for its own system.[3]

M.M. H. P. Shastri says: 'The word Tantra means shortening abbreviation, *i.e.* reducing into something like algebraic forms of *mantras* or formulae that would otherwise run to scores of syllables.'[4] Mantra is the soul of Tantra Śāstra. But it alone does not constitute the whole system. Tantra has many other aspects to be analysed and understood. *Kāmikāgama*, part of the canonical literature of this school, defines Tantra as a system of text 'which promulgates profound matters concerning *tattva* and *mantra* (*tanoti vipulānarthān tattvamantra-samanvitān*).'[5]

Tantra deals with the problem of *tattva, i.e.* study of the Absolute and the First Principle. *Tattva* means pertaining to Thatness (the Cosmic entity). Hence, Tantra is that branch of esoteric cult which brings the realization of *tattva* (Absolute) with the help of Mantra Sādhanā. Tantra stands for the application of the esoteric science for the attainment of spiritual ascendancy.

Various derivative meanings of Tantra have been used to express one's spiritual enlightenment. According to the interpretation of Kāśikāvṛtti, the word Tantra has been derived from the root '*tan*' meaning 'to expand'. Tantra Sādhanā, therefore, means a spiritual path which leads to the expansion of one's mental objectivity and with the expansion of mental objectivity the arena of mental projection is also increased. When a Sādhaka attains the projection of mental arena of 360^0, he becomes one with the Cosmic Mind. This is called qualified Liberation.

Some scholars conceive that the word Tantra has been derived from the root '*tatri*' or '*tantri*' meaning origin of spiritual knowledge. In an esoteric sense Tantra means 'the spiritual cult by which divine knowledge is unfolded (*tanyate vistāryate jñānam anena iti tantram*)'. It is a spiritual discipline in a wide sense, and, when used in a limited sense, it is a mystic form of spiritual Sādhanā.

The mystic definition of Tantra is that it is a spiritual cult which liberates from the bondages of crudeness and ignorance. The word *ta* (त) is the *bīja-mantra* (acoustic root) of crudeness (जड़ता). Tantra is a process of Sādhanā which relieves one from the fetters of crudeness (*ta*). Thus, Tantra is an intuitional science which stands for the progressive realization of the Divine. It liberates one from the cimmerian darkness and leads unto the divine effulgence. It is a path of Salvation. It is a science of the soul. The authoritative definition of Tantra is, that which brings emanicipation from the bondage of Māyā (*tatra ya ayat tārayet yastu sa tantra parikirtitaḥ*).

Origin of Tantra

Ancient India's achievement in the field of spiritual Sādhanā and philosophy is very imperfectly known to the people, generally. From the excavations of Mohenjo-daro and Harappa, we find the historical evidence of a developed urban life dated 600 B.C. The epoch-making discoveries made by the Archaeological Survey of India in the twenties at the city sites of Mohenjo-daro and Harappa have pushed the antiquity of Indian civilization far back into the past. According to Ernest Mackay there were four different races, namely, 'proto-Australoid, Mediterranean, Mongolian and Alpine, although the latter two are represented by only one skull of each type.'[6] From the skeletal material unearthed there, the whole concept of the origin and development of Indian culture has been revolutionized. The Āryans were not the indigenous population of India but came here from Central Asia through the North-West Frontier. They contemptuously imposed the name Anārya (uncultured) on the natives of this land. Anārya does not refer to any ethnic or cultural group; it refers to India's heterogeneous community which is of the Mongolian, Austric and Austrico-Negroid (Dravidian) origin.

The question arises who were the architects of the Harappan culture, and whether they were the indigenous population or immigrants into the Indus Valley, like the Āryans. This question is most vital from both the anthropological and cultural points of view. But anthropological evidence on the subject has proved beyond doubt that heterogeneous ethnic groups were the natives of India and founders of the Harappan civilization. The anthropological research on the skeletal remains recovered from the streets of Mohenjo-daro also reveals four different racial types, *viz.* the Australoid, the Mediterranean, the Mongolian branch of Alpine stock and the Alpine.[7]

The word Harappa is composed of 'hara' and 'appa' which means 'Śiva' and 'father' respectively. The Harappan civilization is the gift of Śaivism or Tantrism. The only male God of the Harappan culture is Lord Śiva. He is characterized by a horned headdress, the symbol of great occult power. A seal showing Śiva seated on a raised throne in the posture of yoga was discovered at Mohenjo-daro (Pl.V.4.). In this he is shown as three-faced which means he is the knower of past, present and future (Trikāladarśī). He is in the '*ūrdhvamedhra*' (*penis erectus*) form which is a proper yogic posture for meditation. (The opposite posture of this leads to impotency.) Four animals are shown on the sides of the god — a rhinoceros and a buffalo on his left, and an elephant and a tiger on his right. Below the throne are two radiant deer with their horns turned inside towards the centre. This symbolizes the great spiritual force of Śiva, in whose presence a tiger and an elephant behave like pet animals. They forget their hostility and reside in the spirit of live and let live. On the basis of this archaeological evidence, of the three faces, the yogic posture, the *ūrdhvamedhrā* form, the trident-shaped headdress and the four animals, Sir John Marshall has said, 'the figure represents a prototype of the historic Śiva.'[8]

From the excavation report of the Harappan culture it is quite evident that both the Śakti cult and Śaivism constituted the spiritual faith of the non-Āryans. While writing about the religion of the Indus Valley civilization Sir John Marshall says, 'Śakti worship was of great antiquity in India; it originated out of the Mother Goddess; and it was closely connected with the cult of Śiva.'[9]

Śaivism and Śaktism are the two aspects of Tantra. Śaktism represents the beginning of Tantra Sādhanā and Śaivism is the culminating point of the spiritual march. Prof. Surendranath Dasgupta, while discussing the origin and development of theistic schools, says: 'In addition to the work of these Vaiṣṇava thinkers there sprang up another class of theistic works which were of a more eclectic nature. These also had their beginnings in periods as old as the *Upaniṣads.* They are known as the Śaiva and Tantra thought ....'[10]

Śaivism and Śaktism, the two schools of Tantra metaphysics, were the official religions of the non-Āryans of the Indus Valley civilization who practised various aspects of Tantra Sādhanā according to their intellectual standards. Śiva and Śakti, the dual deities symbolizing the two schools, were their principal divine beings and worshipped. But in essence Śiva was the goal and god of the non-Āryans.

Among the aniconic objects of worship are the *liṅgas* and *yonis* together with their bactylic forms (Pl. III. 31-33). The *liṅga* (phallus) worship was prevalent amongst the backward classes of the non-Āryans. E.H. Hartland in a detailed and informative article[11] on phallism deals with the subject from a broader view. His central theme is to trace sex-worship as part of the history of religion which has been prevalent in the different strata of culture. Sex-worship was a customary practice and was considered to be part of the religious sacrament by the ancient people belonging to different faiths. With the advancement of civilization it was transformed into a higher religious symbolism. This practice was so universal that it became an integral part of the evolution of human mind, and it seems indigenous with the race.[12] Wall observes: 'All religions are based on sex, some like the ancient Egyptian, Greek and Roman or the modern Brahmanic worship of Śiva more coarsely so, according to modern civilized thought; others like the Christian religion more obscurely so.'[13] Originally sex-worship was not developed for the achievement of any morbid exaltation and ecstasy. The primitive people were mostly engaged in war, and preservation of progeny was their greatest problem. Sex-worship, therefore, reasonably really stands for procreation and not for any sexual indulgence.

Further, Tantra, a positive science, never encourages sexual indulgence. Rather it lays down very strict rules and a severe discipline, which forbids indulgence, even for a family man though it does not restrain him from leading a normal life. The modern man knows the consequences of mental suppression and repression. But Tantra offers an esoteric process, known as Ṣoḍaśī Sādhanā, for the sublimation of the sex instinct.

Another Tāntric symbol prevalent in the pre-historic India is the Svastika (卐). It stands for spiritual victory over mundane existence. The vertical line (।) stands for the Causal Brahman (कारण ब्रह्म), the horizontal line (—) represents the Effect Brahman (कार्य ब्रह्म). The *ka* (क) of Tāntric Varṇamālā is the *bīja-mantra* of the manifest world. Originally *ka* (क) was written as (+). In the Brāhmī script letter *ka* is written in the olden style of the cross (╤). The Svastika (卐) means here the conquering of the manifest world. It has a great mystic significance in Tantra. Madho Sarup Vats is of the opinion that 'the cult of the Mother Goddess and the Svastika symbol were common throughout the ancient world'.[14] The discovery of a seal from Mohenjo-daro depicting a god seated in a yogic posture on a low throne canopied by a snake's hood on either side of him is also of great esoteric significance. The snake symbolizes *Kulakuṇḍalinī* of Tāntric esotericism.

From all this available historical evidence, it can be said with certainty that Tantra is the cult and spiritual faith of ancient India. It is the gift of the non-Āryan civilization.

There is a wrong and biased view about the non-Āryans. Indian culture and civilization fathered by the non-Āryans is the oldest. When the rest of the world had not even seen the twilight of civilization, the non-Āryans of the pre-historic India enjoyed a spiritual form of cultural life. Thus, it will be wrong to believe that all the best elements of Hindu religion and culture came from the Āryans. It will also be wrong to think that whatever is lowly, degrading, or superstitious comes from the primitive, uncultured non-Āryans. On the contrary the Āryan culture, religion, thought and beliefs have been profoundly modified by the superior and subtle Tāntric cult of the non-Āryans. The mysticism and the scientific approach of the Tāntric civilization have had a great influence over the thought and beliefs of the Vedic culture of the Āryans.

Tantra is the outcome of the practical approach in the realm of spirituality. The non-Āryans came into contact with occultism through spiritual discipline. Before the advent of Śiva, the elements of Tantrism were scattered in unsystematic forms. Elements of occultism are found in every ancient religion and tribe. The use of charms and amulets is known to have been a very widespread custom among the primitive people of different ages and lands.[15]

The non-Āryans had spiritual aspirations as well as mystic experiences. They were conversant with the esoteric technique of awakening the *Kuṇḍalinī* though they were not fully aware of the mystic and scientific significance of the Tāntric discipline. It has been mentioned by many scholars that wine and intoxicating herbs were used by the primitive people to attain religious exaltation and ecstasy.[16] The different kinds of physical exercises resembling *mudrās, āsanas* and *nyāsas* of the Tantras were used for the attainment of religious experiences.[17]

It is abundantly clear that Tantrism was prevalent among the primitive people of all the countries. So was the case with India too. Lord Śiva systematized the whole process and gave it the form and content of mysticism and science. From the crude form of black magic, Śiva transformed it into an intuitional science. But Tantrism was unknown to the Āryans. They came into contact with this *vidyā* only when they proceeded towards the eastern region. They not only learnt the Tantra Sādhanā but borrowed the Tāntric male god, Śiva. The cult of Śaivism was the official religion based on mysticism and humanism in the pre-Vedic India. While tracing the religious practices of ancient India, R.C. Majumdar writes: 'Among the male gods the most remarkable figure is that of the deity, seated on a throne with legs crossed in the fashion of a Yogi .... Many scholars regard him as a representation of God Śiva, for the latter is described as Trimukha (three-faced), Paśupati (lord of animals) and Mahāyogin (the great ascetic). They further urge that this god, originally unknown to the Āryans, was later borrowed by them from the people they met in India, a view held on other grounds long before the discovery of Mohenjo-daro.'[18]

There are conflicting theories with regard to the place of origin of Tantra. In the midst of conflicting views and claims, we can clearly notice two main theories — one claiming an extra-Indian and the other an indigenous origin.

Some scholars are of the opinion that the Tantra form of worship was introduced into India by the priests of Iran. M.M. H.P. Shastri opines that Tantrism was imported into India by the priests of Turkestan, who were driven out by the Islamic invasion.[19] According to some Tāntric texts, this form of worship is of trans-Himālayan origin. The cult of Tārā is claimed to have been originated in the country of Bhot in Tibet.[20] The history of Vaśiṣṭha's going to Mahācīna for lessons in Tantra Sādhanā is referred to in more than one Brahmanic Tantra work, like *Rudrayāmālā* and *Brahmayāmālā,* as quoted in *Tārātantra.*[21] *Devībhāgavata* (vii.38, 13) categorically refers to China as the place of origin of Tāntric Goddess Nīlasarasvatī.[22] According to *Kālitantra* (xii.7-10) Vāmācāra and Kulācāra have been imported from China or Mahācīna.

There is no authentic evidence about the origin of Tantra in Iran. It is pure and simple guesswork as there is no mention of Tantra in any Islamic literature. But it is, to a great extent, true that Tantra Sādhanā was prevalent in China. Vaśiṣṭha, one of the great ascetics of India, went to China to learn some aspects of Tantra Sādhanā which is known as Cīnācāra. However, Vaśiṣṭha was well versed in Tantra Śāstra before going to China. He used to perform his Tantra Sādhanā at Tārā-pīṭha, now a railway station similarly named near Rampur Hat, a railway station on Eastern Railway. Since Vaśiṣṭha there was always a great Tantra Sādhaka at Tārā-pīṭha. The last great Sādhaka was Vāmākhepā. (His life and spiritual achievements have been filmed.)

It is also true that some crude processes of Tantra Sādhanā known as Avidyā Tantra were widely prevalent in China, and some aspects of it were imported into India. The word Vāmācāra has been mentioned in this reference.

Nevertheless, the original home of Tantra cannot be said to be China. From the available material, it can safely be said that eastern India was the birth-place of Tantra Sādhanā. There are many scholars in favour of Bengal being the original home of Tantra from where it travelled to other parts of India and Nepal. Prof. Winternitz says: 'The original home of the Tantras seems to have been in Bengal whence they spread throughout Assam and Nepal, and even beyond India to Tibet and China through the agency of Buddhism.'[23] This theory is further supported by a verse which states that 'Tantra Vidyā originated in Bengal, was developed in Mithilā and was found to some extent in Maharashtra and was extinguished in Gujarat.'[24] A similar verse with regard to the spread of devotion is found in *Padmapurāṇa*.[25]

Devotion is the secret of Tantra Sādhanā. Without self-surrender, there is no possibility of success in Tantra Sādhanā. It has been said that the cult of devotion originated in the Dravidian land, *i.e.* eastern India. Kāśī (Vārāṇasī) was the eastern border of Āryāvarta. Some parts of present eastern U.P., Bihar, Bengal, Assam, nay, the eastern India was Dravidian country. The Āryans could not conquer this part of India. There is a legend that if a man took a dip in the river Karmanāśā which divides U.P. and Bihar, his *Saṁskāra* (the reactive momenta) would be wiped out. The Āryans were warned against crossing the Karmanāśā.

According to Jayaratha (twelfth century A.D.), a great commentator of *Tantrāloka* of Abhinavagupta, Kaula Tantras are said to have issued from Kamarūpa in Assam.[26]

There is a reference of Kāmākhyā, the famous Tantrapīṭha in Assam, in *Brahma Yāmālā* where Vaśiṣṭha went to perform Tantra Sādhanā. According to P.C. Bagchi this Tāntric text was composed in the eighth century.[27] Vaśiṣṭha could not attain perfection at Kāmākhyā and was told that Viṣṇu in the form of Buddha alone knew the secrets of Cīnācāra. Vaśiṣṭha, therefore, went to Mahācīna situated on the slopes of the Himālayas. While performing Sādhanā there, Vaśiṣṭha was assailed with many doubts when he saw Him (Viṣṇu) in the form of Buddha, with eyelids drooping as if from the effect of wine. He thought, 'what Viṣṇu is doing these things in his Buddha-form? The *ācāra* (method) is opposed to the teaching of the Veda. I do not agree to it'. When he thus spoke to himself he heard an Ākāśavāṇī (voice from the unknown), 'O, thou who art devoted to good acts, do not entertain such ideas. This *ācāra* (method) is sure to give success in the worship of Tāriṇī. She is not pleased with anything which is contrary to this method. If you have a longing to gain Her grace speedily, then worship Her according to Cīnācāra.'

Brahma Yāmala is of recent origin. There is a clear attempt at Āryanization of the Buddha, who has been described as the incarnation of Viṣṇu. The reference to Viṣṇu who is not a Tāntric deity, here is out of context. Further, it has been said that the Buddha was intoxicated with wine. In Tantra the esoteric meaning of *mada* is the peneal nectar. Hence, the Buddha was not in the drunken state but was in the state of God-intoxication. We shall deal with the subtler and mystic interpretation and significance of the Five Makāras in the subsequent chapter.

It is true that in the course of Sādhanā, a Sādhaka hears Ākāśavāṇī. It comes only to the blessed one and heralds spiritual illumination. The voice from the unknown offers all sorts of allurements and temptations in the beginning. But the Sādhaka who does not waver or drift away by the carnal consideration is showered with blessings. He attains supreme union with Parama Śiva.

In the course of Sādhanā the deity appears before the Sādhaka. There are many Tāntric deities. There are many *siddhis* also. One who performs Avidyā Sādhanā gets *siddhis* in Avidyā. But the wise, the circumspect do not allow themselves to drift or deviate from the path of righteousness and devote themselves whole-heartedly to spiritual liberation.

Tantra was not unknown to China. But the Chinese were practising Avidyā Tantra. The witchcraft has come from China along with other branches of the Avidyā school.

The historical evidence of cultural exchanges between India and China is established by this *Brahma Yāmala* which is being further documented by *Rājataraṅgiṇī* of Kalhaṇa.[28]

Tantra was the spiritual faith and way of life in the Harappan and Mohenjo-daro cultures. India can historically be claimed to be the original home of Tantra. The impact of the Tantra culture in eastern India is greater than in northern and western India. All the great ascetics of eastern India have attained salvation through Tantra Sādhanā. The great Siddha-pīṭhas are associated with great ascetics. Bakreśvara, between Dumka (district headquarters of Santhal Parganas of Bihar) and Suri (district headquarters of Birbhum District of West Bengal), was the Siddha-pīṭha of Aṣṭāvakra. Phullarā was the Tantra-pīṭha of Mahā Prabhu Chaitanya. Tārā-pīṭha has already been mentioned as the place of worship of Vaśiṣṭha. Ramakrishna was also initiated into Tantra Sādhanā by Brāhmaṇī Bhairavī. His place of worship was Dakṣiṇeśvara. Śukadeva has performed Sādhanā near the present Colgong in Bhagalpur District. Mithilā is still very famous for the Śakti cult. Thus, we can conclude on the basis of this historical evidence that the original home of Tantra was eastern India.

However, Tantra Sādhanā was a religious creed of Tibet, Nepal and some parts of China. There are still some renowned Mahā Siddha-pīṭhas in Tibet where many great Tāntrikas of the Buddhistic Mahāyāna cult have performed their Sādhanā and attained salvation, the esoteric unification of Prajñā with Upāya. We find in the teachings of Confucius a reference to the worship of the mystic diagram (yantra of Tantra) and the practice of charms. Confucianism is a curious fusion of the Buddha's Śīla and Tāntric mysticism. The Tāntric mysticism of Confucius provided China with a strong spiritual anchor against the invasion and storms of the alien culture. It preserved its soul and destiny from decay and disillusion. China is alive due to its ancient background of Tāntric mysticism in a socio-moral order of Confucius.

Lord Śiva : Founder of Tantra

Many opinions have been offered with regard to the founder of the Tantra system. (It is, however, an interesting and vital problem for the cultural anthropologists to trace the origin and the founder of Tantra, the literature and the Sādhanā which cover a vast and varied ground.) There is a wild belief among the native Tāntrikas that Tantra is of eternal existence like the Vedas. Abhinavagupta, the chief exponent of Tāntrika Śaivāgamas of Kashmir, has given a philosophical explanation. He observes: 'According to Trikā, creation or manifestation is of two kinds. One refers to speech and the other to substance. Speech is also of two kinds, divine and human. The Śaivāgamas are the divine speech and as such are the grossest manifestation of the Supreme Vimarśa, as different from the individual Vimarśa which is the cause of ordinary human speech. Speech, as we have already shown in the course of our treatment of the Paratriṁśika Vivaraṇa, has an eternal existence in a state of identity with the Para. The Āgamas are but divine speech, and as such they also have a similar eternal existence. According to Trikā, therefore, there can be nothing like an origin of the Śaivāgamas. There is only appearance or reappearance of them at the divine will.'[29]

But from our point of view neither Tantra nor the Vedas are of divine origin. Both embody the intuitive vision of seers. The godhead of the Vedas and of Tantra is an infinite, eternal, formless and transcendental entity. It is not a personal god. It does not have any vocal chord. There is no transcendental validity in the argument that Tantra or the Veda is the Voice of Providence (Āpta Vākya).

The founder of Tantra is Lord Śiva. He is known as Ādi Guru. He is a great ascetic (Mahā Yogi) and a great Tāntrika (Mahā Kaula). He has oneness with the Supreme God. He attained occult powers through Tantra Sādhanā. It is beyond human mind to measure the depth and dimension of his spiritual power and personality. People revered, worshipped and adored him in ancient times. He is conceived to be Guṇātīta and Nirguṇa Puruṣa.

Śiva remains eternally in the state of bliss and beatitude, that is why he is called Sadā Śiva (one who always remains in bliss).

Lord Śiva has later on been conceived to be the Supreme God. He does not remain only the founder of Tantra but becomes the Supreme deity. Śiva is deified in his own lifetime.

The worship of Śiva is as old as Tantra.[30] The paintings of Sadā Śiva at Puri and Bhubaneshwar are of great historical importance. The great Śaṅkarācārya[31] (eighth century A.D.) and Lakṣmaṇa Deśika (tenth century A.D.) have made references to Lord Śiva as the Supreme God.

The worship of Śiva is coeval with the Tantras and the Śaivāgamas. Śiva occupies a supreme position in Tantrika cosmogony. He is the highest and the Supreme Godhead like Vasudeva of the Vaiṣṇavāgamas and Para Brahman of the Vedāntins.

There are different views expressed in *Śākta Tantras* and *Śaiva Āgamas* regarding the position of Śiva and his five faces. In *Śākta Tantras,* Śiva is the manifestation of the Supreme Being. He is Ardhanārīśvara. But, according to *Śaiva Āgamas,* he is the highest and the Supreme Being. He is the embodiment of the Absolute. He is formless, incomprehensible, luminous and ubiquitous.[32] The monograph, *Janma Maraṇa Vicāra,* a treatise on the Advaita Śaiva philosophy of Kashmir, shows that Parama Śiva transcends the space-time universe. He remains in his fivefold power and glory, namely, *Cit, Ānanda, Icchā, Jñāna* and *Kriyā.* But he remains unaffected by it.[33]

The difference between the *Śākta* and the *Śaiva Āgamas* regarding the place of Śiva in their respective systems is apparent and not real. Śiva occupies the supreme position in all the Tāntrika systems.

According to *Śiva Sūtra Vimarśani,* Śiva Sūtra is the basis of all Tāntric Śaivāgamas. Lord Śiva revealed it to Vasugupta in his dream while he was residing in his hermitage below the Mahādeva peak.[34] Lord Śiva observed that the world was immersed in material darkness. He was moved. He, therefore, appeared before Vasugupta and disclosed to him the secret of intuitional science which he was told he would find inscribed on a rock. Vasugupta was also informed about its exact location and that it would be turned downwards to keep it outside the reach of the profane souls. He was also told by Lord Śiva that by his touch the rock would turn over of its own accord and he would be able to read the Sūtras and their deep spiritual meaning and significance. He was directed to disseminate the spiritual knowledge of the Sūtras among his worthy disciples.

This view is supported by *Spanda Vṛtti* of Kallaṭa. He also says that the Sūtras were directly imparted to Vasugupta in his dream.[35] This point of view has been further substantiated by Rajanak Rama, author of *Utpala.* According to Bhāskara the Sūtras were composed by Śiva himself but were taught to Vasugupta by a Siddha—a realized soul with high spiritual attainment. Bhāskara has often introduced the Sūtras with such phrases as शिवसूत्र मरीरचत्:[36] or सूत्रमाह महेश्वर:[37].

According to this version Vasugupta did not find the Sūtras inscribed on a rock as has been narrated by Kṣemarāja. There is a difference of opinion with regard to their authorship. According to Tantra, a pure soul sometimes gets initiation in dream. The esoteric secrets of Tantra are often imparted to mystic beings in dream. Maharṣi Janaka also received initiation in dream. That is why he has no known spiritual guide. Nevertheless he acquired spiritual knowledge and attained oneness with Brahman. In our view Vasugupta also received initiation by Śiva in dream. Śiva is the Ādi Guru (the eternal spiritual guide). Vasugupta states his revelations in Sūtra form. J.C. Chatterjee says: 'It, however, seems certain that although the original version knew nothing of the Sūtras having been found inscribed on a rock and of Śiva himself having given Vasugupta, in a dream, the information of their existence in this form, it did know that either a Sidhha or Śiva himself taught the Sūtras to

Vasugupta not in the ordinary way but in a dream, and that the Sūtras so taught to Vasugupta were the composition of Śiva himself.'[38]

The Śrīmatottara Tantra is also said to have been revealed by Śiva to Pārvatī but has been brought to the mortal world through a human being, Śrīkaṇṭhanātha (e.g., Śrīkaṇṭhanāthāvatarita).[39] Mahākaulajñānavinirṇaya is similarly stated to have been brought down by Matsyendranātha.[40] Yogavijayastavarāja from the *Brahma Yāmla* is said to have been brought down from heaven by Pippalādamuni, though it was originally revealed by Śiva to Pārvatī.[41] *Pāradayogaśāstram*[42], like many other Tantras, is in the form of a dialogue between Śiva and Pārvatī. Tāntric Texts, *Karpūrādistotram*, one of the very old publications of Arthur Avalon, is attributed to Mahākāla.[43]

There is a common belief that there are sixty-four Tantras. According to *Saundaryalaharī*, Śiva brought to this earth this Tantra at the insistence of Devī (Śakti).[44] He had been controlling the cosmos with the sixty-four Tantras. However, it is clear that the chief exponent of the Tantra Śāstra is Śiva, and he is a historical figure.

Another interesting point which we propose to dwell upon is the lineage of Śiva. Sir John Marshall says in the excavation report of Harappa and Mohenjo-daro that Śiva is the male deity of the non-Āryan pantheon of pre-Vedic India. The *liṅga* at Gudimallam is ancient (*c.* 200 B.C.) and it has the figure of Śiva with the Mongolian features carved on it. The deity has plaited hair and no holy thread.[45] M.M. H.P. Shastri says that Śiva is originally the god of the Vrātyas, non-Vedic people.[46]

The pre-Vedic lineage of Śiva is being established by *Saundaryalaharī* also. According to it, Devī, who has been anthropomorphically portrayed as the spouse of Śiva, is an ocean of the milk of poesy. The Draviḍa[47] child of her became the laureate of master poets after sucking her milk of poesy. An Āryan parent could not have a Draviḍa offspring. Śiva comes from the non-Āryan stock. He is an embodiment of spiritual wisdom and asceticism. He is a living symbol of Truth and Dharma in the Indian culture.

Śiva is a great man. He is the god of non-Āryans. It is beyond the powers of a common man to fathom the depth of spiritual wisdom and occult powers of Śiva. He is a miracle for the people. Many superhuman traits have been manifested in Lord Śiva. With all the legendary stories of supernatural powers and origination, Śiva is still a man.

Śiva systematized the whole Tantra Śāstra. He gave it a shape and transformed the magical feats into a perfect intuitional science. He proves by his own Sādhanā that a man can become one with God, and a man is God. There is only a theoretical difference between an ideal man and God. With the passage of time, the Tāntrika and Vedic cultures came closer to each other; this resulted in a cultural metamorphosis. Śiva is later on Āryanized and accepted as a godhead of the Vedic pantheon. An attempt has been made to put an *upavīta* (sacred thread) on his left shoulder to show that he was of Āryan origin and creed. *Śrī Mṛgendra Tantram* of

Kashmir Śaivism is a clear evidence of a cultural blending of the Tāntrika and Vedic ways of life.

Śrī Mṛgendra Tantram is of recent origin. It is not pre-Vedic. According to Madhusudan Kaul Shastri, editor of the present edition of, *Śrī Mṛgendra Tantram*, 'the Śaivaistic cult and the view of life depicted herein seem to have been known in the early centuries of the Christian era.'[48] Here we find that the Vedic deity is narrating the story of the discovery of this Tantram. Indra gives a vivid description about his coming into contact with the sacred and sublime knowledge of Tantra. There is a mythological story that once Indra had to enter into a battle against Vṛtra, a demon, who had two heads and four arms. His one head recited Vedic hymns and the other emptied goblets of wine. In the battle Indra overpowered and killed the demon. In atonement for this sin, Indra offered prayers to Nārāyaṇa. Pleased, Nārāyaṇa blessed him with an armour or Narasiṁha, and instructed him to meditate on the divine glory of Śiva for a period of a thousand years covered with the armour. Nārāyaṇa assured Indra that at the end of this period he would have direct communion with Śiva and with his grace he would attain the objective of his life. Accordingly, Indra meditated for a full thousand years and at the expiry of the period, as assured by Nārāyaṇa, he had a cummunion with Śiva and was metaphysically enlightened. All his anguish and pangs of suffering also ended. Over and above, Indra was blessed with the knowledge of the *Kāmika Tantra. Mṛgendra* is an abridgement of *Kāmika Tantra.* And this is how this Tantram came into existence.

From a rational analysis of the above statements it is clear beyond any doubt that Śiva is the founder of Tantra and is accepted as the Supreme deity by Vedic exegesis. Indra is made only an agency for bringing the sacred knowledge of Tantra to the world after direct contact with Śiva himself. This legend establishes the supremacy of Tantra over the Veda. Indra is a known Vedic deity. The communion of Indra with Śiva symbolizes the blending of the two cultures, non-Āryan and Āryan. The *Mahābhārata* also deals with the Pāśupata Vrata and declares it to be superior to any other Śāstra. In the Śānti Parva of the *Mahābhārata*, while explaining Mokṣa-dharma, Mahādeva says to Dakṣa that 'the Pāśupata Vrata which has been promulgated by him is the quintessence of the Vedas and Sāṅkhya-Yoga. The Pāśupata Vrata is superior to all practices ordained in the Vedas and other Śāstras. It is righteous, beneficial to all castes and creeds (*āśramas*), everlasting, performed in three years and ten days, secret, highly spoken of by men of wisdom, spoken ill of by fools; opposed to *Varṇāśrama-dharma*, prescribed by enlightened persons and it is being practised by men who have risen above the petty considerations of caste and creed.'[49]

To conclude Tantra is the priceless treasure of ancient India. It is the oldest and the most scientific religion of the world. The first spiritual faith laying down ethical norms to be strictly observed for the spiritual enlightenment and integrated development of society, Tantra is the religion of householders. It does not encourage external renunciation (*Saṁyāsa*), and accepts for initiation into Tantra Sādhanā only those who have inner renunciation. Here, we find the first expression of a healthy social order.

Nigama and Āgama

Tantra deals with both the theoretical and the practical aspect of spiritual life. The former is known as *Nigama* and the latter is called *Āgama.* Some scholars have tried to prove that Tantra is the developed form of the Sāṅkhya and Vedānta systems, that the science of Sāṅkhya and Vedānta philosophy has been culminated into the Tāntric cult, that, thus, Tantra is part of the Vedas. P.C. Bagchi says: 'The Tantra is regarded as a *Śruti* or *Āgama,* revelation, as opposed to a *Smṛti* or *Nigama,* "tradition". It is thus classed with the Vedas. It is usually defined as "*Śrutiśākhāviśeṣaḥ*", a particular branch of the Vedas.'[50] This contention is untenable. By no logic or cultural evidence can it be proved that Tantra is a branch of the Veda. Tantra and the Veda are two different currents of India's cultural life. There is no common meeting ground between the two. We shall discuss this in detail in the chapter (2) entitled 'Tantra and Veda'. Tantra is a cult and the Veda a philosophy. Tantra is for the salvation of the soul and the Veda for the enrichment of mind. The difference between the soul and the mind symbolizes the difference between Tantra and the Veda.

According to Dr. Gopinath Kaviraj, one of the greatest living scholars of Tantra, the Veda is *Nigama* and Tantra is *Āgama.*[51] Tantra is the superior and sublime form of spiritual life and Sādhanā. In the process of Āryanization of Indian culture and life, some scholars have cunningly interpolated some verses in the later Tāntric texts to drive home their points of prejudices.

Rudra Yāmala Tantra says that *Āgama* is that class of Tantra which has been addressed to Pārvatī by Lord Śiva and *Nigama* is referred to as the work of Pārvatī spoken to Śiva.[52] *Rudra Yāmala Tantra* is of recent origin. Vedic paṇḍits have doubtlessly interpolated this verse to assert the authority of the Vedas over Tantra. The philosophical and the esoteric exposition of Śiva cannot be classed as the opinion of Vāsudeva. Apart from the differences of the cultural contours and climates of these two greatest of spiritual teachers they belonged to two distinct periods of Indian civilization. Their advent in the cultural life of India represents two periods of evolution and elevation of human civilization. Time perspective has always been an important factor in the shaping of a cultural life. In the present case there is a gap of nearly three thousand years between the advent of these two great teachers. How then can the truth propounded by Śiva be equated with the opinion of Vāsudeva.

Āgama is the esoteric part of Tantra which deals with the problem of awakening the *Kuṇḍalinī* known as *puraścarṇa kriyā* and meditation. It is the Sādhanā part of Tantra. According to Vārāhī Tantra as quoted in *Śabdakalpadruma, Āgama* deals with seven subjects, *i.e.* cosmology, destruction, worship of god, Sādhanā, *puraścarṇa,* the six black rites and fourfold meditation.[53] Tantra, being a science, is amoral. It is a revelation. It unfolds the mystery of mind and soul and takes man to the realization of his own being. The occult powers which one acquires in the course of Tantra Sādhanā can be used for purposes good and bad. And Tantra warns against misuse of the occult science as one would only be exposing oneself to the tortures of animal life. Āgama being the cult or Sādhanā part of the Tantra Śāstra, it is concerned with meditation, *puraścarṇa kriyā* and yoga.

Piṅgalamata (a Tāntric manuscript, dated 1174 A.D., available in the Durbar Library of Nepal) describes Āgama as a śāstra which brings the realization of the objects around and it stands for expansion and salvation of the soul.[54]

Nigama and *Āgama* are two branches of the Tantra Śāstra. Pārvatī inquires from Śiva about the secrets of Tantra Sādhanā. She raises all the possible doubts and seeks clarifications on many problems. This constitutes *Nigama* and forms the theoretical basis for Tantra Sādhanā.

The occult science of Tantra is nothing but Applied Psychology and *Āgama* is a best treatise on Applied Psychology. Psychology being a new science, it is still in the formative stage. That is why Tantra, which is the most developed form of Applied Psychology, has not been fully understood and appreciated. Tantra is full of symbolism. The subtle and esoteric significance of Tāntric symbolism when fully understood will create a revolution in the world of Psychology by making inroads into the dark night of the soul. *Āgama* is the occult part of the Tantra Śāstra. Here Śiva expounds the principles of the Tāntric cult. He lays down certain principles to be strictly followed while practising Tantra Sādhanā. He has enumerated the mystic process of awakening the Serpent Power for the attainment of supreme oneness with Parama Śiva.

REFERENCES

1. *Brahmasūtra Bhāṣya*, II.2.32.
2. *Commentary on the Saptaśatī*, Introduction.
3. *Sāṅkhyakārikā, Kārikā* 70.
4. H. P. Shastri, Notices of Sanskrit Manuscripts. I. Preface, p. xxiv.
5. John Woodroffe, *Shakti and Shakta* (2nd ed.), pp. 18-19. Ganesh & Co., Madras.
6. Ernest Mackay, *The Indus Civilization*, p. 200, 1935.
7. Sir John Marshall, *Mohenjo-daro and the Indus Civilization*, p. 107. Arthur Probsthain, 41, Great Russell Street, London, 1931
8. *Ibid.*, vol. I, p. 52 ff.
9. *Ibid.*, p. 57.
10. Surendranath Dasgupta, *A History of Indian Philosophy*, vol. I, p. 8. Cambridge University Press, 1963.
11. *Encyclopaedia of Religion and Ethics*, vol. IX, pp. 815-31.
12. Brown, *Sex-worship and Symbolism of Primitive Races*, pp. 23, 29-30.
13. Wall, *Sex and Sex Worship*, p. 2.
14. *The Cultural Heritage of India*, vol. I, p. 124. Ramakrishna Mission Institute of Culture, Calcutta, 1956.

15. *Encyclopaedia of Religion and Ethics*, vol. III, p. 392.
16. Taylor, *Primitive Culture*, pp. 410-16.
17. *Ibid.*, p. 419.
18. *Ancient India* (revised edition), pp. 25-26. Motilal Banarsidass, Delhi, 1960.
19. 'Bangiya Sahitya Parishat Patrika', vol. XXXIV, p. 15.
20. एकजठासाधनं समाप्तमार्य्यनागार्जुन पादैर्भोटिषूद्धतम् इति,
    Hirānanda Sastri, *The Origin and Cult of Tārā*, p. 14-16.
21. Appendix to the Varendra Research Society, Rājashāhī edition, 1913.
22. तथा नीलसरस्वत्याः स्थानं चीनेषु विश्रुतम्। *Devībhāgavata*, vii. 33,13.
23. *History of Indian Literature* (English translation), vol. I, p. 592. Calcutta University.
24. गौड़े प्रकाशिता विद्या मैथिलैः प्रबलीकृता।
    क्वचित् क्वचिन्महाराष्ट्रे गुर्जरे प्रलयं गता।। R.C. Chanda, *Indo-Āryan Races*, p. 153.
25. उत्पन्ना द्राविड़े साहं वृद्धिं कर्णाटके गता।
    क्वचित् क्वचिन्महाराष्ट्रे गुर्जरे जीर्णता गता।। *Padmapurāṇa*, Uttarakhaṇḍa, ch. 193, ver. 51.
26. भैरव्या भैरवात् प्राप्तो योग व्याप्त स्ततः प्रिय।
    तत्काशान्तु सिद्धेन मीनाख्येन बरानने।
    कामरूपे महापीठे मच्छन्देन महात्मना। Kashmir Sanskrit Texts and Studies.
27. The only available MS. of *Brahma Yāmala* is dated 1172 (Nepal Saṁvat), *i.e.* A.D. 1052; it is written in Newari. See H.H. Sastri, Nepal Catalogue II, p. 60.
28. *Rājataraṅgiṇī.*
29. *Mālinī Vijaya Vārttika.*
30. One of the oldest Tāntrika MSS. (in Gupta script) discovered is dated A.D. 609. Haraprasad Sastri, 'Report on Sanskrit MSS. 1895-1900', pp. 3 ff, Calcutta, 1901.
31. The well-known Tāntrik scripture *Prapañcasāra* is ascribed to Śaṅkarācārya (published by Woodroffe in *Tantrik Texts*). This work was commented upon by Padmapādācārya who ascribes it to Śaṅkara Bhagavatpādācārya in colophon. (A MS. copy of Padmapādācārya's commentary, showing the final colophon, is in Varendra Research Society, Rājashāhī). As we know only one Śaṅkarācārya who was styled (Bhagavatpāda) and also had a disciple named Padmapādācārya, the authorship of *Prapañcasāra* is to be ascribed to him alone.
    Lakṣmaṇa Deśika has given the names of his ancestors in *Śāradā Tilakam*, paṭal 25, ślokas 86-90. Rājarājeśvari Press, Benaras, 1953. A. Avalon, *Tantrik Texts*, vols. XVI and XVII, paṭal 25, ślokas 83-87.
32. Gopinath Rao, *Elements of Hindu Iconography*, vol. II, pt. II,pp. 361-72.
33. Kashmir Sanskrit Texts and Studies, nos. XIX and XXIV, pp. 1-2. (i) *Janma Maraṇa Vicāra*, (ii) *Amaraṅgha Śāstra*,(iii) *Tantravata-Dhanika.*
34. Illustrations of Śiva Sūtra Vimarśani and Śiva Sūtra-Varttikam by Varadarāja. Kashmir Series of Texts and Studies, no. XCIII. The peak is indicated by an arrow mark.
35. लब्धं महादेवगिरौ महेशस्वप्नोपदिष्टाच्छिवसूत्रसिन्धोः।
    स्पन्दामृतं यद्वसुगुप्तपादैः श्रीकल्लटस्तत् प्रकरोचकर।। *Kashmir Shaivism*, p. 27.
36. Bhāskara, *Śiva Sūtra Vārttika*, pp. 5, 9.
37. *Ibid.*
38. *Kashmir Shaivism*, p. 29. Research & Publication Department, Government of Jammu & Kashmir, Srinagar, 1962.
39. H.P. Shastri, *Nepal Catalogue*, I, p. 255.

40. H.P. Shāstri, *Nepal Catalogue*, I, p. 32.
41. *Ibid.*, p. 236.
42. Published by Motilal Banarsidass & Co., Lahore.
43. *Tantrik Texts*, Luzac & Co., 46, Great Russell Street, London, 1922.
44. चतु:षष्टया तन्त्रैः सकलर्माभसंधाय भुवनं

    स्थितस्तत्तत्सिद्धि प्रसवपरतन्त्रैः पशुपतिः।

    पुनस्त्वन्निर्बन्धादरिबलपुरुषार्थैघटना

    स्वतन्त्रं ते तन्त्रं क्षितितलमतीतरदिदम्।। 3।।

    Saundaryalaharī, p. 60. Cambridge, Massachusetts, Harvard University Press, 1958.
45. T. Gopinath Rao, *Elements of Hindu Iconog,aphy*, vol. 1, pt. I, Introduction, p. 6.
46. 'Journal of the Asiatic Society of Bengal', *Proceedings* 1921, pp. xxi-xxiv.
47. तवस्वतन्त्रं मन्थे धरणिधरकन्येहृददयतः

    पयः पारावारः परिवहति सारस्वत इव।

    दयावत्या दत्तं द्रविडशिशुरास्वाद्यातवयत्

    कविनां प्रौढ़ानामजनि कमनीयः कवयिता।। 75।। *Saundaryalaharī*, p. 78.
48. *Śrī Mṛgendra Tantram*, p. v. Kashmir Series of Texts and Studies, no. L, Srinagar, 1930.
49. Ch. CCXXCIV, Ver. 121-124.
50. *The Cultural Heritage of India* (2nd ed.), vol. IV, pp. 211-12. Ramakrishna Mission Institute of Culture, Calcutta, 1956.
51. *Bhāratīya Saṁskṛti Aur Sādhanā*, p. 1, Bihar Rāṣṭrabhāṣā Pariṣad, Patna, 1963.
52. आगतं शिववक्त्रेभ्यो गतश्च गिरिजानने।

    मतश्च वासुदेवस्य तस्मादागमुच्यते।

    निर्गतं गिरिजावक्त्राद् गतश्च गिरिशश्रुतौ।

    मतश्च वासुदेवस्य तस्मान्निगमुच्यते।।

    Tantras — Studies on their Religion and Literature, p. 2. Punthi Pustak, Calcutta, 1963.
53. *Ibid.*
54. आज्ञावस्तु समन्ताच्च गम्यन इत्यागमो मतः

    तनुते त्रायते नित्यं तन्त्रमित्थं विदुर्बुधाः। H. P. Sastri, *Nepal*, II, p. 69.

2 Tantra and Veda

The evolution of psycho-spiritual philosophy in India is based largely on intuition and mysticism. The irresistible urge for the Beyond is the sheet anchor of the religio-philosophical culture in India. The problems of inner life and the mysteries of the world of becoming and the world of spirit are the *raison d'etre* of philosophical revolution and spiritual renaissance. All Indian philosophical schools are unanimous in their belief that the ultimate Reality is beyond the reach of human words and concepts.[1] The evolution of cult and culture in India is inspired and fed by intuitive vision and subjective realization and not by reason and argument. The orientation to the goal of liberation from the meshes and trammels which connotes total cessation of metempsychosis is both the beginning and the end of the religio-philosophical movement of India.

The original sources of cultural life in India are Tantra and the Veda. When the rest of the world was passing through the dark ages of a barbarian civilization, India was enjoying a most developed and sublime form of cultural life.[2] The cultural heritage of India is to be found primarily in her intuitional science of Tantra and the religio-philosophical schools of the Vedas. Tantra and the Veda are the warp and woof of the cult and culture of India. Tantra is a cult and the Veda a religio-philosophical school. For the development of a robust civilization both spiritual humanism and sublime philosophy are required. There is no doubt that the sources of the philosophical ideas, religious beliefs, social codes lie in the Veda but the spiritual humanism and cult are the discoveries and achievements of pre-Vedic India.

Indian culture has had an extremely long and complex development. It has a longer history of continuous growth than any other living cultural tradition. Historical perspective of cultural tradition is immensely useful in studying and understanding the subterranean cultural spirit of India but it is a very difficult task to present a chronological sequence of the cultural evolution of India. In broad outline, the cultural history of India can be divided into two major periods of development : (i) Tāntric, and (ii) Vedic.

The Tāntric period is dimmed by obscurity but it may be placed approximately between 5000 B.C. and 3000 B.C. This period of Indian culture and civilization is known as pre-historic. The Harappa and Mohenjo-daro civilizations bear the stamp of Tāntric culture. The excavations at Harappa have proved beyond doubt that among the male gods the most remarkable figure is that of the deity Śiva. He has three faces and is seated on a throne with legs crossed in the fashion of a yogi. There are a number of animals such as tiger, buffalo, rhinoceros and deer under the seat.[3] Scholars have regarded him as Lord Śiva for he is described as Trimukha (three-faced), Paśupati (lord of animals) and Mahāyogi (the great ascetic). The idea of three-faced is of great significance. It stands for *Tri-kāladarśī* (knower of past, present and future). The heterogeneous character of the herd of animals signifies the great spiritual power which Śiva possesses and which neutralizes the ferocity of the tiger and renders him harmless even for a deer. He indisputably was a great yogi. Sir John Marshall opines that the huge seal surrounded by four wild animals is proto-Śiva, which has much in common with Śiva of later Hinduism. This rich cultural heritage of India, as described in the words of Prof. Piggot, is 'the unchanging traditions of the temple' and 'not the secular instability of the court.'[4] The prehistoric India had a most developed form of universal religion. The non-Āryans were the first to discover the spiritual cult which makes Tantra the oldest universal religion of the world.

The discovery of the Indus Valley civilization has revolutionized our concept of Indian history and culture. The excavation report has firmly established that the Indus Valley civilization is the oldest living civilization of the world. The indigenous inhabitants of India were highly developed both intellectually and spiritually. And there is no evidence to indicate any affinity between the Indus Valley civilization and the Middle East. A.L. Basham says: 'This great civilization owed little to the Middle East, and there is no reason to believe that it was formed by recent immigrants; the cities were built by people who had probably been in the Indus Valley for several centuries. The Harappa people were already Indians when they planned their cities, and they altered hardly at all for a thousand years.'[5] The most significant feature of the Harappa culture is its inner conservatism.[6] For the survival of any culture some amount of conservatism is essential. Moreover, the conservatism of any great civilization signifies the cultural fullness and richness of the tradition. Only a weak civilization is easily influenced by an alien culture.

We observe that the Tāntric tradition of ancient India contrary to the general belief has greatly influenced the Āryan civilization. This influence can be traced in the Vedic culture. Further, it is generally believed that the Indian culture has its roots in the Vedas. This is not correct. The Vedas are later than Tantras. Recent researches and discoveries have proved this and also that it is wrong to think that the primitive non-Āryans were pagan and uncivilized. On the contrary, many of the sublime forms of religious worship and the concept of deities are of Dravidian origin.[7] The myth of Āryan superiority over the non-Āryans has been exploded by the excavations of the Harappa civilization. When the Āryans (Ārya means cultured) came to India through the North-West Frontier of India, they had contemptuously imposed the name Anārya (uncultured) on the indigenous population. Their misplaced sense of superiority had blinded them to the fact that the native people of India were highly advanced in the fields of philosophy, religion, fine arts and social sciences, which later had a great impact on the Vedic culture of the Āryans.

The Vedas

The Āryans were not the indigenous inhabitants of Bhāratavarṣa whose geographical boundary then was very vast. It encompassed the present Iran (Aranyavraja), Afghanistan (Gāndhāra) and some portion of Asiatic Russia. They came to India from the northern part of Central Asia, their original home. And the Vedas are their greatest contribution. They had, in fact, started the composing of Vedic hymns in their original home. Only the later hymns were composed in India. The *Ṛg-Veda* is supposed to be the most ancient and is considered by European Indologists as a true and only Veda.[8] The hymns of the *Ṛg-Veda* veer round myths and allegories, obscure gropings and immature composings, primitive ceremonials and barbarous propitiatory rites. They are addressed to different manifestations of Nature like Indra, Agni, Varuṇa, etc. But it will be unreasonable to say that all the hymns of the *Ṛg-Veda* are bereft of deep philosophical speculations. We find in the later *Ṛg-Vedic* hymns the speculative transition from the early polytheism to philosophical monotheism and monism. The beginning of rationalization was felt in the *Ṛg-Veda* also. The philosophical doubt is expressed thus: 'Of whom they ask, "where is he", of him indeed they also say, "He is not".'[9]

But the deep philosophical ideas and ideology of the Vedic civilization are the gift of the cultural metamorphosis of the Āryans and non-Āryans. When the Āryans came into contact with the Tāntric Sādhanā of the non-Āryans, exoteric utterances of the Vedic hymns were transformed into esoteric experiences inaccessible to senses and mind. That is why we find in the later hymns a harvest of philosophical richness and subtlety. Sri Aurobindo views: 'Only in the later hymns do we perceive the first appearance of deeper psychological and moral ideas borrowed, some think, from the hostile Dravidian, the "robbers" and "Vedas-haters" freely cursed, in the hymns themselves — and, however acquired, the first seed of the later Vedantic speculations.'[10]

The Āryans had a language but not a script of their own. The Dravidians, on the other hand, had their own script. This explains why the Āryans on coming into contact with the Dravidians wrote the Vedas in the Śāradā script for which they were condemned and cursed, because this was undigestible for the orthodox Āryan mind. The Vedic hymns though inspired are not of divine origin. The Vedas are not the Voice of Providence but are the achievements of human mind, which fathomed the deepest layer of consciousness in the course of deep meditation, an art which they learnt from non-Āryan Tantra. The Vedas were handed down from mouth to mouth from one generation to another from unknown antiquity not because they were taught by God or were themselves revealed to the sages but because the Āryans were profoundly ignorant about the art of writing. The Vedas were called Śruti because they were passed on by one mind to another and not because they were revealed at some unknown period of history at the beginning of each creation. However, the Vedas are considered to be the earliest literary and philosophical monument of the

Indo-Āryan race. It is very difficult to ascertain when they came into existence. Many guesses have been made. Max Müller dates them from 1200 B.C., Hang from 2400 B.C. and Bal Gangadhar Tilak from 4000 B.C.[11] This is speculative and very misleading. For one, all the Four Vedas were not composed at one time or at one place. The *Ṛg-Veda* was composed in Central Asia. It bears the stamp of pure Āryan composition. The *Yajura-Veda* was composed in Aranyavraja (present Iran) and in some part of Asiatic Russia. The influence of Tantra on the Veda starts from the *Yajura-Veda.* The Tāntric tradition and culture greatly influenced the exoteric mind of the Āryan. There is a marked transition, from literature to philosophy, in the composition of the Vedic hymns. The *Ṛg-Veda* speaks about the Āryan sentiment and language. It is a monumental work of literature. Its hymns are famous for their literary grace and poetic depth. The description of dawn (uṣā) is highly suggestive.

The *Yajura-Veda* represents the age of transition. The matter-of-factness of Ṛg-Vāda was transformed into the philosophical monotheism of Brahma-vāda. Philosophy took the place of literature. Speculation subordinated poetic wonderings. The *Yajura-Veda* lays stress on the philosophical speculation and exploration of reality by entering the Beyond that is within, by an ascension of intuition.

The *Atharva-Veda* was composed in the present India. But by that time the Āryans had greatly been influenced by non Āryan Tantra. The racial blending and the cultural metamorphosis had started. In course of time this produced a new healthy and robust civilization, and India reaped the harvest of both cultures, and a new civilization was born. Thus in the *Atharva-Veda* the impact of Tantra Sādhanā is greater than that of the Vedic ritualism. The Āryans were so influenced by the intuitional science of Tāntra that many of them abandoned their ceremonial sacrifices and got initiated into the Tāntric cult. Those (Brahmins) who adopted Tantra were known as Miśras. A large number of them still carry the surname 'Mishra'. This is a clear evidence of the cultural blending of Vedic and Tāntric traditions. P.R. Sarkar says: 'The *Atharva-Veda* was compiled mostly in India and during this period, as a result of their coming in closer contact with the non-Āryans, there emerged a mental or social blending amongst the Āryans who were highly influenced by non-Āryan Tantra. This fact is clearly reflected in the *Atharva-Veda* which cannot be regarded as a picture of Āryan civilization. In the subtle philosophy of the *Atharva-Veda*, particularly in the "Shruti" of Nishingha Tapaniiya, non-Āryan Tantra is more prominent than the Vedic ideal of the Āryan civilization.'[12]

In view of the above we can safely conclude that the philosophical wealth of the Vedas is the product of the cultural blending of Indo-Āryan civilization. And as already said it was due to the influence of intuitional science of Tantra that the teachings of the Vedic hymns became the vehicles more of spiritual illumination than of systematic reflection.

The Śivādvaya school of Tantra philosophy is more comprehensive and coherent than and in a way far superior to the Vedantic school of Advaita. Vedantic Māyāvāda is a negative philosophy. It cannot give any logical explanation of the existence and nature of Māyā and the world of appearance. It declares the world to be an illusion. This is no explanation. The whole world is reduced to illusion. Who is the perceiver of this illusion? Whose projection is this illusion? Certainly it is neither the projection of *jīva* or Īśvara nor of Brahman. But when Brahman is the substratum of all, who except Brahman can be the cause of this original sin. Dr. Gopinath Kaviraj says: 'According to Śaṅkara, Brahman is Truth and Māyā is inexplicable (Anirvacanīya). Hence, the endeavour to show the superiority of Advaita philosophy is turned against its very system. It tarnishes the picture of its philosophical perfection and profundity. He cannot accept Māyā as reality and, therefore, his Advaita becomes exclusive and the whole system is based on renunciation and elimination and is not all embracing. Māyā is the power of Brahman, immanent in Brahman but Brahman is Truth and from the philosophical point of view Māyā is Ṣada-Ṣad-Vilakṣaṇī. And by accepting Māyā as Brahmayī, Nityā and Satyarūpā, Brahman and Māyā (of Tantra) become one and coexistent.'[13] The Śivādvaya of Tantra philosophy means the eternal coexistence of the two (Śiva and Śakti).

Tantra and the Veda are the two aspects of Indian culture. But the impact of Tantra on the life and culture in eastern India is more than in western-northern India. The Āryans called the eastern part as Magadha (मगध) which means the land inhabited by 'Maga'. The word 'Maga' means non-Āryans or those who do not believe in the Veda. The Himālayan region was, therefore, always the choicest abode of Tāntric Sādhakas. That is why the most developed form of the Tāntric school of Kashmir Śaivism originated in Jammu and Kashmir. The impact of the Veda in our socio-religious life is tremendous. There cannot be any ceremony in the Hindu society without the recitation of a Vedic mantra.

Tantra and the Veda are the greatest achievements of Indian culture. They have enriched our socio-spiritual life. The Veda is an idea, Tantra is an ideology. The Veda is a religion, Tantra is a cult. The Veda is a philosophy, Tantra is a science.

Vedic Literature

The word Veda means *jñāna* or spiritual knowledge. The Vedas are called *śruti* not because they are revealed scriptures but because they were handed down from one generation to another by intellectuals who had a photographic memory. It is not *apauruṣeya, i.e.* of divine origin. The great Sāyaṇa has defined it as 'a book which reveals the knowledge of supernatural methods (*alaukika upāya*) for the achievement of the desired object and avoidance of the undesirable'.[14] According to Hindu mythology the real Veda, first revealed by God to the seers, consisted of one hundred thousand verses, and had four divisions. According to the *Viṣṇu Purāṇa,* in the beginning of the Dvāpara Yuga, Kṛṣṇa Dvaipāyana revived the Vedic study and classified the monumental work into four ancient divisions: Ṛg, Yajura, Sama and Atharva. To resuscitate the Vedic literature and give it a proper form, he imparted the teachings of the Veda to his four principal disciples. He taught the *Ṛg-Veda* to Paila, the *Yajura-Veda* to Vaiśampāyana, the *Sāma-Veda* to Jaiminī and the *Atharva-Veda* to Sumanta. And thus Kṛṣṇa Dvaipāyana became known by the name of Veda Vyāsa, the classifier of the Vedas.

The Vedic literature is divided into four great works, *i.e. Ṛg-Veda, Yajura-Veda, Sāma-Veda* and *Atharva-Veda.* Each of these again has four divisions, *viz.* Saṁhitās, Brāhmaṇas, Āraṇyakas and Upaniṣad. The great Vedic commentator Yāska divides the Veda into two, *i.e.* Saṁhitās and Brāhmaṇas. The Āraṇyaka and the Upaniṣad form part of the latter. According to him the Upaniṣads are part of the Āraṇyakas. There are some Vedic scholars who include Kalpa-sūtras also in the body of the Vedic literature. The Saṁhitās and the Brāhmaṇas are loosely called Karma-Kāṇḍa and the Āraṇyakas Upāsanā-Kāṇḍa and the Upaniṣad Jñāna-Kāṇḍa.

The Ṛg-Veda

The *Ṛg-Veda* comprises one thousand and seventeen hymns. It is divided into ten books (*maṇḍals*), and represents the earliest phase of the evolution of literary and religious consciousness of the human mind. Naturalism and anthropomorphism constitute the beginning of Vedic culture. In the first phase of the Vedic thought, we find no trace of religio-philosophical consciousness. The Āryans were pagans. They had no religion. They worshipped Nature out of fear, the force dominating their personalities. They thought that through sacrifices they could influence Nature through gods, of their own creation and representing the different elements, like Indra, Marutas, Vāyu, Agni, Sūrya, Uṣā, etc. They conceived that these gods would be pleased by their ceremonial rites and, in return, shower blessings on them. Thus every Āryan chieftain hired the services of priests to please those gods. J.N. Farquhar, commenting on Ṛg-Vedic people, says: 'Men believed that the sacrifices were mighty to influence the gods and bring down gifts from them. Therefore, every chieftain and noble among the Āryans was eager to secure the help of a skilled priest, and was glad to pay him handsomely for services which brought victory and wealth from the gods.'[15] Almost all the hymns were composed in the praise of different gods who presided over the different elements of Nature. Unlike the Greek gods or the mythical gods of the Purāṇas, the Ṛg-Vedic gods represent the divine powers of Nature. The Ṛg-Vedic deities are neither personal nor impersonal gods. We think that the Āryans of the Ṛg-Vedic age had no conception of God as such. They were simply wonder struck by the cosmic arrangements. Nonetheless the Ṛg-Vedic age was the age of great cultural turmoil when the nomads were being tamed and domesticated by Nature herself. It has rightly been said that, 'It was the forces of nature and her manifestation on earth here, the atmosphere around and above us, or in the Heaven beyond the vault of the sky that excited the devotion and imagination of the Vedic poets. Thus with the exception of a few abstract gods of whom we shall presently speak and some dual divinities, the gods may be roughly classified as the terrestrial, atmospheric and celestial.'[16] The Ṛg-Vedic seers offered prayers to nature gods with awe and reverence. The hymns of the *Ṛg-Veda* are primeval worship.

Indra is the most prominent of gods in the *Ṛg-Veda.* He is primarily a deity of the thunderstorm. He is praised for his power and heroism, and as the god of war. The anthropomorphism of the Ṛg-Vedic hymns is evident. Indra has been extolled as a heroic person who could cut asunder the earth and sky.[17] He has been identified with Sūrya, the Sun-god. He is a deliverer from the darkness.[18]

Indra has been given the most prominent place in the Ṛg-Vedic pantheon as he delivers man from the black hued darkness. The night was the most horrible and was considered to be the nightmare. In that age of twilight of civilization, people were exposed to prey of animals at night. Life was most miserable after sunset.

Uṣās (dawn) is the goddess of the *Ṛg-Veda.* It is evident from the hymns that it is the sense of security and survival which is the motive force behind the native prayers, the ceremonial and the allegorical expressions of Ṛg-Vedic culture. Uṣās has been described as the daughter of sky, lady of the light and giver of wealth and joy.[19]

Sūrya (the Sun-god) is another Ṛg-Vedic deity. He has been described as the shelter of all creatures.[20] Sūrya thwarts the darkness and hence he liberates mankind from the wail of miseries. Agni (the Fire-god) is another deity who occupies a place of distinction in the Vedic pantheon. Here also we find the same yearning for wealth and joy. The *Ṛg-Veda* says that one can obtain wealth and happiness through the worship of Agni.[21]

The Atharva-Veda

The *Atharva-Veda* is a monumental work of Hindu Tantra. Composed in India, it is quite different from the *Ṛg-Veda* both in content and form. The influence of Tantra is felt on every mantra of the *Atharva-Veda.* It gives the whole picture of life. It is not an isolated work of philosophy or religion but deals with the ideal of man's ultimate beatitude, the intuitional science (Vidyā Tantra), witchcraft (Avidyā Tantra), statesmanship, warfare, etc. But due to the influence of Tantra, the orthodox Āryan does not recognize the *Atharva-Veda* as part of the revealed scripture (Śruti).Dayānanda Saraswati, the founder of Ārya Samāj, also condemns it as a heretical literature. The word 'travyi', which is commonly used to signify the Vedic scriptures, denotes that the orthodox section of the Hindus does not recognize the *Atharva-Veda* as the fourth Veda. Pāṇini, the greatest grammarian of India, also supports the orthodox view and describes the Veda as 'trayi'.

The *Atharva-Veda* is a landmark in the history of intuitional science. It is a sacred text. Many of its hymns are benevolent and pregnant with deep philosophy. The content of many of its *mantras* is borrowed from the *Ṛg-Veda* and the *Yajura-Veda,* yet it became the victim of the strong wave of aversion only because it was of non-Āryan origin. It could not escape the blight of contempt because it was a textbook of

Tantrism. An Atharvan has been contemptuously described as 'a lean black man, sharp, irascible, and amorous'.[22]

The *Atharva-Veda* mainly deals with the Tāntric cult, and covers all the branches of Tantrism. Tantra is a science of psychic power. It lays down certain principles and techniques for exploiting the unfathomable potentialities of human mind. Thus, it is double edged. It can be utilized for the betterment of human society but when it falls in the hands of anti-social elements, it becomes dreadful. The class of esoteric formulas designed to establish harmony in family village life, victory in war, development of intellect, reconciliation of enemies and the royal duty (Rāja Karma) are obviously auspicious and sublime in their form and content. Even the class of charms which are meant to cure *takman* (fever)[23] are scientifically dealt with in it. On the basis of Atharvanic literature, we have developed mesmerism, hypnotic suggestion, self-hypnotism, mental healing, etc., which are employed in curing many diseases.

The *Atharva-Veda* is a compendium of Vidyā Tantra, Upa-Vidyā Tantra and Avidyā Tantra. As a work of Vidyā Tantra, it propagates the philosophy of Brahma Vāda. It is said Vaidarbhi, the son of Bhṛgu approached sage Pippalāda and asked: 'What is Brahma Vidyā? What is the relation between Brahman and the world? Do kindly enlighten me on this subject.' In reply, the sage said that the nucleus of the cosmological order is Brahman.[24] Just as the spokes are attached to the nave of a wheel, similarly every object of this cosmo is Brahma-centric. Ṛk, Yaju and Sāma are all dependent on Brahman.

Ṛṣi Pippalāda while throwing light on the mysticism of the *Atharva-Veda* tells Sukeśa, the son of Bhāradvāja, that as the nave of a wheel controls the spokes, similarly Brahman controls all the sixteen basic factors (*kalās*) of the universe. Ten organs (five sensory and five motor), five vital principles or *prāṇaḥ* (Prāṇa, Apāna, Samāna, Udāna and Vyāna) and the ego constitute the sixteen *kalās* — the basic factors of the universe — and are completely dependent on Him. They are the causes of life and death. The Supreme One can be known only through intuition or Prajñā. By knowing Him one bypasses death.

The mysticism of the *Atharva-Veda* is like Bergson's 'open religion'. It is a spiritual stream in whose holiness the Āryan and non-Āryan minds used to take a dip to refresh and restore their divine beings. The esoteric experiences are not to be confused with the instinctive experience. It is not a drift into unreason or obscurity. The mysticism of the *Atharva-Veda* lays stress on the intuitive realization of Brahman, the supreme unification of Self with Brahman, which is the sole objective of Tantra Sādhanā.

Schweitzer also says that 'becoming one with the Infinite is 'a pure act of the spirit which has nothing to do with ethics'.[25] Some of the Atharvans might have been disillusioned by the astounding achievements of a mental voyage. These Atharvans have simply laid down the esoteric process for the unfolding of the hitherto closed mental chamber. But it is up to the Sādhaka to utilize these mental propensities which when utilized for some intellectual or material gain without doing any harm to others are known as Upa-Vidyā Tantra. Most of the charms and sorceries of the *Atharva-Veda* belong to Upa-Vidyā.

The spell blows hot and cold from the same mouth. It is neither moral nor immoral. When it is used against inimical and demoniac forces, it is a moral practice; when the same is employed in inflicting injuries on noble souls, it is condemned. The *Atharva-Veda* takes this view. Hymn II.12.[26] stops the bitterest enemy who tries to thwart the holy sacraments. But at the same time it does not prevent anybody from frustrating the evil designs of an enemy (VII.70.). Hymn II.7. promises protection against curses and sinister plottings.

Yātu Vidyā (esoteric practices) of the *Atharva-Veda* was very popular among the non-Āryans. Many Āryans also were enamoured of this Vidyā and could not resist getting themselves initiated in this cult. But they were cursed and condemned. The orthodox Āryans, in fact, condemned everything non-Āryan. Yātu Vidyā was also condemned. The *Ṛg-Veda* (VII,104,15,16) says: 'May I die today if I am a sorcerer.' Here Tantra is declared as devilish, yet, in response to their conscience, the Āryans, at one time, had to recognize the greatness of Yātu Vidyā. In *Śat. Br.* (X,5,2,20) Tantra was accepted in principle as one of the holiest forms of literature. 'Those skilled in sorcery' were given an honourable place. But the hatred of the Āryans was so deep seated that they were not ready to accept even *bheṣajam* (the science of medicine) as it belonged to the altruistic province of the Atharvan. It could not escape the blight of sneer. The *Tait S.*, V1,4,9,3 (cf. *Maitr S.*, IV,5,2; *Śat. Br.*, IV,15,14) says, "a Brahman shall not practise medicine."[27] The non-Āryans were advanced in the field of physical and intuitional sciences. The Atharvans have always kept contact with the depths. They were never satisfied with the superficial life. They were aware of Tantra Sādhanā (Yātu Vidyā) and knew that the fountain of life, from which the creative instincts sprang forth, was not psyche but Self. Man is a spiritual being. He becomes truly human only when his intuitive self is awakened. So long as his life is confined to Vedic rites and sacradotal ceremonies, his life is incomplete and insipid. The Vedic rituals might have some social value, but they are the sign of spiritual homelessness. Only ascension to consciousness could bring the realization of total being. According to Tantra there is no salvation by proxy. But Vedic rituals can be performed by hired priests (who gradually became professionals and social parasites). But there was no scope for priesthood in Tāntric culture. The Brahmanical literature naturally, therefore, started a tirade against Tāntric tradition.

Nārāyaṇīya Tantra says that the Vedas have been originated from the Yāmalas, authoritative works of Tāntric literature. According to it the *Sāma-Veda* has been originated from *Brahma Yāmala* and the *Ṛg-Veda* from *Rudra Yāmala.* The *Yajura-Veda* reflects *Viṣṇu Yāmala* and the *Atharva-Veda Śakti Yāmala.* The verses, referred to by the great Siddha Sarvananda in his compendium called *Sarvallāsa Tantra* are a clear evidence that Tantra preceded the Vedas.

To our view neither the Vedas have been originated from Tantra nor the latter forms part of Vedic exegesis. Śrī Gauḍapāda has written another Tāntric text named *Śrī-Vidyā Ratna Sūtra* to propagate the mysticism of the Śrī Vidyā cult.[28] *Prapaṁcasāra* is also ascribed to Śrī Śaṅkarācārya. Rāghava Bhaṭṭa in his commentary on *Śāradā Tilaka* has also supported this view.

Śrī Vidyārṇava[29] gives a detailed account of the hierarchy of Guru and disciples of Śrī Śaṅkarācārya. It is a Tāntric literature belonging to the Śāktāgama school. According to this book Śaṅkarācārya was not a grand disciple of Gauḍapāda. In between Gauḍapāda and Śaṅkara, there were five *ācāryas.* The names of the seven *ācāryas* are given in the following order: Gauḍapāda, Pāvaka, Parācārya, Satyanidhi, Rāmacandra, Govind and Śaṅkarācārya.

On the basis of available research material it can be safely concluded that Śaṅkarācārya was a great admirer and follower of *Tantra Śāstra.* The mystic power that he had cannot be achieved through the Vedantic method. Śaṅkarācārya has displayed occult power to defeat his adversaries on many occasions. This power can be achieved only through Śakti Sādhanā. Śaṅkara was a profound devotee of the Śrī Vidyā cult, Śrī-Cakra is still being worshipped in his Śṛṅgerī Muṭṭa. Dr. Gopinath Kaviraj is of the opinion that Śaṅkarācārya will have to be recognized as one of the greatest exponents of the Tripurāgama branch of the Śākta school.[30]

The Veda is a religio-philosophical system. Tantra is a science of religion and philosophy of science. Tantra does not believe in the lifeless Vedic rituals. Truth cannot be attained through the exercise of intellect. Tantra is Sādhanā. It is reduced to esotericism and *siddhi* or realization attained as an experimentally verified fact. There is a famous story about Maharṣi Śāṇḍilya, who studied the whole of Vedic literature but could not attain salvation. After this he went through the literature of the Pañcarātra School of Vaiṣṇava Tantra and performed Sādhanā according to the Pañcarātra system and attained enlightenment.

REFERENCES

1. यतो वाचो निर्वतन्ते अप्राप्य मनसा सह। *Taittirīya Upaniṣad, 11.4.1.*
2. *The Wonder That Was India,* pp. 4-9, Sidgwick and Jackson, London, 1956.
3. *Ibid.*, p. 22.
4. *Pre-Historic India,* p. 155. Harmondsworth, 1950.
5. *Ibid.*, p. 15.
6. *Ibid.*
7. *Ancient India,* p. 19.
8. Sri Aurobindo, *On the Veda,* p. 4. International University Centre, Pondicherry, 1956.
9. *Ṛg-Veda,* II. 12, *A Source Book in Indian Philosophy,* p. 4.
10. *On the Veda,* p. 3.
11. *A History of Indian Philosophy,* vol. I, p. 10.

12. *Cosmic Society — An Anthology*, p. 16. Renaissance Universal Publication, New Delhi, 1967.
13. *Bhāratiya Saṁskṛti aur Sādhanā*, vol. I, p. 5.
14. *Black Yajura-Veda.*
15. *Outline of Religious Literature of India* (2nd ed.), p. 7.
16. *A History of Indian Philosophy*, vol. I, p. 17.
17. 'I will extol the most heroic Indra who with his might forced earth and sky asunder.'— R. T. H. Griffith, *Hymns of the Ṛg-Veda* (3rd ed.), p.x.89. E. J. Lazarus & Co., 1920-26.
18. 'Sūrya is he : throughout the wide expanses shall Indra turn him, swift as car-wheels, hither, like a stream resting not but ever active : he hath destroyed with light the black-hued darkness.' — *Ibid.*
19. 'Dawn on its with prosperity, O Uṣās, daughter of the sky. Dawn with great glory, goddess, lady of the light, dawn thou with riches, bounteous on'— *Ibid.*, 1.48.
20. 'Aloft as beams now bring the god who knows all creatures that are born, That all may look upon the Sun.'— A. A. Macdonell, *Hymns from the Ṛgveda*, p. 150. Oxford University Press, London, 1922.
21. (i) 'Agni, worthy to be magnified by the ancient ṛṣis and by the present ones, may he conduct the gods hither'.

    (ii) 'May one obtain through Agni wealth and welfare day by day, which may bring glory and high bliss of valiant offspring.'— Hermann Oldenberg, *Sacred Books of the East XLVI*, Vedic Hymns, part II, p. 2. Clarendon Press, Oxford, 1897.
22. Rajendralal Mitra, *Gopatha-Brāhmaṇa*, introduction, p. 4.
23. *Hymns of the Atharva-Veda*, p. 1.
24. अराइव रथनाभो कला यस्मिन् प्रतिष्ठिति।
    त्वं वैद्यं पुरुषं वेद यथा मा मृत्यु परिव्यथः।। *Atharva-Veda.*
25. S. Radhakrishnan, *Eastern Religion and Western Thought* (2nd ed.), p. 95. Oxford University Press, 1940.
26. *Atharva-Veda.*
27. ब्राह्मणेन भेषजम न कार्यम्। *Atharva-Veda.*
28. *Tripura Rahasya*, p. xi.
29. The manuscript of this book is lying at the famous temple of Raghunath at Jammu. See Steins catalogue of Raghunath Temple Library.
30. *Bhāratiya Saṁskṛti aur Sādhanā*, vol. 1, pp. 13, 115.

3 Buddhist Tantra and Hindu Tantra

Buddhist Tantra is mystic Sādhanā which brings the realization of the Supreme God, where Prajñā (Pure Wisdom) and Upāya (Incomprehensible Activity) are one, undivided and indivisible whole. The Absolute is described in Hindu Tantra as Parama Śiva and in Buddhist Tantra as Bodhi-Sattva or Vajra-Sattva, which are free from all categories of existence and non-existence. In the words of Dr. Gopinath Kaviraj: 'This ideal is described in one word as *Samarasya*, which implied obliteration of all traces of all kinds of existing differences, not by a process of transcendence as in Sāṁkhya or of sublation as in Vedantic Māyāvāda but by a positive process of what may be described as mutual interpenetration.'[1]

Vajra-Sattva is the Supreme Being. According to Buddhist Tāntric practices, salutation is offered to this Lord Supreme in the same way as Hindu Tantra offers oblation to Parama Śiva. There is no difference between Vajra-Sattva and Parama Śiva.

The Vajrayāna school of Buddhist Tantra conceives the Self as a transcendental being. The Absolute is both transcendental and immanent. The attainment of Nirvāṇa means the mystic unification of Prajñā and Upāya. According to Vajrayāna the realization of Vajra-Sattva means the realization of Śūnyatā in its pure nature, which is the cause of all existence and being. Śūnyatā of Śūyavādin is the same as the Brahman of Brahmavādin. The moment a Sādhaka attains this state of Bodhi-Sattva, he is called Arhat. According to Jñāna-Siddhi our Bodhi-intuition, which is of the nature of Vajra, is itself the Buddhahood; hence Buddhahood can be realized by one who conceives all things as the Self.[2] In such a state of spiritual enlightenment a man becomes one with the Cosmos and realizes himself in all things, everywhere, in all aspects, Eternal, Omniscient and Universal Self.[3]

Like Brahman, Vajra-Sattva is the noumenal cause of the phenomenal existence and the Ultimate Principle as the unity of the universe. Vajra means Śūnyatā and Sattva stands for pure knowledge and the identity of the two follows from the nature of Vajra-Sattva. Śūnyatā is Vajra, and all manifestation in form is Sattva, and Vajra-Sattva implies the unity and identity of the two. Vajra-Sattva is the Abhūtaparikalpa of Vijñānavādins, when both Śūnyatā and the manifest world remain unified and identical.

A close study of Buddhist Tantra removes many a doubt about Buddhist philosophy. Buddhism is a way of life. It was never confined to ethics only. It is primarily a cult which was employed for swimming across the stormy sea of existence.

Sādhanā is a raft with the help of which one can cross the ocean of existence which is full of snares of false subjectivity.

Vajrayāna is rightly characterized as the Divine path. It is unity of all religions. The cult of Vajrayāna is most secret. It is a religion of non-substantiality and purity. It is one without second.[4]

Vajrayāna harmonizes monism and dualism. Its central objective is to grant salvation to *jīva*, who is wrapped in subjective illusion or nescience, and to bring about the realization of monistic truth. It opens the door of divine effulgence by changing duality into unity. And thus a Sādhaka feels and enjoys the divine play of Prajñā who is the spouse of Upāya. Prajñā and Upāya are anthropomorphically portrayed as an ideal married couple. They are ever together in the cosmic *uṣanisakamal.* In Hindu Tantra *uṣanisakamal* is called *sahasrāra.*

Sahasrāra or the penial gland is said to be the abode of Śiva and the lowest Mūlādhāra Cakra is said to be the seat of Śakti — generally known as *Kulakuṇḍalinī.* This lower region where the Serpent Power is sleeping is known to be the region of *pravṛtti* while the higher region of pure intuition is called the region of *nivṛtti.* Tantra Sādhanā consists in awakening the dormant divinity residing in the region of *pravṛtti.* It unites the self with Śiva residing in the region of *nivṛtti* which results in the attainment of the Supreme Bliss. *Gandharvamālika* says: 'Sahasrāra is the beautiful and auspicious place of Sadā Śiva. It is free from sorrow and divinely beautiful with trees which always bear and are adorned by flowers and fruits. The Kalpa tree adds to its beauty. This tree contains all the fine elements and is possessed of the three *guṇas.* The four Vedas are its four branches. It is laden with beautiful unfading, flowers which are yellow, white, black, red, green, and of variegated colour. Having meditated on the Kalpa tree in this manner, then meditate upon the jewelled altar below it. O Beauteous One, on it is a beautiful bed adorned with various kinds of cloth and mandāra flowers and scented with many kinds of scents. It is there that Mahādeva constantly stays. Meditate upon Sadā Śiva, who is like the purest crystal, adorned with all kinds of gems, long armed, and of enchanting beauty. He is ever gracious and smiling. In His ears are ear-rings, and a chain of gems goes round His neck. A garland of a thousand lotuses resting on His neck adorns His body. He has eight arms and three eyes like the petals of the lotus. On His two feet He wears twinkling toe ornaments, and His body is Śabda-Brahma. O lotus eyed one, meditate thus on Him. He is the quiescent, corpse-like Deva within the Lotus who is void of all action.'[5]

It is said when the *Kuṇḍalinī* awakens and embraces Parama Śiva residing in *sahasrāra* it drinks the penial nectar. It then returns from the eternal bliss. This state of eternal bliss can be attained only by a Sādhaka who is adept in Yama and Niyama Sādhanā, and with the grace of a Dikṣā Guru (spiritual teacher).[6]

The Sādhaka, who has attained the unification of *jīva* with Śiva, leads a normal life and remains unsoiled even though living in the mud of worldly existence. His mind is not swayed by the material objects.

In Buddhist Tantra, it is said that when Prajñā or Śūnyatā commingles with universal compassion, *karuṇā*, it is called Bodhicitta — perfect wisdom. It is a general belief that Vajra-Sattva eternally coexists with his consort known as Vajra Vārāhi, and Prajñā-pāramitā.

Vajra-Sattva is the metaphysical absolute of Buddhism and the Supreme Lord of Buddhist Tantra. It is the collective name of Śūnyatā and Karuṇā, and is known as Hevajra and Heruka.

According to the Citta-viśuddhi-prakaraṇa the pure and perfect wisdom is the product of the union of Prajñā and Upāya as the fire, which is pure in the beginning, in the middle and in the end and which illumines everything, is the product of two logs of wood rubbed together. Similarly Dharma-dhātu, which extinguishes the fire of both pleasure and pain, can be obtained only by a proper churning of the milk of Prajñā and Upāya.

Prajñā and Upāya

Suzaki traces the concept of Prajñā and Upāya to the time of Aśvaghoṣa. He says that Enlightenment has two attributes: (i) Pure Wisdom (Prajñā), and (ii) Incomprehensible Activity (Upāya or Karuṇā). Nāgārjuna has also used the word *upāya* for *karuṇā*.[7]

Prajñā stands for perfect knowledge which liberates an individual mind from the miseries and torments of life and removes the veil of ignorance; *karuṇā*, a strong emotion of deep compassion, is a dynamic force, a source of human inspiration, which compels one to live and die for the suffering mankind. This spiritual awakening prompts, guides and leads to mystic oneness which is a state of wisdom and liberation. Prajñā has been conceived as a passive force. That is why one has to take the help of Upāya for the realization of salvation. In Śākta and Vaiṣṇava Tantra, Śiva is conceived as a passive being and Śakti as an omni-active force. Śakti is the immanent principle of Śiva. Surprisingly enough when Śiva is recognized anthropomorphically as the husband, and Śakti as the wife, and they are amorously sporting in Śrī-cakra[8] or in Sahasrāra, it has been said that a man who is submerged in the ocean of rebirth can escape from this bondage only with the aid of Devī. The cause of the misunderstanding is the mistaken conception of the *Kuṇḍalinī*. The *Kuṇḍalinī* has been wrongly identified with *Prakṛti*. The greatest difficulty as regards the meaning and understanding of the different words and symbolism of Tantra is that they carry more than one meaning. In the Tāntric cult sometimes misleading words have been used so that only those who have insight and foresight can understand the real meaning and spirit of the different symbols used in Tantra.

The cardinal principle of Tantra is the unification of Prajñā and Upāya from both metaphysical and esoteric points of view. The fundamental basis of the Buddhistic Trinity — Buddha, Dhamma and Saṅgha — is that *citta* can shine and enjoy the Supreme Bliss only when Prajñā and Upāya are united, which is really a state of non-duality from the logical point of view of Tattva and Tattvatitta, *i.e.* the One and the Beyond.

Some scholars think that Nāgārjuna, the founder of the Mādhyamika school, is the real exponent of the Buddhist esotericism. There is a general belief that he was initiated into the Tāntric cult, Buddha Vairocana, with the grace of Bodhi-Sattva at the 'iron tower', in South India. But, according to a Tibetan account, Nāgārjuna was imparted Tāntric Sādhanā by Siddhācārya Sarahapāda and he attained *Vajrakāya Siddhi.*[9]

To our view it is the Buddha himself who is the founder of Tāntrism in Buddhism. It is said when Siddhārtha was moving about in Bihar in search of Truth, he met Sañjaya, a great Tantrist, near present Gaya and was initiated by him into Tantra Sādhanā. Further it is a well known fact that Tantra is performed in a cremation ground or a lonely place. And when it is performed under a *kula*-tree, the progress is accelerated. According to the accepted Tāntric belief and usage, the banyan tree is one of the five trees recognized as *kula*-trees. It is, therefore, not without any reason that Siddhārtha performed his Sādhanā under the famous banyan tree at Bodha Gaya and attained spiritual enlightenment (Buddhahood).

This is further confirmed by the characteristic occult power which the Buddha obtained along with *Parinirvāṇa* which is manifestly of Tāntric origin. Also Tantra Sādhanā is kept secret, and is imparted only to its rightful claimant. Obviously, therefore, it was due to this reason that the Buddha maintained mystic silence. It is said that the Buddha himself practised *āsphānaka-yoga*[10] (yoga of psychic expansion) when he was in search of the Eternal Truth. The *Vinaya Piṭaka*[11] says that the Buddha's own disciple Bharadvāja rose into the air and brought down the begging bowl which was held high above by Seṭṭhi. Dr. B. Bhattacharya says: 'Buddha recognized the *ṛddhis* or supernatural powers and mentioned four *iddhipadas*[12] conducive to the attainment of supernatural powers.'[13] But, the Buddha warned his disciples against any wanton display or misuse of the occult power gained in the course of its practice.

This is further supported by the concept of Bodhi-maṇḍala or the mystic circle round tide famous tree beneath which the Buddha practised meditation and attained *bodhi.* This belief and cult of Bodhi-maṇḍala is a necessary practice to draw circles or other mystic diagrams in a place selected for meditational Sādhanā. The *maṇḍala* of Buddhist Tantra is nothing but Yantra of Hindu Tantra. 'Even the formulas of refuge and worship, which were current at all times and in all the countries of Therevāda Buddhism, possess a mantric character. Their perfect parallelism of sound, rhythm and idea, their concentration on the highest symbols, like Buddha, Dhamma, Saṁgha, and their underlying devotional attitude, in which Saddhā (devotion) and Metta (love) occupy the first place, make their *mantras* in the best sense. That their formal expression is as important as their idea is emphasized by their threefold repetition and by the fact that some of these formulas are repeated twice three times with a slightly different pronunciation within one and the same ceremony (be it *pūjā, paritta, upasampadā, patimokkha* recitals or at similar occasions) in order to be sure of the proper form, the proper reproduction of the sound symbol, which is sanctified by tradition and, therefore, charged with psychic power.'[14]

Mantra, Mūdrā and Maṇḍala (Yantra) are the basis of Buddhist Tantra Sādhanā from its very inception and thus a new introduction was made to revise and resuscitate the lost science of Tantra by the Buddha.

Forms of Buddhistic Tantra Sādhanā

There is a controversy regarding the founder of Buddhist Tantra. According to traditional belief Asaṅga, the advocate of the Yogācāra school, is the exponent of 'Tantrism in Buddhism. In *Mahāyāna-Sūtra-laṅkāra* of Asaṅga, there is a clear evidence of and reference to Tantrism. But there is great confusion over the word *paravṛtti.* According to some scholars, 'in the *paravṛtti* of sexual union supreme greatness is obtained'. Sylvian Lévi suggests that '*paravṛtti* of sexual act' means 'the mystic coupling of Buddhas and Bodhi-Sattvas' which have much importance in Tantrism. Dr. P.C. Bagchi is of the opinion that the Tāntric sexo-yogic practice means the enjoyment of bliss similar to that arising from the sexual act-which is evident in *Sūtra-laṅkāra* itself.[15] He seems to be correct and we find that the word Ātma-rati is profusely used to convey the intensity of enjoyment which one experiences at the time of the unification of finite mind with the Infinite Self. The Buddha revolted against the traditional rituals and religiosity of the Brahmanical school. He denounced the Vedic rituals as useless and a time-killing process and the chanting of Vedic verses without understanding as a fruitless labour.

Dr. S. Radhakrishnan says: 'Buddha does not like the idea of basing the reality of Brahman on Vedic authority, for whom once we admit the evidence of revelation, there is no end to it. So in the Tevijja Sutta, Buddha compares those who believe in Brahman on the authority of the Vedas and seek union with Him to those who build a staircase at the junction of four roads to mount up to a high mansion as to which they can neither see nor know whether it exists at all.'[16] But it is certainly not the ethical obsession of the Buddha which is responsible for his indefiniteness on metaphysical problems. The Buddha had a firm faith in meditation. His conviction of barrenness of intellectual flapping of wings in the vacuum prevented him from becoming a metaphysician.

The dormant divinity when awakened with the ideation and incantation of *mantra* opens the gate of *bhūmi* (consciousness). This divine power is known in Buddhist Tantra, as Herukā, Vajra-Tārā, Vajra-yoginī, Vajra-caṇḍikā. Herukā is known in Hindu Tantra as *Kulakuṇḍalinī.*

There are three chief forms of Buddhist Tantra,[17] *i.e.* Vajra-yāna, Kālacakra-yāna and Sahaja-yāna. According to Tattva-ratnāvalī (collected in the Advaya-Vajra-Saṁgraha) Mahā-yāna has been divided into Pāramitā-naya and Mantra-naya. We find that Buddhism was divided into Mahā-yāna and Hīna-yāna on the acceptance of Tantrism. Those who are satisfied with the theoretical aspect and lack courage and determination are declared Hīna-yāna which means 'a sect of inferior ideology'. Mahā-yāna is decidedly the superior and sublime form of Buddhism.

Mantra-Yāna

Mantra-yāna is a science of psychic power. Its principles are accessible only to persons of higher intellectual calibre and spiritual bent of mind who can understand and appreciate the esoteric doctrine of *mantra-śāstra,* a priceless treasure of Tāntricism. According to *Gāyatrī-Tantra,* 'that is called Mantra, by the meditation (*manana*) on which the *jīva* acquires freedom from sin, enjoyment of heaven and liberation and by the aid of which he attains in full the fourfold fruit (*Caturvarga*).'[18] Mantra Sādhanā is an essential part of the ethical and spiritual discipline. Like Hindu Tantra, Mantra-yāna is the cornerstone of Buddhist Tantra. It is the most powerful way to create an ideational climate and awaken the dormant Divinity.

The world is a seething mass of forces. It is left to the human ingenuity to discover the secret technique for their progressive utilization. When the surging currents of a mighty river are captured in the arms of a hydro-electric plant, several megawatts of electricity is produced. In the present scientific age we can catch and transmit a vibration from one end of the solar system to its other end if our instrument is sophisticated. Similarly, through Sādhanā mind is sharpened and made subtler with the help of ideation and meditation of *mantra.* It makes an individual consciousness eligible for stepping into the Kingdom of Divinity. According to Buddhist Tantra the finite mind, with the help of Mantra-yāna, links up with the Infinite Vajra-Sattva. Mantra-yāna not only awakens a Sādhaka to his inner spiritual wealth of Bodhi-Sattva, which ordinarily remains unperceived instead of being caught and harnessed, but it ushers in an unfoldment of the Divine.

The concept of *bīja-mantra* is also found in Buddhist Tantra. It is a mono-syllabic *mantra* and stands for different manifestations commonly known as Devatā. *A* (अ) is the *bīja mantra* of creation which is represented in Buddhism by Vairocana. *Ba* (ब) is the *bīja-mantra* of Dharma which represents here Amitābha. Being the first letter and the *bīja mantra* of creation, *A* (अ) is said to be the representative of Śūnyatā or Prajñā. The letter *A* is an indeterminate letter. In the Mahāsukhaprakāśa of the Advaya-Vajra-Saṁgraha it has been said that the *bīja* proceeds from Śūnyatā knowledge, and from the *bīja* is produced the reflection or the form of particular gods and goddesses.[19] Dr. Benayatosh Bhattacharya has given the history of *bīja-mantra.*[20] In the Mantra-paṭala of *Hevajra Tantra* we find that the *bīja-mantra* of Tathāgata is *oṁ ḥa huṁ phaṭ svāhā*; that of the goddess, *krūm aṁ jiṁ khaṁ huṁ,* and that of Heruka, *taṁ maṁ paṁ taṁ baṁ oṁ deva picuvajre huṁ huṁ huṁ phaṭ svāhā.*[21]

According to Vasubandhu the real significance of a *mantra* lies in its being meaningless,[22] the constant meditation of which brings the realisation of the absolute void or Śūnyatā. Here meaningless means non-understanding of the esoteric significance of the *mantra*, for the common man. But, for a Sādhaka *mantras*, which stand for the deeper and richer significance of Tantrism, are highly meaningful. Mere repetition of a *mantra* cannot bring any fruitful result. When repetition or meditation (*japa*) of a *mantra* is coupled with ideation it gives the desired result. The meditational form of a *mantra* is rhythmic and ideational. It starts with a single note and develops into chord and symphony. When the musical vibration created by the *mantra-jap* becomes one with the inner cosmic vibration, man hears the hitherto unheard sound of Praṇava and sees the unseen effulgence of Vajra-Sattva. He is lost into the utter state of motionlessness, the tranquil void which is the origin of all waves and vibrations. The process of repetition of a *mantra* is not mechanical. When a *mantra* is rehearsed over and over again with the ideation of God it produces the spiritual condition essential for the ascent of consciousness. After a long practice and devotion, the meditation of a *mantra* can be perfected and mastered. The *mantra* is not to be read and re-read or to be recited without any esoteric and ethical discipline but it is to be worked out and every *devatā* must be made a living *devatā*. The potential power of a *mantra* is made kinetic when it is vivified and drenched with consciousness and incantation. With the incantation of a *mantra*, mind becomes pure and sublime, and the Sādhaka penetrates into the mystic and richer realm of consciousness and is united with the Bodhi-citta. John Van Manen has rightly observed: 'I do not know of any literature which in its nature is so absolutely symphonic, so directly akin to music, as this, as this sample of a Tibetan meditational exercise.'[23]

We find an elaborate and scientific arrangement and method laid down for the worship of deities, *mudrā* (pose) and *maṇḍala* (mystic diagram) in *Mañjūśrī-mūlakalpa*, a stupendous work of Mantra-yāna. The Mūlakalpa is said to be the basis of Guhyasamāja Tantra. According to scholars of Buddhism, this Tantra is the product of the first century A.D.

Buddhist Tantra has also adopted the Hindu element of *mudrā* which is used to express different esoteric and subtler ideas and ideologies. The word *mudrā* is sometimes used in the sense of Mahāmudrā which is Prajñā or the great woman to be adopted in the yogic practice, not for libidinous phallic necromancy but for the sublimation and conquest of the sex instinct.

Spiritual waves or divine vibrations are sent forth for the benefit of disciples and people in general by those who have attained liberation. These waves, which emanate from the Siddhas, Seers and Arhatas, are of untold help for the beginners and Sādhakas. The Buddha himself has employed different *mudrās* to shower blessings and benediction on his disciples. His Varabhaya Mudrā, Dharma-cakra-paribarttana Mudrā, Bhūmisparśa Mudrā, etc., are not only very popular but are of immense mystic importance. In both Hindu and Buddhist Tantra, Varābhaya Mudrā is of great importance; with its help Ādi Buddha and Ādi Śiva shower blessings on their disciples.

Vajra-Yāna

Like Hindu Tantra, Buddhist Tantra has been wrongly stigmatized as a sexo-yogic practice. Grünwedel, writing about Tibetan Tantra, says: 'To work out these things will be, indeed, a *sacrificium intellectus,* but they are, after all, no more stupid than the Brāhmaṇas on which so much labour has been spent.'[24] Waddell writes: 'In the tenth century A.D., the Tāntrika phase developed in Northern India, Kashmir and Nepal into the monstrous and poly-demonic doctrine, the Kāla-cakra, with its demonical Buddha, which incorporated the Mantra-yāna practices, and called itself the Vajra-yāna or the Thunderbolt-Vehicle, and its followers were known as Vajrācārya or followers of the Thunderbolt.'[25]

Vajra-yāna which is the most scientific and positive approach to spiritual awakening and enlightenment, was misunderstood due to the exhibition and misuse of occult powers by some degenerate disciples like Avidyā Sādhakas of Hindu Tantra. That is why the Buddha put so much emphasis on the strict observance of *śīla* (ethical norms). Śīla is not the *summum bonum* of life, but a stepping stone to the realization of Buddhahood, with the help of Vajra-yāna It is the backbone of Tantra. Adherence to this supreme moralism is fundamental; its neglect must result in catastrophic repercussions on the Bodhi-sattva.

Mañjūśrī-mūlakalpa and *Guhyasamāja* are the earliest canonical literature on Tāntric Buddhism. Apart from the method of worship of *mudrās* (facial and finger expressions), *maṇḍalas* (mystic diagrams) and *mantras* (mystic spells), *Mañjūśrī-mūlakalpa* lays down the ethical disciplines, to be strictly practised, like *Śīla* (moralism), *Caryās* (do's of the disciple), *Kriyā* (rites), *Vrata* (vows), *Śaucācāra* (cleanliness in acts), *Niyama* (regulation of mind), *Japa* (incantation) and *Dhyāna* (meditation). *Guhyasamāja* deals with yoga (ordinary esoteric practice) and *anuttarayoga* (Tāntric forms of Sādhanā).

Like *Mahānirvāṇa Tantra, Guhyasamāja Tantra*[26] also believes in the happy blending of spiritual and physical existence. A man cannot achieve the state of Supreme Blessedness or Buddhahood by starving his senses and desires. *Nirvāṇa* cannot be achieved by subjecting the mind and body to suffering; or by keeping aloof from all worldly enjoyments. It views that emancipation can be obtained by satisfying the unfulfilled wishes and thereby exhausting them and not through processes which are painful and difficult. It echoes the voice of Tathāgata. The Buddha is against penance and physical suffering.

Vajra-yāna is, however, not the Thunderbolt-Vehicle. Vajra stands for Śūnyatā, which means that which is indestructible, which undergoes no change, *i.e.* which is eternal. The Reality is called Śūnyatā because it is beyond the dualism of subject and object. It is beyond the reach of the senses and mind. Yāna means path. However, Śūnyatā of Vajra-yāna is quite different from the Śūnya of the Madhyamikas (nihilist) or the Vijñānavādins (dialecticians) which is based on negativism and is opposed to any positive philosophy. The philosophy of both the nihilist and the Vijñānavādins is denial of all existence and non-existence and if we apply the same tenets to them, then they stand as philosophies denied by themselves. Whereas the Śūnyatā of Vajra-yāna includes three principles, *viz.* Reality Śūnyatā Consciousness (Vijñāna) and Bliss (Mahā-sukha).

Guhyasamāja Tantra, which is recognized by some scholars as the Bible of Buddhist Tantra, lays down a fourfold method (*upāya*) for the realization of Vajra-Sattva and deities, namely, Sevā, Upasādhanā, Sādhanā and Mahā-sādhanā. The *uttama sevā yoga* includes *pratyāhāra, dhyāna, prāṇāyāma, dhāraṇā, anusmṛti* and *samādhi*. These are the same that have been professed by Hindu Tantra. The realization of Śūnyatā or Vajra-Sattva is the supreme ideal of Vajra-yāna All the deities are an expression of Sūnyatā.[27] The different manifestations are only the unfoldment or externalization of Śūnyatā. Everything from *bīja*, deity to the crude manifest world issues from Śūnyatā. The process of evolution is that of dependent origination.

Sādhanā is a process of psychic transformation of a deity into the spiritual being. The conception of different godheads is the spiritual realization of different aspects of Vajra-Sattva. Sādhanā should be practised in solitude. When a Sādhaka enters the higher spheres of the Conscious in his deep meditation, he forgets about the physical existence but remains awakened and alive about the inner world of Vajra-Sattva. In the life of a devoted and determined soul, a stage comes during the course of meditational practice when his *bodhicitta* achieves unification with the Infinite Consciousness, and lie is amazed to visualize the stupendous beauty of the sparkling *bījākṣara. Guhyasamāja Tantra*[28] has given a detailed description of the inner vision that Sādhakas have had in their deep meditation. However, we like to remove some doubts and misunderstandings regarding the dreadful visions and the mystic experiences associated with deities. There is no such deity like demoniac Buddha or ghost. However, the question arises why some Sādhakas have two visions of deities, one benign and the other ferocious. These are subjective experiences and the projection of one's own inner psyche. Environment plays an important role in the making of a man. One gathers impressions or beliefs, both good and bad, according to the time and clime, and mentally superimposes them. These superimpositions are the important factors in the formation of the mental health and image of a man. Sādhanā helps him clean his mind of all the dirt of his past actions; not even a trace is left. The visions of benign and dreadful deities disappear since they are nothing but the thought projections of one's own mind. At this stage, the Sādhaka becomes free from the bondage of past actions, *Karma*, and realizes Buddhahood.

The individual soul is called Bodhi-citta and the Transcendental Self is known as Śūnyatā or Vajra-Sattva. Under the veil of ignorance a Bodhi-citta is a finite being like Jīvātman of Hinduism. The Bodhi-citta is Infinite in his transcendental aspect. The realization of the transcendental nature of the Bodhi-citta is called *Nirvāṇa*.

Due to the apparent nature of finitude worship of different deities is prescribed. When a Bodhi-citta goes into deep meditation his experiences vary according to his own individual nature and mental disposition, according to the reactions of his psychic power which manifest in the different deities. This is the psychological cause of a large number of deities in the pantheons of both Buddhist and Hindu Tantra.

Mantras (mystic syllables) are the basis of Vajra-yāna. They are pregnant with great psychic powers and can confer Mokṣa or Buddhahood on the meditators. The mystic syllables or *mantras* are made living with the constant repetition which leads to the mystic experience of the deity. When *mantras* are dynamized they create an acoustic vibration which commingles with Absolute Śūnyatā. It generates spiritual waves which are perceived by the meditators as different deities according to their own mental disposition. The deities have no objective existence, nor are they the imaginative flights of superstitious minds. They are the creation of acoustic vibrations.

Śakti-Tattva in Buddhist Tantra

Śiva and Śakti are inseparable in Tantra. Śakti is the immanent principle. Without Śakti one cannot attain the state of Buddhahood. The fundamental position of Hindu and Buddhist Tāntric pantheons is the same. According to Buddhist belief men and women are Upāya and Prajñā in their ultimate nature.

In *Hevajra Tantra, prajñā* is addressed as *yuvati* (young woman), *janani* (mother), *bhaganī* (sister), *rajaki* (washer woman), *nartaki* (dancing girl), *duhitā* (daughter), *dombī* (doma girl). *Prajñā* is called *janani* because she is the cause of creation. She is called *nartaki* because the manifest universe is but a cosmic dance of *prajñā* and every object is in a dance posture (*nṛtaratā*). She is dombi because she is beyond the touch of human mind and senses. In the *Atharva-Veda* Brahman is called Vrātya (untouchable). It is so called because it cannot be grasped by the senses.

In *Guhyasamāja Tantra* Śakti has been introduced. But one should not be mistaken that before this there was no element of Śaktism in Buddhist Tantra. Śakti has been the inevitable principle of practice for obtaining liberation since the origin of Tantra. *Guhyasamāja Tantra* has only introduced the new idea of five Dhyāni Buddhas presiding over the five *skandhas* or factors of which the universe is composed along with Śakti. These five *skandhas* are: Rūpa (form), Vedanā (feeling), Saṁjñā (name), Saṁskāra (impression) and Vijñāna (consciousness). *Sādhanamālā*[29] describes the names, colours and symbols of the different Dhyāni Buddhas. The names are: Vairocana, Ratna Sambhava, Amitābha, Amoghasiddhi and Akṣobhya. Their colours are: white, yellow, red, green and blue; and they are depicted in different *mudrās* namely: *Bodhyaṅgī* (teaching), *Varada* (grace), *Dhyāna*, (meditation), *Abhaya* (protective) and *Bhūmisparśa* (earth touching).

The female (Śakti) counterparts of the five Dhyāni Buddhas are: Locana, Vajradhātvisvarī, Pāṇḍārā, Māmakī and Tārā. These five consorts of Dhyāni Buddhas belong to the five families of *dveśa, moha, rāga, cintāmaṇi* and *samaya.* The names of the five Bodhi-sattvas of the Dhyāni Buddhas are: Vajrapāṇi, Samantabhadra, Padmapāṇi, Ratnapāṇi and Viśvapāṇi.[30]

According to *Ekalla-vīra-Candamahā-rośana-tantra* Lord Candarosana says to his Lady that all men are of the nature of Upāya and all women are of the nature of Prajñā and the whole world is of the nature of Prajñā and Upāya. According to Buddhistic belief, the Buddha was the incarnation of Upāya and his wife Gopā of Prajñā or Prajñā-pāramitā, and he attained *Parinirvāṇa* which is a state of Supreme Bliss (Mahā-sukha) in union with Prajñā-Gopā.

In *Caryā-pādas* of the Siddhācāryas the divine love of yogin and yoginī has been symbolically expressed in the form of a metaphor of ordinary courtship and sex union of lover and beloved. Here the individual self is male, or lord and the Śūnyatā (Cosmic Self) is female or lady. Kukkurlpāda says[31] in his divine intoxication, 'Desireless am I and the void-mind is my husband.' Tillopāda says, 'The mind is the Lord, and vacuity (śūnyatā) is the Lady; they should always be kept united in the *sahaja.*'[32] Like Sri Ramakrishna, Kaṅhupāda[33] says that when the Lord-mind merges himself in his wife vacuity, he becomes one with her as salt after dissolving in water.

Tantra is full of symbolism. The concept of Dhyāni Buddha has great esoteric significance. All Dhyāni Buddhas are consorting amorously at every *padma* or *cakra.* Like Hindu Tantra, these Dhyāni Buddhas have been described with colour, form and bāhana. Those who are adept in practical Sādhanā can alone understand the deeper meaning of the mystic symbols which have been employed in both Hindu and Buddhist Tantra.

The elements of Śaktism are distinct and important. Only different names have been given to the principle of Śakti in Buddhism.

Ādi Buddha

Tāntric Buddhism is wedded to the philosophy of non-duality. The five Dhyāni Buddhas have sometimes been wrongly represented by five primordial gods which certainly smack of polytheism. Like the monotheistic philosophy of Hindu Tantra. Tāntric Buddhism belongs to the Śivādvaita school. In accordance with the monotheistic spirit and tradition of Tantrism, the concept of Ādi Buddha, the Supreme deity like Ādinātha or Sadā Śiva of Hindu Tantra, came into being. According to Dr. B. Bhattacharya[34] this theory of Ādi Buddha or Vajra-dhara (the primordial monotheistic Buddha) was originated in the Nālandā monastery in about the tenth century. According to Alexander Csoma de Koros[35] also the theory of Ādi Buddha was introduced at Nālandā in the beginning of the tenth century. *Svayambhū Purāṇa* says that Ādi Buddha first expressed himself in Nepal in the form of a flame of fire, and Mañjūśrī erected a temple over it in order to preserve his glory and grace. The temple is known as Svayambhū Caitya.

There is some confusion regarding the place, form and concept of Ādi Buddha. The identification of Vajra-dhara with Ādi Buddha is not acceptable to all. According to some scholars one among the Dhyāni Buddhas is Ādi Buddha; according to others

Bodhi-Sattvas such as Samantabhadra and Vajrapāṇi, are Ādi Buddhas. Only those who are initiated into Tantrism can understand the non-dualistic significance and profound importance of the esoteric symbolism of Ādi Buddha and Dhyāni Buddha which are one in essence.

There are two forms — Single and Yab-yum — of Ādi Buddha in Vajra-yāna. When he is conceived single, he is well ornamented, bedecked with jewels and sitting crosslegged in deep meditation. He holds *vajra* in his right hand and *ghaṇṭā* in his left. Vajra is the symbol of Śūnyatā and *ghaṇṭā* stands for *prajñā* the sound of which spreads far and wide.

Ādi Buddha in his Yab-yum pose remains the same except that he is locked in love with his Śakti which is known as Prajñā- pāramitā. Śakti is richly dressed and profusely jewelled. She carries the *Kartri* (knife), which symbolizes the cutting of the veil of nescience, and the Kapāla (skull) which stands for the absolute union. The Yab-yum represents both dualism and non-dualism.

Kālacakrayāna

Kālacakrayāna is the development of Vajra-yāna This school of Tāntric Buddhism was misunderstood by many. As we have already discussed, whenever a Sādhaka has an illusion because of the mantric fog created due to the violation of Śīla, he is bound to fall and take recourse to Avidyā Tantra. These Avidyā Tantra Sādhakas display their occult power for self gratification and material gains. Whereas true Sādhakas perform their Sādhanā in solitude and carefully preserve their spiritual gains and employ them for the attainment of the Supreme. They never make any publicity of their spiritual wealth and live in the world with the stoic attitude of self negation. That is why the Avidyā Tāntrikas were wrongly acclaimed to be the only custodians of Tāntric Vidyā. Avidyā Tantra came before the public gaze with all its demoniac gods and goddesses. Thus, it is no wonder that Waddell did not understand the true spirit and the grand system of Kālacakrayāna which is one of the finest forms of Buddhist Tantrism.

Dr. B. Bhattacharya says: 'The Kālacakrayāna seems to be a later development of the Vajra-yāna. This concerns itself with the Yoga Tantra and Anuttarayoga Tantra and incorporates doctrines of the Sahajayāna also.'[36] According to Kālacakra Tantra and its commentary, *Vimalaprabhā*, Kālacakra is a deity. It bespeaks of the monotheistic. attitude and belief. It is the union of Śūnyatā and Karuṇā. The deity is embraced by Goddess Prajñā or Śakti. The *maṇḍala* (mystic circle) of the deity consists of all the planets and stars. The textbook of Kālacakra deals with subjects like astronomy and astrology. The introduction of Kālacakra Tantra[37] is attributed to *Mañjūśrī*, and the commentary, *Vimalaprabhā*, was written in one thousand and two hundred *granthas* by one Puṇḍarīka.[38]

Dr. S.B. Das Gupta mentions *Śrī Kālacakra Tantra*[39] as the only text available on this form of Buddhist Tantra. According to him this is the only way of liberation in the Kali Age.[40] It puts more emphasis on the control of vital winds (*prāṇa* and *apāna*). There is a detailed discussion on the control of these vital winds which can cure many diseases. However, Prāṇāyāma, is a *sādhanāṅga*, and is not Sādhanā. It is a process for keeping the mind in a state of pause in which it comes into contact with the stream of Consciousness. It helps in deep meditation and concentration.

The *maṇḍala* of a deity constitutes the whole universe. It simply conveys the idea of the omniscient being and the all-pervasive nature of the deity. Further, it has been said that it is the only method in the Kali Age.

Abhinava Gupta has dealt with the theory of Kālacakra in his celebrated work *Tantra-loka*. The exposition of both *Śrī-kāla-cakra-tantra* and *Tantra-lōka* regarding the concept and esoteric importance of Kālacakra is the same. The reality is Kālātīta (timeles). Realization of the Reality in the realm of relativity is impossible. Therefore, to realize the Absolute, which according to Buddhism is Vajra-Śūnyatā or Vajra-Sattva, and according to Kashmir Śaivism Parama Śiva, one will have to go beyond Time. To achieve this both systems emphasize control of the vital wind through *prāṇāyāma*, which enables one to suspend one's mind and go above the influence of Time and become one with the timeless entity.

According to *Sekoddeśa-ṭīkā*,[41] a commentary on *Kāla-cakra-tantra's* Sekoddeśa, the deity Kālacakra is the same as Vajra-Sattva, the godhead of the Vajra-yāna. Kāla is here defined as immutable and unchanging and is itself the realization of this transcendental principle. Thus, the Kālacakra[42] is the emblem of the unity of Prajñā and Upāya.

Further, it is said that all the letters and syllables of Kālacakra imply certain mystic meanings; *ka* is the *bīja-mantra* of effect Brahma (kārya Brahma). Thus Kālacakra stands for the merger of unit consciousness into the original cause-potency, which is Śūnyatā, *i.e.* the Pure Consciousness, the Supreme Subjectivity. Like the Vajra-yāna, Kālacakrayāna aims at the attainment of spiritual salvation, for the individual as well as the mankind. Thus, it is a cult of collective welfare like Hindu Tantra which can be summarized in one sentence: *Ātma mokṣārtaṁ jagathitāyaca.*

According to Dr. B. Bhattacharya[43] the Kālacakrayāna embodies in its teachings and practices all the best of Vajra-yāna Nāthism and Sahaja-yāna. Dr. Gopinath Kaviraj[44] is of the opinion that the Kālacakrayāna which implies the unity of Prajñā and Upāya technically known as Vajra-Yoga, represents in fact the state of Supreme Oneness.

Thus, Śrī Kālacakra represents the metaphysical concept of Reality which is one, eternal and transcendental. In *Sekoddeśa-ṭīkā*[45] at salutation offering to the deity Kālacakra, he has been addressed as 'Prama-kṣara', '*Śūnyatā-karuṇā-bhinnaṁ bodhi-cittaṁ yad akṣaram*'. We find here a strong insistence on the ideal of oneness of Śūnyatā and Karuṇā which constitute Kālacakra or Vajra-Sattva. The word Akṣara[46] means that which undergoes no change. It conveys the sense of Reality which is indestructible.

Nevertheless we must observe that the monotheistic concept of godhead of Kālacakra-yāna is analogous to what we find in the Tāntric school of non-dualistic thought of both Hindu and Buddhist Āgamic systems.

Sahaja-Yāna

According to Dr. B. Bhattacharya, Lakṣmīnkarā Devī (729 A.D.), sister of Indrabhūti, the king of Uddiyāna, is the exponent of Sahaja-yāna.

We don't subscribe to this view. Indrabhūti is one of the eighty four Siddhas[47] of Buddhism according to the Varṇaratnākara of Jyotirīśvara. Sahaja-yāna. is not a separate and distinct school of Tāntric Buddhism. It is only another name of Vajrayāna. Sahaja means straight. Here it signifies the straight path of Herukā (*Kuṇḍalinī*) which brings the Infinite Bliss (*Mahāsukha*). The perfection is possible only by the help of Vajra-Tārā (another Buddhist name of the *Kuṇḍalinī*) whose path is Avadhutikā. The path of Avadhutikā is straight and not zig-zag like that of Lalanā and Rasanā. In Hindu Tantra, Kuṇḍalinī Sādhanā is also known as Ṛju Mārga (straight path). And those who attain perfection with the help of Herukā are known as Siddhas. *Lalita Sahasranāma* mentions three forms of spirituality: *divya, mānava* and *siddha.*

The different *cakras* (wheels or nerve plexuses) have been conceived to be the abodes of different mystical gods and goddesses, who grant different types of mystic power (*siddhi*), and are known as different places of pilgrimage. The top-most *cakra* is known as *Mahāsukha Cakra.* The sole objective of Tantra Sādhanā is to cross these different *cakras* and reach the *Mahāsukha Cakra,* the fountainhead of Infinite Bliss and Beatitude.

A psychological analysis will show that these *cakras* or nerve plexuses control certain human tendencies. When a Sādhaka crosses a certain *cakra,* he acquires mastery over the human tendencies controlled by this particular *cakra.* This gives the Sādhaka tremendous mental strength which in common parlance is known as occult power. That is why these different stations are known as sacred places of pilgrimage like Uddīyāna, Jālandhara, Pūrṇagiri and Kāmarūpa.

The word Uddiyāna here stands for the mystic kingdom of pilgrimage and not for the historical place of which Indrabhuti styled himself as king. Uddīyāna, here means the (Mahāsukha). Cakra which Indrabhuti conquered with the help of Herukā and thus became Siddha (the Perfect Being).

The main aim of Sahaja-yāna. Vajra-yāna. and Kālacakra-yāna is the realization of salvation. The state of spiritual sublimity which remains ever unpolluted by the humming of the longings and desires is known as *Sahaja.* It is a state of desirelessness and motionlessness. This state of Sahaja is created only when a Sādhaka buries his individual ego consciousness and merges into the Cosmic Consciousness. When this state is attained, the objective multiplicities are merged into the Supreme

Multiple and everything else dwindles into non-existence. The Sādhaka comes to the realization of Buddhahood, which is totality of all beings and existence.

REFERENCES

1. *Philosophy of Gorakhanath,* Prefatory Note, p. xxv.
2. *bodhicittam idani vajraṁ sarva-buddhatvam ātmanaḥ, tasmāt sarvātma sarva-buddhatvam āpunute. — Jñāna Siddhi,* ch. XV.
3. *Sarvatra sarvatāḥ sarvaṁ sarvathā sarvadā svayam, Sarva buddhamayaṁ siddhaṁ svamātmānaṁ prapaśyati — Ibid.*
4. *Vajra-yānam anuttarain, Sarva-dharma-samekatvam yat tvayā bhāṣitaṁ prabhu aho guhyātiguhyasya vajra-yanasya deśanā, niḥsvabhāvasya śuddhasya vidyate yasya no'pamā — Guhya Siddhi.*
5. *The Serpent Power* (6th ed.), Ganesh & Co., Madras, 1958.
6. *Ṣaṭcakra Nirupaṇa,* vv. 51-54.
7. *Mādhyamikavṛtti* (La Vallu Poussin'a edition), p. 2.
8. *Saundaryalaharī,* vv. 9,11,34.
9. 'A Tibetan Account of Nāgārjuna,' an article by S.C. Sarkar in the '*Sino-Indian Journal,*' December, 1948.
10. *Lalitavistara,* edited by Rajendralal Mitra, p. 315.
11. *Sacred Books of the East,* vol. XX, p. 78.
12. They are: Chando (will), Viriyam (effort), Cittam (thought), Vimaṁsā (investigation). See R.C. Childers, *Dictionary of the Pali Language,* p. 157.
13. *The Cultural Heritage of India,* vol. IV, p. 260.
14. Lama Angarika Govind in an article on Mantra in the 'Stepping Stones', vol. II, no. 1, published from Kalimpong.
15. Dr. P.C. Bagchi, *Studies in the Tantras.*
16. *Indian Philosophy* (seventh impression), vol. I, p. 467. London, 1956.
17. According to some experts on Buddhism, there are four schools of Buddhist Tantra for four different types of disciplines, namely: (1) Carya Tantra, (2) Kriyā Tantra, (3) Yoga Tantra, and (4) Anuttarayoga Tantra. See *The Cultural Heritage of India,* vol. IV, p. 265.
18. John Woodroffe, *The Garland of Letters* (4th ed.), p. 247. Ganesh & Co., Madras, 1963.
19. *Śūnyatā-boddhito bījam bijād bimbaṁ prajāyate — Advaya-Vajra- Saṅgraha,* p. 50. Gaekwad Oriental Series, Baroda, 8 — 1909B.
20. *Introduction to Buddhist Esotericisn.*
21. MS., Royal Asiatic Society of Bengal, no. 11317, p. 5(A).
22. *Bodhisattva Bhūmi.*
23. A Tibetan Tantra, 'The Theosophy', July, 1919.
24. *Mythology,* p. 106.
25. *Lamaism,* p. 15.
26. *Guhyasamāja Tantra,* Gaekwad Oriental Series, Baroda, no. 53, p. 27.
27. *Sphūrtiśca devatākārā niḥsvabhāvāḥ svabhāvataḥ;*
    Yathā yathā bhavet sphurtiḥ sā tathā śūnyatāmikā.
    Advayavajra Saṅgraha, Gaekwad Oriental Series, Baroda, 1927, p. 5I.
28. *Guhyasamāja Tantra,* Gaekwad Oriental Series, Baroda, 1931, XVII, pp. 162-65.

29. *Jino vairocano khyāto ratnasambhava eva ca,*
Amitābha-amoghasiddhir-akṣobhyośca prakīrtitaḥ,
Varṇa amisam sitaḥ pito rakto harita-mecakan,
Bodhyaṅgī varado dhyānaṁ mudrā abhaya-bhūsparśni.
30. For details see B. Bhattacharya, *Indian Buddhist Iconography*. Oxford University Press, 1924.
31. *hāuṁ ninãsi kha-maṇa-bhatāri,* Song no. 20.
32. *Citta Khasamā Jahi Samasuha palaṭṭai (india-visā tahimatta) na disai.* Doha no, 5, Dr. P.C. Bagchi, Ed.
33. *manaha (bhāvā) khasamā bhāvi (divaratti sahaja rahiai).* Doha no. 17. *Ibid.*
34. *The Cultural History of India,* vol. I, p. 530.
35. *Journal of the Asiatic Society of Bengal* (1833), II, p. 57 ff.
36. *The Cultural Heritage of India,* vol. IV, p. 270.
37. *Ibid.*, p. 271.
38. See the '*Laghu-Kālacakra-tantra-raja-ṭīkā*' given by M.M. Haraprasad Shastri in 'Descriptive Catalogue of the Government Collection' (Asiatic Society of Bengal), 1, pp. 73 f.
39. Preserved in the Cambridge University Library (Cambridge MS. Add. no. 1364).
40. *Ibid.*, p. 1(B).
41. Gaekwad Oriental Series, Baroda, edited by Mario E. Carelli.
42. *Karuṇā-Śūnyatā-mūrtiḥ-kālaḥ-samvṛtti rūpinī, Śūnyatā-cakram ity uktaṁ kāla-cakro dvaya kṣaraḥ* — p. 8.
43. *The Cultural Heritage of India,* vol. IV, p. 271.
44. *Philosophy of Gorakhnath,* Prefatory Note, p. xxvi.
45. *namaste kāla-cakrāya sarva-varana hānaye*
parama-kṣara-sukha-pūrṇa jñāna-kāya namo (sic) *state*
śūnyatā-karuṇa-bhinnaṁ bodhi-cittaṁ yad akṣaram'
tena sekena me nātha prasādaṁ kuru sampratam.— p. 24.
46. *Kṣaraṁ pradhānamamṛākṣaraṁ haraḥ,*
Kṣarātmānaviśate deva ekaḥ.
Tasyābhidhyānād yojanāt tattvabhāvad
bhū-yaścānte viśvamāyā nivṛttiḥ. — *Ibid.*
47. 1. Lāhipā, 2. Lilāpā, 3. Virūpā, 4. Dombipā, 5. Sābara (Sābaripā), 6. Saraha (Rāhulabhadra), 7. Kaṅkāli, 8. Mīna, 9. Gorkṣā,10. Cauraṅgī, 11. Vīnā, 12. Śānti, 13. Tānti, 14. Carmari, 15. Khaḍga, 16. Nāgārajuna, 17. Kāṅhupā, 18. Kānarī (Āryadeva), 19. Thagana, 20. Nāda pāda, 21. Śālipā (Śṛgāla-pāda), 22. Tiḷo-pā (Tailikapā), 23. Chatra, 24. Bhadra, 25. Dvikhaṇḍī, 26. Ajogi, 27. Kada-pāda, 28. Dhovī, 29. Kaṅkaṇa, 30. Kambala, 31. Tenki, 32. Bhāde, 33. Tandhī, 34. Kukkuri, 35. Cujbi (Kusūli), 36. Dharma, 37. Mahi, 38. Acintya, 39. Babhani, 40. Nalina, 41. Bhusuku, 42. Indrabhūti, 43. Meghapāda, 44. Kutharī, 45. Karmāra, 46. Jālandhari, 47. Rāhula, 48. Garbharī, 49. Dhakari, 50. Medinī, 51. Paṅkaja, 52. Ghaṇṭā, 53. Yogi, 54. Celuka, 55. Vaguri (Gundari), 56. Luñcaka, 57. Nirguṇa, 58. Jayānanda, 59. Carṣati, 60. Campaka, 61. Viṣana, 62. Bhali (Telī Taite), 63. Kumari, 64. Carpati, 65, Maṇibhadra, 66. Mekhalā, 67. Mankhalā, 68. Kalakala, 69. Kanthaḍi, 70. Daṇḍi, 71. Udhaḷi, 72. Kapāla, 73. Kila, 74. Puṣkara, 75. Sarva-bhakṣā, 76. Nāgabodhi, 77. Dārika, 78. Puttali, 79. Panaha, 80. Kakilā, 81. Anaṅga, 82. Lakṣmīnkarā, 83. Sāmudra, 84. Bhalipā.

4 Principles of Tantra Philosophy

The philosophical system of Tantra is known as the Śivādvaita school. Behind the theocratic culture of Tantra is an evolved and consistent school of philosophic thought. According to the Śivādvaita school, the Supreme Reality is of the nature of pure consciousness, self-luminous and all-pervading. The Supreme Reality is called Parama Śiva.[1] Parama Śiva is endowed with Śakti which is held to be identical with Himself by virtue of which He is described as the Pūrṇahantā. Parama Śiva is both transcendent and immanent. Śiva is the Jñāna-Śakti and Devī is the Kriyā Śakti. Śakti is the non-material principle. She is known as Cit-Śakti.

The theory of Tāntric evolution is known as Ābhāsavāda. According to this the world is real, in the sense that it is an aspect of the Supreme Reality. Dr. Gopinath Kaviraj says: 'The peculiar metaphysical position of the Tantra consists in the theory of Ābhāsa; which is consistent with this position. It rejects the Vivartavāda of neo-Vedānta, because the world is not originally a false appearance due to Error. It is real in the same way as an image is real but it has no existence apart from the medium in which it is manifested .... To the Vedantist the world appears as such, to the ignorant owing to his ignorance and in the last analysis it is resolved into Māyā which is not identical with Brahman and is materialistic; but to a Tāntrist the world is real and is the expression of the Cit-Śakti or Free Will of the Lord and is really spiritual in essence like the Lord Himself.'[2] From Tāntric point of view the entire creation is an Ābhāsa. The appearance of limitation is the manifestation of non-Self. The Supreme Reality is split spontaneously into subject and object. However, Parama Śiva suffers no change. He always remains Pure, Undivided and Absolute. The universe of appearances is the unmanifest nature of the Absolute from which the process of involution emanates which is perceived by the subject as different from itself.

The quintessence of Tantra philosophy is the attainment of the supreme unification of Self with Parama Śiva. This state of Self-realization is both an enjoyment and liberation. Tantra rejects the philosophy of nihilism and pessimism. To a Tantra Sādhaka world is nothing but the manifestation of Reality. With the gradual ascent to God-path, one experiences Him both in animate and inanimate objects. This realization of divine presence puts an end to all physical, mental and spiritual sufferings and inspires one to live up to the ideal and glory of man. According to Tantra the world is neither an illusion nor reality. Tantra puts emphasis on the spiritual realization without ignoring the material aspect of life.[3]

Tantra philosophy makes a fundamental departure from all the existing philosophical systems, in its novelty, originality and verifiability.

The Absolute

Parama Śiva is the Absolute of Tantra philosophy. He is unsubjectivated Transcendentality. He is the Pūrṇahantā self-luminous and Pure Consciousness. Just as light and heat coexist in fire, in the same way Śiva, the universal *I*-ness (Ahantā), and Śakti coexist in Pure Consciousness (चैतन्य). The Pūrṇahantā is the essence of Parama Śiva.

The Absolute of Tantra is of the nature of Pure Consciousness. It is unaffected by the limitations of Time, Space. and Causality.[4] It has absolute freedom. It is unrestricted by its Vimarśa Kriyā. Vimarśa Kriyā is identical with Parama Śiva. It remains involved in Him. The Absolute is endowed with Power which is identical with Itself and by virtue of which It is described as the Free Agent. Freedom is the essence of Consciousness.

Śiva and Śakti are the two aspects of the Absolute.[5] It is unchanging, eternal, infinite, one and uncaused. It is the Supreme Reality. It is beyond the categories of existence and non-existence, being and non-being. Parama Śiva does not come within the scope of the thirty six *tattvas* of Śaivism.

Parama Śiva is the Supreme Reality. He is of the nature of Bliss and complete in Himself. He holds in Himself the unmanifested universe as an idea. At the same time, He transcends the ideal universe. He is the transcendental Reality, Pure Intelligence as well as the one all including Supreme Experience. J.C. Chatterjee says: 'He is logical first principle but not in time.'[6]

Parama Śiva is pure intelligence, real, limitless and infinite from the transcendental point of view. But empirically considered, He is omniscient and omnipotent, creator, sustainer and destroyer of the universe. He, in this aspect, is known as Śiva. He is possessed of infinite divine qualities and is the object of worship.

Parama Śiva is both transcendent and immanent. Śiva tattva is the transcendental aspect and Śakti-tattva is the immanent principle of Parama Śiva. Śiva and Śakti eternally coexist in Him. They constitute the Absolute of Tantra philosophy. The collective name of Śiva and Śakti is Parama Śiva. Tantra maintains the spiritual monism of Śiva and Śakti. The duality, involved in the admission of Śiva and Śakti, is due to the analytical approach of mind. Śakti is identical with Śiva, as salt is with the sea water.[7]

Parama Śiva in His transcendence is beyond Time, Space and Form and in His immanence is manifested in the universe in the limitations of the sixty four *tattvas.* In His immanence, He is transformed into the manifest world and in His transcendental aspect He is beyond it. Śiva is consciousness as *stasis* (Cit), Śakti is consciousness as dynamics (Cidrupinī).

Parama Śiva is the Supreme Cognitive Principle. He is the Supreme Subjectivity

(परम प्रतिसंवेदी), He is the Eternal and the Absolute (अपरिणामी). He undergoes no change. He is One and uncaused. He is beyond Time, Space and Person. There is nothing outside and beyond Him.

Parama Śiva is consciousness force (चितिशक्ति). He is the ultimate base of existence. 'The absolute *citi* is the cause when the universe is in the process of becoming perfected.'[8] Parama Śiva is not a passive principle. He is the noumenal cause of this phenomenal world. He is the ultimate cause of the manifest universe.

Parama Śiva is the fundamental stuff out of which the whole manifest and unmanifest universe has been created. By the power of consciousness (चितिशक्ति), He creates the cosmos. *Mahānirvāṇa Tantra* says: 'I bow to Thee, the pure consciousness who art in the form of universe.'[9]

Parama Śiva is called Mahā-Bindu. He is without colour (अवर्ण) and formless (निराकार).[10] Bindu has position but no magnitude. It means Parama Śiva exists but He cannot be conceived. He is beyond the question of existence and non-existence. He is logically indemonstrable. He is beyond the reach of speculative mind and thought. He is the composite form of Śiva (Consciousness) and Śakti (Operative Principle). Śiva and Śakti are an inalienable concomitance.[11] They are dualistic in theory but monistic in spirit. To separate them is as impossible as to separate moving wind from steadfast ether in which it blows. The Absolute of Tantra is Ardhanārīśvara. Parama Śiva is Yāmalarūpa. The Tāntric concept of the Absolute resolves the philosophical dilemma of Monism and Dualism. It resolves the scientist's enigma of mind and matter and the Vedantin's problem of Brahman and Māyā.

The inalienable concomitance of Śiva and Śakti is called Abinābhāvī. The word Abinābhāvī means inseparable. It means the existence of one cannot be proved in the absence of the other. There is no Śiva without Śakti and no Śakti without Śiva.[12]

Parama Śiva is called Parā-Saṁvit. In the transcendental state of Parā-Saṁvit, the dualism of subject and object is indistinguishably merged in the unitive consciousness of Parama Śiva. His divine sublimity remains unpolluted and spiritual tranquillity undisturbed. Śakti, the immanent aspect of Parama Śiva, does not get the scope of Her manifestation. Here Śakti is known as Mūla Prakṛti. Before the manifestation of the universe, there was one Infinite Being, the embodiment of Bliss and Consciousness.[13]

Parama Śiva is Truth, Consciousness and Bliss. He is Truth because He is an unchanging, unsubjectivated and transcendental entity. He is one. He ever is. He is the Reality and Truth. He is the Supreme unity without a second. He is luminous and self manifest. He indeed is alone. Śakti is the cause of the transformation of Śiva from real to relativity. However, the change is not physical but spiritual.

Śākta Tantra calls the Absolute Parā-Devī. Parā-Devī of the Śākta school is the composition of Prakāśa and Vimarśa. The Absolute is Prakāśa-Vimarśa-Sāmarasyarūpinī.[14]

The absolute of Tantra is Truth, Consciousness and Bliss.[15] 'He is without change, self-existent and ever the same, serene, above all attributes. He beholds and is the witness of all that is, omnipresent, the Self of everything that is. He, the Eternal and Omnipresent, is hidden and pervades all things. Though devoid of senses, He is the Illuminator of all the senses and their powers.[16] Parama Śiva is witnessing entity. Mind is an ever changing functional organism. It has two chambers — subjective and objective. For the common man it is the eye which perceives. But the student of medical science and physics will say that it is the retina which receives the colour vibrations from objects and transmits them to the brain. The metaphysician will say that the brain transmits these vibrations to the objective mind which takes the form of the vibrations and the subjective mind does the act of perception. Further introspection proves that the subjective mind perceives only because of supreme subjectivity. Parama Śiva is the subjective counterpart of our mind. Mind perceives only because Parama Śiva is the witnessing force behind our all mental activities.

Parama Śiva is supreme and paramount. He alone is the sovereign entity. 'Through fear of Him the wind blows, the sun gives heat, the clouds shower rain and the trees in the forest blossom.[17] The whole universe lives, moves and has its being in Him. The whole universe has come into being from Him, and unto Him it will return. He is the illuminator of senses and mind. 'There the sun does not shine, neither do the moon and the stars; nor do these flashes of lightning shine. How can this fire? He is shining, all these shine; through his effulgence all these are variously illumined.'[18]

The authorship of the entire manifest and unmanifest world lies with Parama Śiva. He is the nucleus of this cosmic cycle.[19] The material cause of the entire Cosmic Cycle is Śiva. He is the Supreme Controller of the world process. Kurt F. Leidecker says: 'The difference of the Īśvarādvaya system from the Brahmavādins consists here in that the Cit-like Exalted One always retains the authorship of the fivefold world process.'[20]

Parama Śiva is the fundamental reality. He is the indeterminable and transcendental existence. He is beyond all divisibility and separability. He is all comprehensive. He is Advaitam (Supreme Unity). In Tantra, Advaita (Supreme Unity) means the eternal coexistence of Śiva and Śakti.[21] To make any real distinction between them will be a logical abstraction. Arthur Avalon says: 'All that is manifest is Power (Śakti) as Mind, Life and Matter. Power implies a Power-Holder (Śaktimān). There is no Power-Holder without Power or Power without Power-Holder. The Power-Holder is Śiva The Power is Śakti, the Great Mother of the Universe. There is no Śiva without Śakti or no Śakti without Śiva. The two as they are in themselves are one.'[22]

Tantra accepts Māyā as a Brahmayī, Nityā (Eternal) and Satyarūpā (Truth). In Tantra philosophy Brahman and Māyā become one and coexistent.[23] By accepting the principle of Māyā as a reality, the Absolute of Tantra philosophy becomes all-embracing. Unlike Śaṅkara's Brahman, which is based on the principles of renunciation and elimination, Parama Śiva of *Āgama Śāstra* is the perfect and profound principle. The plurality and diversity represent the spiritual and essential oneness of the Absolute.

All things of the universe are made of the same Cosmic Consciousness (Śiva). The transcendental aspect (Śiva) of Parama Śiva is the fundamental stuff of the cosmos. Śakti, the creative matrix, is the cause of multiplicities. She is the immanent (Vimarśa) aspect of Parama Śiva. The Absolute of Tantra is the composite of Śiva and Śakti. They are two for the sake of argument but they can under no circumstances be separated from one another in the Cosmic Entity. Śiva is witnessing consciousness. Śakti is the binding principle. Śiva is Cosmic Consciousness and Śakti is Cosmic Principle.

The material cause (उपादान कारण) and the efficient cause (निमित्त कारण) are the cardinal principles of creative ideation. Every object has these two causes. Over and above these, there is a conjunctive principle which acts as a catalytic agent between the material and the efficient cause. Śiva is the material cause. Śakti is the linking force. As the efficient cause Śiva is the primary and Śakti the secondary factor. Śiva is the consciousness force and all-pervading entity. None else than Śiva can be the material cause of the universe. Śakti is always merged in Śiva. She activates the process of creation only when Śiva offers an opportunity and grants divine permission. Hence, the *doership* lies with Śiva. As an efficient cause Śiva is the primary principle and Śakti the secondary.[24] Parama Śiva of Tantra is the fundamental stuff and the Supreme Doer. He is the nucleus of all the nuclii. He is the soul of the soul, and the life of the life. He is the ultimate, eternal and infinite reality.

Parama Śiva is beyond the triple bondage of Time, Space and Person. Time, Space and Person are imbedded in relativity. They constitute the relative manifest world. Time is a mental measurement of any action. Time entails the existence of Space and Person. Parama Śiva is outside and beyond the scope of relativity, yet there is nothing beyond and outside Him. There is no difference and distinction between one part and another. He is eternal. He does not shed the character of eternity in present, past and future. There is no past and future for Him. He always is. He is an eternal existence. He does not admit any internal differentiation. He is free from any empirical distinction.

Parama Śiva is beyond the question of 'is' and 'is not', and existence (चित्) and non-existence (अचित्). The ideas of existence and non-existence are positive and negative psychic concepts, whereas Parama Śiva is inconceivable to human reason. Reason is an analytical process. It involves dualism of subject (ज्ञाता) and object (ज्ञेय). Parama Śiva is the Supreme Cognitive Principle. He is singular and unitary in character. 'One' and 'two' are positive mental conceptions. To say Parama Śiva is one does not mean that He is within reach of the speculative mind. He is described as one because He can be realized by making mind one-pointed. With the constant meditation on Parama-Bindu mind is apexed. An apexed mind realizes Parama Śiva in the state of deep meditation. Mind is dissolved into the Divine Consciousness. Mind ceases to be mind. It becomes consciousness. It is called the mystic oneness of Śiva and Śakti, Kuṇḍalinī and Parā-Bindu. Parama Śiva is attainable with the help of 'intuition'. Intuition is a divine power and mystic faculty. The awakening of the

Kuṇḍalinī opens the gateway to intuition. It brings the realization of Parama Śiva which is the *summum bonum* of Tantra philosophy and Sādhanā.

Śiva-Tattva

Śiva is the first principle and supreme religious godhead of Tantra. He is the identity of 'being', 'bliss' and 'consciousness'. He is devoid of any form and colour. He is Pure Awareness. He is limitless, self luminous and absolutely without any differentiation. It is in Him that the whole universe of the created and when uncreated remains in a potential form. He is the ground of all existence. He is the ultimate cause and the fundamental stuff of the cosmos. It is in Him that the whole universe becomes manifest.

Śiva means Cosmic Consciousness. He is transcendental by nature and eternal by character. He is the Supreme Subjectivity and the Prime Cause of all objectives. He is the noumenal cause of the phenomenal existence.

Śiva is Citi Śakti (Consciousness Force). Consciousness is the very cause of the universe which is in the process of becoming perfect. Kurt F. Leidecker says: 'When the universe is in the process of becoming perfected means as much as when [all suchness] from Sadāśiva to the earth emerge.'[25] We observe that the process of becoming perfected means mergence or reabsorption of the world process into Śiva. When all our loves and longings, aspirations and desires are directed unto Him, we attain perfection by becoming one with Him.

Prof. Surendranath Das Gupta[26] makes three divisions of Śiva-tattva on the basis of *Vatula-tantram*,[27] namely: (1) Niṣkala, (2) Sakala, and (3) Niṣkala-sakala. Śiva is called niṣkala when He is without kalā. Das Gupta has used the word in the sense of parts or organs. Kalā has been used in Tantra metaphysics to signify the different waves which constitute the world process. Niṣkalatva means the pure state of Śiva which remains unaffected by the omni active Śakti. There takes place no humming up of the waves and, therefore, the spiritual sublimity of Śiva remains unpolluted. Both macrocosm and microcosm remain merged and mingled in the undifferentiated whole. Sakalatva means the qualified state of Śiva. When Śiva allows his immanent principle to act and manifest, he undergoes a metamorphosis. Śiva becomes the cosmos.

Sakala-niṣkala is the tangential point of Sakala and Niṣkala. This tangential point is the abode of Parā-Bindu who resides within the scope of both Nirguṇa and Saguṇa Śiva. At the time of creation Śiva associates Himself with mayopadāna. This *bindu* represents the force of liberation. Those who aspire for non-qualified liberation get out of the cycle of birth and rebirth at this point.

The nomenclature used for Śiva, Sakala, Niṣkala and Sakala-niṣkala is only indicative of different moments in Transcendentality. There is no real transformation of Śiva for He always remains unchanged and transcendental in himself. It is only due to the activation of Śakti that Śiva, the Supreme Entity, appears to have lost his transcendentality.

According to *Vatula-tantram,* Śiva has three forms: (1) Subrahmanya-Śiva, (2) Sadā-Śiva, and (3) Maheśa. According to others Śiva has five forms: (1) Dakṣiṇāmūrti, (2) Īśāna, (3) Kalyāṇasundarama, (4) Kālāgni, and (5) Vāmadeva. Again Śiva can be studied in ten ways: (1) Tattva-bheda, (2) Varṇa-bheda, (3) Cakra-bheda, (4) Varga-bheda, (5) Mantra-bheda, (6) Praṇava, (7) Brahma-bheda, (8) Aṅga-bheda, (9) Mantra-jāta, and (10) Kitā.

It is said that from Śiva-Tattva comes Śakti-Tattva and from the latter issues Sadākhyā Tattva. It is further said that from Sadākhyā-Tattva evolves Īśvara-Tattva. Śiva is described as Saccidānanda.[28]

In Rudra-saṁhitā of *Śiva-mahāpurāṇa*[29] Śiva says that there is no differentiation between the Self and the Brahman. The highest reality is Pure Consciousness, the realization of which brings about liberation. Śiva identifies *bhakti* (devotion) with *jñāna* (knowledge). It is through bhakti (the longing for Śiva) that the true knowledge and inner renunciation are possible. Salvation is granted by Śiva alone because He is *guṇātīta* (beyond all the *guṇas* of Māyā).

Śiva is described as the Eternal Being (*nirvikārin*). The non-qualified liberation (*kaivalyamūkti*) can be attained only by the knowledge of Śiva and his ultimate nature. With the disappearance of ignorance (*avidyā*), one is freed from the veiling (*āvaraṇa*) and projecting (*vikshepa*) influence of Māyā and becomes pure. Through the grace of Lord Śiva one becomes what one really is, that is, Śiva.

Śiva is without any quality and condition. He is impersonal and Supreme Lord of the cosmos. Words cannot describe him; mind cannot reach him. He is the Para-Brahman. The whole universe comes out of him, returns to him and is pervaded by him. He knows all but none knows him. Though Śiva is the whole of the world yet he does not enter into this world of change. All the subtle and the gross manifestation is Śiva. Śiva alone remains the unchangeable transcendental reality. He is said to be qualified only when one considers him as being the possessor of Śakti.

The theory of the Śivādvaita school has been propounded in Kailāśa-saṁhitā of *Śiva-mahāpurāṇa.*[30] According to this view the Original Cause of the world must be the unity of male and female principles as all beings are constituted of *he* and *she* parts; the Śivādvaita system forms the basis of the Sāṁkhya conception of Puruṣa and Prakṛti.

Parama Śiva with the elimination of the feeling of the ideal universe is known as Śiva-Tattva. J.C. Chatterjee writes: 'But, in order that there may be a universe, He brings into operation that aspect of His Śakti which manifests itself as the principle of Negation and lets the Ideal Universe disappear from His view and allows Himself, as it were, to feel the want of a universe, but for which feeling there could be, as said above, no need of a manifested universe on the part of one who is all complete in Himself.'[31]

In our opinion Śiva is not a logical entity. Logic is a psychic survey. Its scope is limited. It being the system of thought of psychic survey it can deal and discuss only that which comes within the scope of intellectual pursuits. But Śiva Tattva, being Aprameya,[32] according to Śrī Kṣemarāja, one of the exponents of Kashmir Śaivism, does not come within the purview of logical thinking. Secondly, to say that Parama Śiva employs the principle of Negation 'to feel the want of universe' will invite logical inconsistency. The entity which is absolute and transcendental can never suffer from any feeling of 'want' which is a characteristic feature of relativism. Thirdly, to say that Parama Śiva 'holds in Himself the still unmanifested universe, as an idea, rather, as an experience of his own', will amount to qualifying the Unqualified Reality (Parama Śiva) with the act of subjectivization of 'experience'.

Unlike the dry-as-dust doctrine of Śaṅkara's monism, the pantheistic school of Tantra is a happy blending of spirituality and materialism. The world is a personification of Śiva. The universe is both an ideal and real, whereas in the Vedānta the reality is Brahman and everything else is but an imposition on the reality of Brahman. They are ultimately unreal and their unreality is exposed when the person attains salvation. There will be a moment when the phenomenal world will completely cease to exist before the liberated person. However, in Tantra, the universe as such in all its various forms of the animate and inanimate is regarded as different real forms of Śiva. These are thought projections of Śiva, and are created for the benefit of the soul.

In *Prāṇa-toṣiṇī*[33] Śiva has been described as both Nirguṇa (unsubjectivated) and Saguṇa (subjectivated). It is said that unsubjectivated Śiva is the origin of the three bindus, namely, Brahma-Bindu, Viṣṇu-Bindu and Rudra-Bindu.

Śiva occupies a prominent place in Tāntric cosmogony. Śiva worship is coeval with the Tantrās.

According to the Śaiva Agamas, Sadāśiva is the highest and the Supreme Being — formless, beyond the comprehension of anyone, subtle, luminous and all pervading.[34] There are, however, some differences among the Śākta Tantras, Śuddha Śaiva Āgamas and the Purāṇās regarding the position occupied by Śiva and the disposition of the Five Faces of Śiva. But there is general agreement that Śiva is the supreme godhead and Īśāna (Sadā-Śiva) represents the Ākāśa-Tattva (space). He is spotlessly white in colour. This is only symbolical since white is not a colour but only the effect of the combination of all the colours of the rainbow in a certain proportion and under certain conditions. He is said to be spotlessly white, because He is the origin of all the colours and forms.

Śiva-Tattva is Pure Consciousness. He is the universal principle common to all the pure and limited *cit.* He is universal (Sāmānya) and holds within himself all the Viśeṣas (particulars) whereas Parama Śiva is transcendent and above both Sāmānya (universal) and Viśeṣa (particular). Hence, Śiva-Tattva may be more properly described as Pure caitanya in its general but conditioned form, free from all *vikalpas* and is to be distinguished from the Absolute proper.[35]

Śakti-Tattva

Śiva is Cosmic Consciousness and Śakti a Cosmic Principle. Śiva is a witnessing force, knowing entity but without the activation of Śakti, He remains objectless, unmanifested. Śiva is a Jñāna-Tattva and Śakti is a Kriyā-Śakti. But Śakti is neither absolute nor an independent entity. She is an immanent principle of Śiva.[36] Without Śakti, Śiva is inactive. Śakti is known as Devī and Mahā-Māyā. Śiva, being a supreme subjectivity, remains as a witnessing force. Śakti is the primordial force.[37] Reality is one and Eternal but due to the activation of Śakti the Absolute Reality appears to have taken different forms and colours. It means that when Śakti gets the scope of her manifestation, Śiva (Cosmic Consciousness) undergoes a metamorphosis. The singular Self (Śiva) is transformed into innumerable finite entities but remains the essence and the fundamental stuff of all physical and metaphysical entities. However, due to the operation of Śakti, Śiva does not lose his transcendentality.

Where Śakti does not get the scope of expression due to the density of Consciousness, she remains merged in Śiva. But it does not mean that in the state of Parama Śiva there is total absence of omni-active Śakti. Śakti exists at all levels of manifestation and unmanifestation — simply there is no clash within or without Parama Śiva. The transcendentality of Śiva remains uncontaminated. He is unaffected by his impersonal exhibition.

Śāradā Tilakam of Lakṣmaṇācārya expounds the philosophy of monism. Śiva-Tattva and Śakti-Tattva are inseparable (Sanatan Samavāyinī), the latter being only the immanent aspect of the former. John Woodroffe[38] and J.C. Chatterjee[39] have wrongly conceived Śakti as Negation, which is a logical principle, whereas Śakti-Tattva of Tantra is a spiritual principle. The Principle of Negation as explained by Spinoza and Hegel is a logical dichotomy where 'being' and 'non-being' live together in an unholy alliance. 'Being' and 'non-being' are psychic concepts, and have nothing to do with the mystic and metaphysical principle. A logical principle is conceptual and of dependent origination, whereas a spiritual principle is real and self-existent. As Vimarśa-Śakti, she does not negate Śiva (Cosmic Consciousness) in the Western sense; rather she fulfils the desire of Śiva by creating the world. She is said to be Niṣedha vyāpāra-rūpā Śaktiḥ. Here Niṣedha means the veiling and projecting (*vikṣepa*) *kriyā* of Śakti which is quite different from the Principle of Negation.

In the causal stage, she is called Icchā-Śakti ever associated with Śiva. She is the seed of the manifest and the unmanifest, things and beings. All the moving and stationary things remain absorbed in her.[40]

Śakti is thus called the womb (*yonī*), or seed (*bījāvasthā*) and the heart of the Supreme Lord (*hṛdayaṁ paramisitaḥ*). In *Yoginī-hṛdya Tantra,* Śakti is described as Yoginī because she is a relational principle between cause and effect. Śakti is the heart of the universe and Śiva the Lord.

When Śakti, the causal matrix, gets the scope of expression, the visible and the invisible world with all its forms and colours comes into being.

Śakti and Māyā are almost one and the same. There is only a conceptual difference between the two. When Śakti is merged into Śiva and does not get the scope of her manifestation due to the density of consciousness, she is called Mūla-prakṛti. Śakti or Prakṛti is the combination of three attributes or *guṇas, i.e.* Sattva (sentient), Rajas (mutative) and Tamas (static). In the state of Mūla-Prakṛti all the three *guṇas* remain in equilibrium and hence Śakti is a mere operative principle. She is unmanifested. But the moment the equipoise is disturbed, due to the belligerent nature of the three *guṇas*, Śakti, the primordial force, is transformed into Māyā, the creative principle. And thus is heralded the era of creation.

Māyā is the mother of all beings and existence. Śakti has been addressed as *jananī*[41], *mātrī*[42] and *ambā.*[43] In the absence of a creative principle; or motivity, there cannot be any creation. If Śakti or the primordial force had not been transformed into the creative principle, the cosmos would have remained in Comic Consciousness in a potential form. Śakti is polymorphic. That is why she is addressed in Tantra as Cosmoform Mahāmāyā. The phenomenal world is the manifestation of her heterogeneous forms. It is nothing but her playful motivation.

If Śakti had remained inexplicit, primordial and merged in Śiva, the diverse manifestations of different beings and existence would not have taken place. Creation means that the three components of Śakti are not in equilibrium. There is a disparity. Either the sentient or the static force is dominant. If the sentient force is predominant, Śakti is known as Vidyāmāyā and if the static force is pronounced, then she is known as Avidyāmāyā. 'She is Vidyā-Śakti when She reveals in the Paśu state of Ātma whose true nature is Lordship but when She veils then She is called Māyā.'[44]

Generally, Śakti or Devī is identified with Vidyāmāyā. With the help of Vidyāmāyā, *jīva* proceeds towards spiritual sublimity. Śakti or Devī helps *jīva* in racing towards Parama Śiva. Without the help of Śakti (Vidyāmāyā) it is not possible for *jīva* to attain the supreme oneness with Parama Śiva. Māyā is reduced to nothing. But when *jīva* attains the state of spiritual sublimity, he has to say good-bye to Śakti (Vidyāmāyā) also. Vidyāmāyā disappears due to divine exaltation.

One of the greatest difficulties in explaining Śakti-Tattva is due to the highly poetic and phraseological expressions. Further, due to the manifold characteristics of Śakti, it is really very difficult to differentiate between the symbolic, esoteric and literal meanings of Śakti.

In *Mahānirvāṇa Tantra*, Śakti has been addressed as Kālī, Tāriṇī, Durgā, Ṣoḍaśī, Bhuvaneśvarī, Dhūmāvatī, Bagalā, Bhairavī, Chinnamastakā, Annapūrṇā, Vāgdevī, Kamalālayā, and Śivā.[45]

In *Saundaryalaharī*,[46] Śakti has been called Aruṇā, Aparṇā, Pārvatī, Caṇḍī, Umā, Bhavānī, Satī, Paracit, Samayā besides Jananī, Mātrī Devī and Ambā. In *Hymn to Kālī*,[47] Śakti has been described as Mahāvidyā — a composite form of Śiva and Śakti. The forms of Mahāvidyā are divided into two groups, namely, Kālikulā and Śrīkula. Kālī, Tārā, Raktakalā, Bhavanā, Mardinī, Triputā, Tvarita, Durgā and Vidyā

Pratyaṅgīrā belong to the Kālikula. Sundarī, Bhairavī, Bālā, Bagalā, Kamalā, Dhūmāvatī, Mātaṅgī, Vidyā, Svapnāvatī, Mahāvidyā and Madhumatī belong to the Śrīkula.

In *Lalita Sahasranāma*, Śakti has been named Kālī, Karālī, Kalyāṇi, Kalāvatī, Kamalā, Kālidarpāghni, Kaparddīśakṛpanvitā. Śakti is the origin of the world, but She herself is uncaused.[48] Devī has sometimes been used in the sense of Ātman. Devī is called Tripurasundarī. 'Tripura' literally means three cities. Here Tripura symbolically represents three bodies of the microcosm — crude, subtle and causal. The crude body or the Kāmamaya-koṣa deals with the physical aspects of human desires. That part of the mind which controls the sensory and motor organs is known as Manomaya-koṣa. It is related with the psychic recollection and contemplation. Higher or the subliminal mind is all knowing. It is known as the causal mind. It is the combination of Supramental (Atimānasa), Subliminal (Vijñānamaya) and Hiraṇyamaya spheres (Koṣa). Beyond the spheres of the crude, subtle and causal mind is the kingdom of Ātman. Ātman is rightly called Tripurasundarī. Śakti or Kālī has been addressed as the spouse of the Destroyer of the Three Cities.[49] Śiva alone can grant liberation to *jīva* by destroying the veil of nescience.

Kālī worship is part of Śaktism. Kālī is called Mahādevī.[50] The deity symbolically represents the causal matrix. She is said to be beauteous with the beauty of a dark rain-cloud.[51] She has been compared with a black cloud, because she is formless and colourless. Black is no colour. Want of colour is black. She is said to be adorned with a garland of beads which is known as Akṣa Mālā. The different beads of the garland represent different expressions of creation. These expressions, fifty in number, are again represented by fifty letters, from *a* (अ) to *kṣa* (क्ष). Kālī or Mahādevī, being the creative principle, is the origin of creations. Hence, She is adorned with the Akṣa Mālā. She is without any clothing (निःवस्त्रा) because she is uncaused. Clothing her would have conveyed the sense of limitation. She has been further described as dancing on the corpse of Śiva.[52] Śiva is said to be inactive (अकर्त्ता). The corpse of Śiva conveys the sense of inactivity. Śiva or the Cosmic Consciousness has willingly gone into the bondage of Śakti so that He can enjoy the cosmic dance of Śakti. The cosmic dance of Śakti is nothing but the rhythmic expression of different forms, colours and vibrations of the Cosmos.

Śakti is the causal matrix. Cause and effect are really one. What is cause in the first phase becomes effect in the second phase and this effect again becomes cause in the third phase.

J.N. Farquhar has wrongly interpreted Śakti as 'far more important than Śiva'. According to him, 'The genetic idea is this that, since the eternal, inconceivable Supreme, Śiva-Brahman, is altogether inactive, while his spouse is pure activity, Śakti, the creation and re-creation of the world and all the work of divine grace and liberation are her functions.'[53] He forgets that there cannot be two Supreme or Absolute entities. Śiva is certainly Supreme and Paramount. Śakti is symbolically represented as the spouse and hence, She is the immanent principle of Śiva. She does the act of creation and re-creation but only to the extent of Śiva's concurrence and kind approval.

Evolution

Bindu, Nāda and Kalā are the three phases of Tāntric evolution. Involution is the process of crudification of Cosmic Consciousness, which undergoes metamorphosis. Consciousness is transformed into crude matter. According to the variation in the degree of bondage of Śakti, Śiva, the Consciousness, has taken different forms, but the fundamental stuff is one and the same.

When Śiva undergoes a metamorphosis, he is known as Saguṇa. Saguṇa means the qualified form of Śiva. *Śāradā* says that the eternal Śiva should be known both as Nirguṇa, when Prakṛti (Śakti) remains dormant in Śiva, and Saguṇa, when Prakṛti, the operative principle, is transformed into the creative principle.[54] This Saguṇa Śiva is another name for Saguṇa Brahma.

The creation is nothing but the thought projection of Saguṇa Śiva. Śakti the *magna mater* is Mahādevī who conceives, bears and nourishes the entire world. Śiva is pure consciousness and Śakti is the activating principle. The whole world has sprung from her womb. As a dynamic aspect of Śiva, she ideates the world. This world is nothing but the creative ideation of the causal matrix. *Yoginī-hṛdaya Tantra* says that the world is designed by her own will.[55] Bhagavan Śiva was very pleased to see it. In *Kubjikā Tantra* it is stated that it is not Brahmā, Viṣṇu and Rudra who are the Creator, Preserver and Destroyer of the world but their Śaktis — Brahmāṇī, Vaiṣṇavī and Rudrāṇī.[56] The idea behind this is that Śiva, Pure Consciousness though, being Transcendental and Supreme, is inactive and helpless without the creative ideation of omni-active Śakti.

Śiva and Śakti coalesce into one undivided unity of transcendentality. The former is the Illuminating (Prakāśa) and Knowing entity and the latter the Veiling (Vimarśa) and Activating entity. So long as Śakti remains merged in Śiva, and does not get any scope of her activation, Śiva is unqualified and objectless. The theoretical dualism of Śiva and Śakti is symbolically represented in Tantra by a grain of gram (*canak*) having two seeds closely joined and covered with the sheath of Māyā. The creation starts only when they come apart.[57] When Śakti starts acting and reacting, the differentiation is started. This differentiation between Śiva and Śakti is the cause of creative ideation (*Sṛṣṭi-kalpanā*). By differentiation is meant objectivization of the Supreme Subjectivity.

Tantra expounds the philosophy of thirty-six Śaiva-Śākta Tattvas. Tattva means the created being. The stages of the creation are the stages of involution of the macrocosm and evolution of the microcosm. In the process of involution, consciousness is metamorphozed, due to the operation of the creative matrix, into causal, subtle and gross Tattvas. J.C. Chatterjee writes: 'The process of the production of the Tattvas may, therefore, be spoken of, as it indeed is, as one of involution, the Reality of Parama Śiva being more and more involved, stage at which it appears as the physical.'[58]

Involution is the process of analysis; the one, Infinite Self, is transformed into innumerable entities. In the course of an analysis, the higher principles are involved in the lower principles. Each Tattva remains involved in its lower Tattva. The cruder Tattvas develop from the subtler Tattvas. The subtler Tattvas have a wider scope for the manifestation of the Spirit; the cruder Tattvas have increasingly greater restrictions. In the crudest Tattva all the causal, subtle, ideal and spiritual principles are present. 'That is to say', remarks J.C. Chatterjee, 'wherever there exists a lower Tattva, *i.e.* a Tattva of greater restriction (being produced from one of a wider scope), there are also all the other and higher ones, in full manifestation and holding the lower, as it were, in their bosom, they existing as so many concentric circles of gradually decreasing extent – or, from another point of view, standing like a number of mathematical points occupying the same position and yet somehow maintaining their individuality, in the heart of the lower as its very life and soul.'[59]

In *Pratyabhijñā-Hṛdayam*[60] it is said that Śiva animated by the desire of having a manifest universe which is one with Himself first of all shines forth as the one Cit which is the very void detached from Māyā. This state of isolation of Cit is known as *anāśṛtaśiva* (Śiva who is attached to nothing). Therefore, he is metamorphozed in the totality of suchnesses, worlds, entities and Tattvas.

'From Sakala Parameśvara vested with the wealth of Sat, Cit, Ānanda issued Śakti, from Śakti came Nāda and from Nāda issued Bindu.'[61] Parameśvara is here Saguṇa Brahman. He is Śiva Tattva. When Parama Śiva is encircled by the three belligerent forces of Śakti, he is known as Śiva Tattva and Śakti is here called Śivānī. He is called Sakala because he is metamorphozed. He is no more Parama Śiva, *i.e.* unsubjectivated. He has been subjectivized by the creative matrix. And hence he is associated with the expressed creative ideation (*kalā*). When Śakti is individualized She is called *kalā*. Śiva is always with Śakti. In the state of spiritual sublimity (Parāsaṁvit) Śakti is unmanifest and exists in her own form as pure Being-Consciousness-Bliss (Saccidānandamayī, Cidrūpiṇī). It is said that Śiva is endowed with the spiritual wealth of pure Being-Consciousness-Bliss to prove that he does not lose his transcendentality even when he associates himself with the creative matrix (Māyā). Śiva has two aspects. In his unchanging aspect, he is Saccidānanda. It is called Parā-Saṁvit. In the changing aspect, he transforms himself into the world process and the apparent change is being experienced by *jīva*. But the ultimate cause of this change, involution and evolution is he himself; which is known as Śiva-Tattva inseparably associated with his immanent principle Śakti-Tattva. In this way from Parama Śiva or Parā-Saṁvit. has emerged Śiva-Tattva and Śakti-Tattva. But Śiva-Tattva and Śakti-Tattva are neither different nor alien to Parama Śiva.

Śakti-Tattva means here Mūla Prakṛti. Śakti is the combination of three principles or forces, *i.e.* Sentient, Mutative and Static. In the state of Parā-Saṁvit all the three belligerent forces of Śakti exist in a dormant stage. They form an infinite geometrical figure but cannot form a triangle of forces due to the density of Consciousness. But with the activation of Śakti-Tattva, three belligerent forces form a triangle of forces known as Śiva-Tattva. Śiva is enclosed by this triangle. Śiva-Tattva is under the theoretical bondage of Śakti. In this state of equilibrium, no resultant is formed due to the proper adjustment in the triangle of forces. Proper adjustment means the constant exchange or transformation of identities of the three fundamental principles. This inter-exchange of identities amongst the forces of the triangle is the causal state of creation.

The great commentator of *Śāradā Tilaka,* Rāghava Bhaṭṭa, says that like the Saṁkhya concept of appearance of realities from realities (Sadutapattivāda), Śakti which remains in the dormant stage in Parā-Saṁvit becomes manifest (Ucchunāvasthā).[62] Śakti is without any cause. She is beginningless. Here Caitanyadhyasena means the eternal coexistence of Śiva and Śakti. The eternal flow of Śakti is there but they are flowing without any feeling. Thus, Nirguṇa Śiva does not mean Śiva without Guṇa (Śakti) but it means the Guṇātīta state of Śiva. This Śakti-Tattva issues from Śiva-Tattva. It is further said that from Śakti evolves Nāda and from Nāda issues Bindu. From the causal Bindu proceeds the effect (*kārya*) Bindu, Nāda and Bīja.[63]

The scientific explanation of the Tāntric interpretation of creation will be like this. After the formation of the triangle of forces, the three fundamental principles could not maintain the state of equilibrium due to their belligerent nature. As a result of a constant clash amongst the three principles, it is but logical that the balance would be disturbed and the triangle of forces would burst from one of the vertices. The point from which the triangle of forces bursts out is Bīja. It is called *kāmavīja.* It is the seed of creation. When this seed of creation is expressed in a metaphysical straight line it is called Nāda. It is dominated by the Sentient principle. But due to the activation or domination of the Static principle, the expression takes the form of a curvature known in Tantra as Kalā. With the creation of the curvature of Kalā, the phenomenal world comes into being. In the scientific language the universe is nothing but a collection of different waves or curvatures.

Woodroffe writes: 'Thus, the Tantras speak of the development of the straight line (Ṛju-rekhā) from the point which, when it has gone its length as a point, is turned (Vakra-rekhā aṁkuśākāra) by the force of the spiralling sack of Māyā in which it works so as to form a figure of two dimensions, which again is turned upon itself, ascending as a straight line into the plane of the third dimension, thus forming the triangular or pyramidal figure called Sṛgataka.'[64]

Mādhavācārya, while enumerating the philosophy of Paṇini, says: 'The eternal word is called *sphoṭa* . . . .'[65] Sphoṭa is nothing but the bursting of the Kāmabīja. It is the first sound. That is why it is said that in the beginning there was nothing but word and the word was God.

Parā-Bindu is the synonym of Parā-Saṁvita. It is the undivided and undifferentiated state of Śiva-Śakti. But when Śiva and Śakti are differentiated due to the 'bursting' of Kāmabīja, Parā-Bindu is transformed into three forms, of Bindu, Bīja and Nāda. Bindu is Śiva, Bīja is Śakti and Nāda is Śiva-Śakti from the point of view of cause. *Śāradā Tilaka* says: 'That which is supreme Śakti again divides itself into three, Bindu, Nāda and Bīja.'[66]

Bindu is of the nature of Śiva and Bīja of Śakti and Nāda represents the mutual relation of the two. This is held by all those who are versed in the Āgamas.[67]

The Nāda or Śabda is the first expression of creation. The Śabda Brahman is the cause of the manifest and differentiated word and meaning or the subtle and crude objects. Without understanding the meaning and significance of *sphoṭa* or the eternal word, one cannot become one with Brahman. The Supreme Bliss is accomplished only after the removal of Nāda-Bindu ignorance. Tantra prescribes Nāda-Bindu Yoga for the attainment of supreme oneness with Parama Śiva. Nāda-Bindu Yoga is an intuitional practice of tearing the veil of ignorance and establishing oneself in the realm of Divinity. Mādhavācārya in summarizing the philosophy of Pāṇini says: 'And thus we establish the facts that the "exposition of words" is the means to final bliss.'[68]

Nāda is called Sadākhyā-Tattva and Bindu is known as Īśvara-Tattva. Bindu and Nāda are the stages of creative ideation. The dormant germ of creation gets the scope of its expression due to the activation of Sadākhyā and Īśvara-Tattva. Bindu has been described as the massive (Ghanavasthā) state of Śakti.

Bindu is both void (Śūnyatā) and Guṇa.[69] In the void aspect of it, Bindu is Supreme Brahman and in its Guṇa aspect, it is Śakti. According to J.C. Chatterjee the experience of *I am* is the Sadākhya-Tattva which has issued from Śiva-Śakti-Tattva.[70] Sadākhyā-Tattva has been named as Sadā-Śiva-Tattva also. Further in the process of impersonal exhibition, Śiva creates the ideal universe. The Cosmic Mind or the Divine Experience in the process of emergence transforms *I* into *This.* This is called Īśvara-Tattva. The Śudhya-Vidyā-Tattva is the equalization of subject and object, *I* and *This.* 'This experience of equalizing the realization', says J.C. Chatterjee, 'of the two sides of the relation of identity, namely, "I and This", and also of what may be called possession—of one of the two sides as belonging to the other—is called the Sad-Vidyā or Śudha-Vidyā—the state of Experience (or Knowledge) in which the true relation of things is realized."[71]

It is said that Śiva, Śakti, Sadākhyā, Īśvara and Śudha-Vidyā are the spiritual manifestation of Parama Śiva. According to Kashmir Śaivism these are the five powers of Parama Śiva. These are the pure states of expressions. Śudha-Vidyā is called Mahāmāyā. It is predominant with Sentient principles.

When Śakti, which is an operative principle, becomes the creative principle it is known as Māyā. Māyā is a causal matrix. It is the cause of physical manifestation. Māyā is the Śakti of Parama Śiva, which brings about metamorphosis or transformation in Cosmic Consciousness. Śiva is individualized in many. According to Kashmir Śaivism Parama Śiva has two forms of Śakti—Cit-Śakti and Māyā-Śakti. They may be called Vidyā-Māyā and Avidyā-Māyā. The nature of Vidyā Māyā is to help in the attainment of Parama Śiva with her power of *hlādinī* (ह्लादिनी) and *samvita* (संवित). It accelerates the process of evolution. Whereas Avidyā-Māyā brings about the crudification of Self. It creates the phenomenal world. With the power of her veiling (*āvaraṇa*) and deflect (*vikṣepa*) it obscures, limits and binds the Self. But these two powers or functions of Śiva are not independent and separable. Woodroffe explains: 'Śiva has two functions, namely, Tirodhāna, that by which He yields to His worshipper, and Anugraha whereby He, through His grace, reveals Himself by the "descent of Śakti" or grace (Śāktipāda).'[72] Śakti has been described as both Madhumatī (honey) and Māyā.[73] She is the liberator from the trammels of primeval ignorance. She is the beacon of light with whose help one can swim across the ocean of worldliness. And at the same time she is the basis of false universe (Mithyā Jagadadiṣṭhāna).[74]

Māyā is all-pervasive, because it is the causal matrix. It is subtle because it is incomprehensible to the intellect. It is, eternal because it is the immanent aspect of the Absolute. *Mālinivijayottara* says: 'She is one, pervasive, undivided, the origin of the world, without beginning and end, and it is also called the Īśānī of Śiva.'[75]

Māyā is the creative principle of Parama Śiva. It is a principle of obscuration and limitation. It limits the true nature of both subject and object, the Self and the universe. Parama Śiva is the Absolute. He is Truth, Consciousness and Bliss, No limitation or obscuration is admissible in his Transcendentality. With the activation of Śakti , Parama Śiva does not lose his Transcendentality. Dr. K.C. Pandey remarks: 'The supposition of Māyā as a principle of obscuration is both necessary and logical. For, if the ultimate Reality possesses all the five powers Cit, Ānanda, Īcchā, Jñāna and Kriyā — and so is perfect in every way, and the universe is identical with it, it has to be explained where does the plurality and selves with all their limitations come from; and what is the cause of the limited creation which form, the object of experience of the limited beings. To account for these facts or rather to answer these questions, it is that the Māyā is supposed to be the force of obscuration. As such Māyā-Tattva hides the true nature of the Self so that not only all its, five powers are obscured but the universe also, which was in relation of identity with it, disappears. Thus, there arises the occasion for the other aspect of Māyā, *viz.* as the cause of the limited universe to come into play and produce limited universe in all its parts almost simultaneously such as emblic myrobalan (*amalākī*), being forcefully struck with a stuff, lets fall its fruits.'[76]

Māyā is the efficient cause of the universe. She is a force of obscuration and limitation and is responsible for the transformation of Infinite Self into innumerable finite beings. The Universal Self is metamorphozed into innumerable empirical selves. Due to the influence of Māyā, the Real Self erroneously identifies itself with the lower self. Due to ignorance Self becomes the victim of Svarupakhyāti. Māyā creates five principles or powers known as *Kañcukas* (sheaths) which limit the Knowledge and Power of the Universal Self. These five evolutes are Kāla, Vidyā, Rāga, Niyati and Kalā. They obscure interest, knowledge, power, space and time.

The five *kañcukas* or sheaths envelop the Universal Self. Kalā limits the omnipotent powers of the Supreme and reduces the power of Puruṣa to the doing of only few things. *Tattva-Sandoḥ* explains *kalā* thus : 'That which was His power of all-doingness, the same being contracted and capable of accomplishing but a few things and reducing him to the state of a little doer is called *Kalā*.'[77]

Kāla produces limitation of time and makes an individual mortal. Niyati snatches the freedom, the will to do everything and anything, regulates and restricts the movement and action. Rāga creates a sense of attachment with the mundane objects. The individual pines for the mundane possessions. The transcendentality and omniscience and omnipotence of Self are circumscribed by the *kañcukas*, and Puruṣa is reduced to a little 'doer' and 'knower'.

A view of the evolutes of Māyā Śakti :*

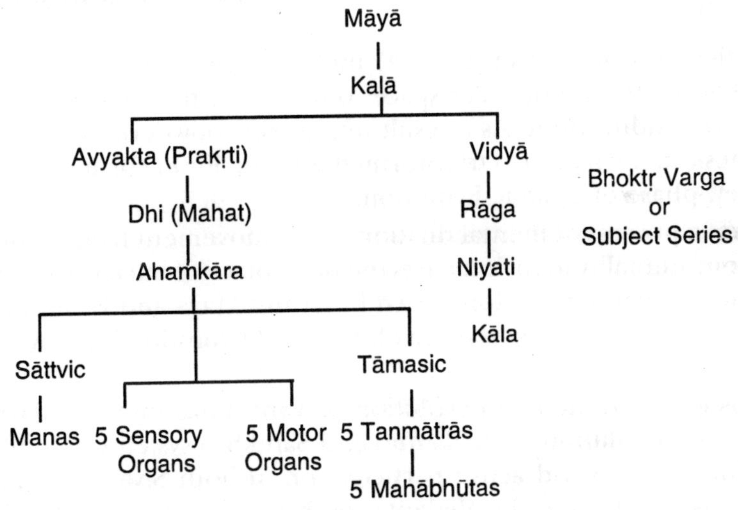

*Taken from *Mālinivijayottara.*

It is with these *kañcukas* that Māyā enwraps Puruṣa. The microcosm goes into deep slumber and forgets his Divine nature and origin. According to Tantra every microcosm is a hybernated macrocosm. Tantra lays down the principles of intuitional practice (Sādhanā) to arouse the dormant divinity in man and to make him realize that he is Śiva, the Absolute.

Prakṛti is the creation of Māyā Śakti. It is the origin of the emergence of twenty-four objective *tattvas* almost in the same manner as we have in the Sāṁkhya system. Unlike Sāṁkhya Prakṛti, Prakṛti of Kashmir Śaivism is not an independent reality but is one of the lower powers of Parama Śiva.

In our opinion Śiva-Śakti-Sattva forms the universal nucleus. Every structure has a nucleus. In the atomic structure, we know that electrons, protons, etc., move round the nucleus which maintains the structural solidarity. In case of our solar system, sun forms the nucleus, round which other planets and satellites revolve like electrons. This is not the only solar system in our cosmos. There are innumerable solar systems. Hence there must be some cosmic nucleus. That cosmic nucleus is Śiva-Śakti Tattva. That alone is the ultimate source of life of the entire universe.

In the process of Involution, the Cosmic Consciousness undergoes transformation in form of first subjectivity (Budhi-Tattva), second subjectivity (Aham-Tattva) and objectivated *I* (Citta). This objectivated *I* or Cosmic Citta is the physical world constituted of the five fundamental factors — Ether, Air, Luminous, Liquid and Solid. It has been said that 'Consciousness (*cetanā*) which is qualified by the contraction of Citi has been formed of the contracted universe.'[78]

The solid (Pṛthvī-Tattva) factors is the crudest manifestation; there is no further scope of crudification. But the push and pull of the Māyā (Avidyā Māyā) is there. Due to the internal clash and external pressure, there is a change in intra-molecular space.

Crudification of Consciousness (Śiva) means increase in the chemical affinity and decrease in the intra-molecular space. But beyond the solid factor there is no further scope of crudification. As a result matter gets powdered down. Due to this clash and cohesion, the matter is transformed into the lower form of mind and thus ushers in a new phase of Cosmic Evolution.

Evolution is a process of mental dilation. It is a movement from imperfection to perfection, from animality to divinity. It is the birth-place of microcosm. It is a stream of consciousness. Involution is dominated by Avidyā-Māyā and Evolution is guided by Vidyā-Māyā. The whole process of Involution and Evolution is known as Brahma-Cakra.

The philosophy and theory of evolution of Tantra has some similarity with the Sāṁkhya system of Evolution. Both Tantra and Sāṁkhya systems hold the view that for the creation of the world active participation of both Śiva (Puruṣa) and Śakti (Prakṛti) is required. Unlike the Vedānta, both systems profess that the world is neither real nor unreal. It is not unreal like man's horn, nor real, since it passes away.[79] According to Tantra, the universe is neither real nor an illusion. It is a relative truth.

However, the Tantra theory of Evolution is nearer to the Sāṁkhya than the Vedānta. It stands in between the Sāmkhya and the Vedānta. According to Tantra, universe is the thought projection (Sṛṣti-kalpanā) of Saguṇa Brahman. It is real for the microcosm but unreal for Saguṇa Brahman. In the process of Involution Śiva (Cosmic Consciousness) is metamorphozed into crude physicality. In the process of Evolution, the Crude physicality is transformed into psychic being. Here Tantra agrees with the materialists that mind is the by-product of matter but contrary to the objective thinkers, Tantra holds that matter itself is nothing but the transformed stage of Consciousness.

Thus, the Tantra theory of Evolution is most logical and scientific. It solves all the intricacies of both science and philosophy. Tantra is, in a way, the meeting ground of both science and philosophy.

Parama Śiva has no externality. The appearance of universe in Cosmic Consciousness is the action of Avidyā. Due to the activation of Avidyā, Parama Śiva suffers no change. He remains always pure and undivided. However, the phenomenal world is not a false appearance due to original Error. The world is neither Māyā nor Reality.

According to Tantra the entire creation is Ābhāsa. The phenomenal world is real in the sense that it is the manifestation of Parama Śiva. Evolution is the result of self-movement (Spanda) on the part of Śiva-Śakti. The world of waves and vibrations, things and beings, is the self-manifestation of the non-dual Cosmic Consciousness. The Supreme Reality splits itself spontaneously into two sections— subject and object. Māyā a essentially identical with Cosmic Consciousness. She creates infinite forms but never swerves from the essence. Gopinath Kaviraj states: 'When the universe comes into being it does so as only an image within the unique Self. The universe as such is varied but underlying it is the pure and simple unity of Caitanya revealing itself to the eye of diligent search (अनुसंधान). The manifestation of the universe, due to the Free Will (स्वातन्त्र) of the Absolute, is thus a process of Ābhāsa and for the initiation of this process nothing beyond the play of the will is needed ....'[80] The world of appearance is real in the same way as an image is real but it has no existence apart from the consciousness in which it is manifested. Its existence is only the existence of the Absolute.

REFERENCES

1. तावान्पूर्णस्वभावोऽसौ परमः शिव उच्यते।
   तेनात्रोपासकाः साक्षात्तत्रैव परिनिष्ठिताः।।108।। *Tantrāloka*, vol. I, ch. I, ver. 108, p. 151.
2. *Tripurā Rahasyam*, pp. 11-12. Sarasvatī Bhavan Granthamālā, vol. 15. Varanasi, 1965.
3. *Malinivijayottara Tantram*, ch. I, ver. 7, p. 1. Srinagar, Kashmir Sanskrit Series, 1922.
4. *Tripurā Rahasyam*, pp, 7-8.
5. शिवशक्त्यात्मसंघट्टरुपे ब्रह्मणि शाश्वते। ii. 19
   Yoginī Hṛdaya, p. 105. Sarasvatī Bhavan Granthamālā, vol. 7. Varanasi, 1963.
6. J.C. Chatterjee, *Kashmir Śaivism*, p. 63. Research & Publication Department, Srinagar, 1962.
7. शक्तिमदैक्यात्म्यलक्षणात्लवणारनालवत्परस्परमेलनात्। *Tantrāloka*, 11, 192.
8. चितिः स्वतन्त्रा विश्वसिद्धि हेतुः।
   Pratyabhijñāhṛdayam, p. 20. Adyar Library, Madras, 1938.
9. *Mahānirvāṇa Tantra*, ch. II, ver. 59.

10. निराकारं परं ज्योतिबिन्दु चाव्ययसंज्ञकम्।
    बिन्दु शब्देन शून्यं स्यात तथा च गुणसूचकम्। तोडलतन्त्रे *The Serpent Power.*
11. *Ānanda Sūtram*, p. 1. Ananda Nagar, Purulia (W. Bengal).
12. तयोयद यामलं रूपं स संघत्त इति स्मृतः
    आनन्दशर्त्तिः शैवोक्त यतो विश्वं विसृज्यति
    न शिवः शर्त्तिहितो न शक्ति शिववर्जिता। *Tantrāloka*, Āhnika 3.
13. अहं प्रकृतिरूपा चेत चिदानन्दपरायनः *The Kulacūḍāmaṇi Nigama*, vol. 6. ch. I
14. शिवशतयात्मसंघट्टरूपे शिवशक्तंयात्मनोः
    प्रकाश विमर्शममयोः सघंट्टः सामरस्य तद्रूपे........1 *Yoginī Hṛdaya*, p. 105.
15. *Mahānirvāṇa Tantra*, ch. I, ver. 34.
16. *Ibid.*, ver. 36.
17. *Ibid.*, ver. 14.
18. न तत्र सूर्यो भाति न चन्द्रतारकं
    नेमा विद्युतो भान्ति कुतोऽयमग्निा।
    तमेव भान्तमनुभाति सर्वं
    तस्य भासा सर्वमिदंविभाति *Kaṭha Upaniṣad*, II.ii.15.
19. परमः शिवः पुरुषोत्तमः विश्वस्य केन्द्रम्। *Ānanda Sūtram*, p. 4.
20. *Pratyabhijñāhṛdayam*, p. 50.
21. शिवशक्तिसामरस्यमयजगदानन्दरूपमित्यर्थ। *Tantrāloka*. Āh. XXIX, 84.
22. *The Serpent Power*, p. 28,
23. *Bhāratiya Saṁskṛti aur Sādhanā*, vol. I, p. 5.
24. *Ānanda Sūtram*, p. 3.
25. *The Pratyabhijñāhṛdayam*, p. 20.
26. *A History of Indian Philosophy*, vol. V, p. 38.
27. MS., Adyar Library, Madras.
28. *Śāradā Tilakam*, ch. I.
29. *parattvaṁ vijānīhi vijñānaṁ parameśvarī dvitiyaṁ smaranaṁ yatranāhaṁ brahmeti śuddhadhiḥ.* — II.2.23.13.
30. *utpatya ajñāna-sambhutaṁ saṁsayakhyaṁ visa drumam Śivādvaita-mahā-kalpa-urkṣa-bhūmir yathā bhavet.* — II, 1.6, iic.d-12.
31. *Kashmir Shaivism*, p. 64.
32. अप्रमेयं ततो जेयं शिव तत्त्वं वराणने *Svacchanda Tantram*, vol. V. (part B). p. 281, 1933
33. *Nirguṇa Saguṇas citi śavo jñeyaḥ sanātanaḥ*
    Nirguṇaccaiva saṁjata bindavas traya eva ca
    Brahmabindura viṣṇubindu rudrabindura maheśvarī. — p. 13
34. Gopinath Rao, *Elements of Hindu Iconography*, vol. II. pt. II, pp. 361-72.
35. *Tripurā Rahasyam*, pp. 15-16.
36. शक्तिः सा शिवस्य शक्ति। *Ānanda Sūtram*, ver. 2, p. 3.
37. *Kāma-kalā-Vilāsa*, (3rd. ed.) p. 6., ver. 2, Ganesh & Co., Madras, 1961.
38. *The Garland of Letters*, p. 97.
39. *Kashmir Shaivism.*
40. *Iccā śaiva svacchā santatasamavāyani saḥ śaktiḥ sacarācarasya jagato bījaṁ nikhilasya nijanilinasya — Tattva Sandoḥ.*
41. *Saundaryalaharī*, vv. 17, 29, 32, 51, 64, 76, 77.

42. *Saundaryalahari.*, vv. 65, 84, 90.
43. *Ibid.*, ver. 74.
44. *Īśvara-Pratyabhijñā,* III. ii. 7.
45. *The Great Liberation,* pp. 66-67.
46. *Saundaryalaharī,* p. 10
47. *Hymn of Kālī,* p. 33.
48. *Tantrasāra,* edited by Rasik Mohan Chatterjee, p. 596.
49. *Karpurādi-stotra,* ver. I., p. 49, Ganesh & Co., Madras.
50. सैव काली महादेवी जीयते लोकवेदयोः।
    इतिहासेषु तन्येषु सिद्धान्तेषु कुलेषु च।। *Mahārtha Mañjarī,* p. 107, 1919.
51. *Ibid.*
52. *Ibid.*, p. 67.
53. *Outline of the Religious Literature of India* (2nd ed.), p. 200.
54. *Nirguṇaḥ saguṇaśceti śivoḥ jñeyaḥ sanātanaḥ,*
    Nirguṇah prakṛteranyaḥ saguṇaḥ sakalaḥ smṛtaḥ.
55. *Svecchā-viśvamayollakha-khachitaṁ.* *Yoginī-hṛdaya Tantra*
56. *Kubjikā Tantra,* ch. 1, Prantoṣṇī-9
57. शित्वं शक्ति विभागेन जायते सृष्टि कल्पना। *Ṣaṭcakra Nirupaṇa,* p. 76.
58. *Kashmir Shaivism,* p. 148.
59. *Ibid.*
60. *Pretyabhijñā-Hṛdayam,* p. 30.
61. *Saccidānanda-vibhavāt sakalāt parameśvarāt asic-chaktis tato nādo nādād bindu-samudbhavaḥ* — *Śāradā,* ch. 1, ver. 7
62. *Yā anādirūpā caitanya-dhyāsena mahāpralaye sūkṣma sthitā.* — *Śāradā Tilaka.*
63. *Asmacca kāranabindoḥ sākṣāta krameṇa kāryabindrotato nādastato bījam iti trayaṁ utpannaṁ tadidaṁ parā sūkṣmasthūlapadam apy ucyate.* — *Śāradā Tilaka.* ver. 132.
64. *The Serpent Power,* pp. 35-36.
65 *The Sarva-Darśana-Saṅgraha,* p. 211.
66. *Śāradā Tilaka,* I.1.9.
67. *Śāradā Tilaka.* ch. I. 8, 9.
68. *The Sarva-Darśana-Saṅgraha,* p. 220.
69. *Toḍala Tantra,* ch. VI.
70. *Kashmir Shaivism,* p. 67.
71. *Ibid.*, pp. 73-74.
72. *The Garland of Letters* (4th ed.), pp. 136-37. Ganesh & Co., Madras, 1963.
73. *Lalitā Sahasranāma,* ver. 139.
74. *Ibid.*, ver. 10.2.
75. सा चैका व्यापिनी रूपा निष्कला जगतो निधिः।
    अनाद्यन्ता शिवेशानी व्ययहीना च कथ्यते। — ch. I, ver. 26.
76. Abhinavagupta, *A Historical and Philosophical Study,* pp. 235-36. Chowkhamba Sanskrit Series, Benares, 1935.
77. *Tattva-Sandoha,* ch. V, ver. 8.
78. *Pratyabhijñāhṛdayam,* Sūtra 4, p. 30.
79. *Indian Philosophy,* vol. II, p. 274.
80. *Tripurā-Rahasyam,* p. 11.

5 Kuṇḍalinī -Yoga

Tantra-Yoga stands for the realization of Parama Śiva. Mantra, Yantra and Kulakuṇḍalinī are the cardinal principles of Tāntric culture. Mantra and Yantra are the warp and woof of the Tāntric cult. Tāntrism is a scientific approach towards the realization of Truth, which is transcendental in nature. It brings about a spiritual renaissance and psychic revolution. Life cannot be made fuller and richer by a logical approach alone. Mind is not the ultimate category of the existence and being. There is something which transcends reason for which the term 'intuition' is used. That is why reason is subordinated to intuition. Reason cannot comprehend the Absolute, which is beyond the dualism of subject and object. According to Tantra morality is the base, intuition the way and life-divine the goal. When a man enters into the realm of intuition, he has not only the vision of the Divine, but he himself feels extended and illumined. Mantra is life. The Kuṇḍalinī is the soul and Yantra is the body of Tantra Śāstra. Mantra Sādhanā makes a man pure and Kuṇḍalinī Sādhanā leads to the mystic oneness of Śiva and Śakti. Mantra Sādhanā prepares an esoteric background for the arousal of the Kuṇḍalinī. However, they are not independent schools of Tantra. They are complementary to each other.

The Kuṇḍalinī is the greatest discovery of Tāntrism. It is the backbone of the Tāntric cult. The whole esoteric science of Tantra veers round this mystic spiritual force. The awakening of the Kuṇḍalinī is the sole objective of Tantra Sādhanā. It ushers in a new era of spiritual experience and brings about a total transformation of an individual. It deepens the consciousness and sublimates intellect into intuition. It brings the realization of Parama Śiva, the Supreme Godhead, which is the nucleus of all the psychic and physical nuclei.

The Kuṇḍalinī is a dormant divinity in animality. It is an esoteric concept, a spiritual force latent in every being. Without the arousal of the Kuṇḍalinī, there cannot be any development of divinity. Every man is God. *Jīva* is Śiva. '*Jīva* is Śiva and Śiva is *jīva*; the only difference is that one is in bondage and the other is free.'[1] In *jīva,* the divinity is in a dormant condition. This dormant divinity is known as Kuṇḍalinī.

For the awakening of the Kuṇḍalinī following three factors are required: *Mantrāghāta, Mantra-caitanya* and *Mantra-dīpinī.* The awakening of the Kuṇḍalinī is known as Puraścarṇa. The Kuṇḍalinī-Yoga is an aggressive form of spirituality. It is pre-eminently an esoteric science. The attainment of the four objects of life, *viz. Dharma, Artha, Kāma and Mokṣa,* is the main purpose behind the Kuṇḍalinī-Yoga.

The Kuṇḍalinī can be made conscious by constant incantation of the Īṣṭa-Mantra. With the awakening of the Kuṇḍalińī the Sādhaka starts losing the feeling of *I*-ness. It has the consuming effect. The individual loses his own individuality. As fire is latent in wood and on the rubbing of wood is made kinetic and burns its very source, similarly when the Kuṇḍalinī becomes conscious, it burns the very seed of individuality. It cuts asunder the bondage of nescience and *jīva* becomes Śiva. To achieve oneness with Śiva is the central objective of making the Kuṇḍalinī conscious.

Kulakuṇḍalinī

Man is wrapped in nescience. He has erroneously identified himself with the lower self. Unless he neutralizes the positive effect of nescience, he cannot retrace his way against the singular and positive current of macrocosmic creative ideation. One can retrace one's way against the positive force of nescience only with the help of some negative force. Kulakuṇḍalinī the spiritual force with its fundamental negativity[2]—offers this help. The Kuṇḍalinī is the negative force of every individual being. It is not universal in character. The Kuṇḍalinī is a negative force of individuation. It differs from one individual to another.

The Kuṇḍalinī is Parā-Śakti.[3] It is the spiritual force behind all mental and physical activities. Dr. Gopinath Kaviraj says: 'The name of the Kuṇḍalinī is Ādhāra-Śakti. It is the substratum of all realities and remains the primordial basis of all beings. When it awakens it becomes one with consciousness by becoming unsubjectivated (*nirādhāra*) and the moment the Kuṇḍalinī becomes objectless the whole universe becomes objectless. When the Kuṇḍalinī becomes conscious the whole world takes the form of consciousness. The awakening of the Kuṇḍalinī and the realization of "Sarvaṁ Khalvidaṁ Brahman" (All is Brahman) of Śruti and the Sādhanā of spiritual experience of all-pervasiveness of consciousness are one.'[4]

The Kuṇḍalinī remains in a sleeping state. When it is awakened, the Sādhaka attains the intuitive power to visualise the Absolute. According to Tantra the Absolute is both Transcendent and Immanent. The transcendental aspect of the Absolute is Śiva and the immanent part of it is Śakti. However, it will be wrong to think that the transcendental aspect (Śiva) is real and the immanent part (Śakti) unreal. Both Śiva and Śakti constitute the Reality. This eternal co-existence or Samarasatā of the two is known as Parama Pada or Mahā-Bindu. The division of the two is the origin of creation. The transcendental aspect of the Absolute remains as a witnessing entity and the immanent part of it becomes the manifest universe. The transcendental aspect (Śiva) is one and unchanging Reality. Śiva remains always as the nucleus of both manifest and unmanifest universe. This Parā-Bindu acts and controls, both within and without the periphery of the cosmic order.

The Parā-Bindu has sub-centres in all created beings. These sub-centres are also the Parā-Bindu. In Tantra, the cosmic sub-centre is called the Sahasrāra Cakra. It is the seat of Parama Śiva. The Parā-Bindu is the starting point of cosmic creation. The starting point of the cosmic being is known as *Kāmavīja.* This is the point of origin of the fundamental positivity. In Tāntric esotericism it is said that Parama Śiva resides on the back of Śambhu Liṅga. The Kuṇḍalinī Śakti lives on the back of Svayambhū Liṅga. The Kuṇḍalinī being the force of fundamental negativity, its starting point is negative *Kāmavīja* of created being. Mūlādhāra Cakra, being the controlling station of the crudest matter (solid factor), is the starting point of negative *Kāmavīja.* Mūlādhāra is the lowest nerve plexus. Herein resides the Kuṇḍalinī, the Serpent Power. Tantra Sādhanā is mainly devoted to the awakening of the Kuṇḍalinī. Its whole purpose is to bring about the unification of Kuṇḍalinī Śakti, with Parama Śiva, whose abode is Sahasrāra. Only with the mystic unification of Śiva and Śakti, the non-qualified liberation (*Mokṣa*) can be attained.

There is, however, great misunderstanding about the concept of the Kiṇḍalinī. Some modern scientists have tried to locate the Kuṇḍalinī in the physical body. They have tried to identify the Kuṇḍalinī with the Vagus nerve. Vasant G. Rele writes: 'To our mind the Kuṇḍalinī interpreted as the serpent power, is the Vagus nerve of modern times, which supplies and controls all the important vital organs through different plexuses of the sympathetic portion of the autonomic (nervous) system.'[5] We differ from Rele's views. The Kuṇḍalinī has been wrongly identified with the Vagus nerve by him. This nerve has a physical existence and can be located in our body whereas the Kuṇḍalinī is a spiritual concept. It has no physical form. There are two kinds of the Vagus, right and left. But the Kuṇḍalinī is a singular principle. Research has been done on the location of the Kuṇḍalinī at the Yoga Research Centre of the All Indiạ Institute of Medical Sciences, New Delhi. According to Dr. B.K. Ananda and Dr. Balbir Singh Chinna, the Kaṇḍalinī cannot be identified with the Vagus nerve. It is in a sleeping condition at the Mūlādhāra Cakra. It is coiled, anti-clockwise (Dakṣiṇāvrata), three and a half times around the Svayambhu Liṅga. In both the Tāntric manual, *Ṣaṭcakra Nirupaṇa,* and *Haṭh Yoga Pradīpikā* it is said that the pericarp of the Ādhāra Lotus is a triangle or Kaṇḍa. The Kulakuṇḍalinī is said to be sleeping, closing the mouth of the Brahmadvāra.

When the Kuṇḍalinī is awakened and made conscious, it forces its passage through the different *cakras* and excites them to action and, piercing them, rises up. With the rising of the Kuṇḍalinī, the mind opens up and all mystic visions and esoteric powers come to the Yogi. When it reaches the pineal gland, the Yogi goes beyond body-mind consciousness and the soul becomes free in all respects. *Gandharva-Malikā* says: 'Meditate upon the Devī-Kuṇḍalinī who encircles the Svayambhu-Liṅga. Lead the Devī with the aid of the Haṁsa-Mantra to the Sahasrāra, where, O Parameśvarī, is the great Deva Sadāśiva. And then place there the beautiful Kuṇḍalinī who is excited by Her desire. Kuṇḍalinī, O Beloved, then wakes up and kisses the lotus-mouth of Śiva, who is gladdened by the scent of Her lotus-like mouth, and O Deveśi, she then enjoys Sadāśiva but after a very little while immediately, O Devī, Parameśvarī, then issues nectar. This issuing from their union is of the colour of lac. With this nectar of Deveśi should the Para-devatā be satisfied. Having thus satisfied the Devatās in the Six Cakras with that ambrosial stream, the wise one should by the same way bring her back to Mūlādhāra. The mind should in this process of going and coming be dissolved. O Pārvatī who practises this Yoga day by day is freed from decay and death, and is liberated from the bondage of this world.'[6]

The Kuṇḍalinī-Yoga is a physico-psycho-spiritual process of understanding the Transcendental Self which is beyond the dualism of subjectivity and objectivity. The esoteric process of awakening the Kuṇḍalinī and its gradual piercing of different *cakras* brings about the change and revolution in the metaphysical stratum of the living being. With the rising of the Kuṇḍalinī, the objectivated *I, i.e., citta,* is transformed into second subjectivity, i.e. *Ego,* and again *Ego* is transformed into *First Subjectivity, i.e., Buddhi-Tattva.* This process of transformation does not stop here; it goes one step further and the very first subjectivity is transformed into the Transcendental Self. Thus, the oneness of the Kuṇḍalinī and Śiva is essential for the realization of the Absolute which is not possible through intellectual pursuits because intellectual understanding is a process of knowing the causal relation of the given problem. Reason or intellect is embedded in dualism. It cannot go beyond the bounds of relativity. It has no access to the realm of Transcendent existence.

Slumbering Serpent Power

The awakening of the Kuṇḍalinī is the great event in the life of a man. When the Kuṇḍalinī is made to work, the trammels of Māyā are cut asunder, and the Soul becomes free from the bondage of individuation. We have already said that the Kuṇḍalinī is aroused with the help of Mantrāghāta, Mantra-dīpinī and Mantra-caitanya. By the incantation of *bīja-mantra,* a part of the Mantrāghāta process, an acoustic vibration is produced in the psychic body which has a whipping effect on the Kuṇḍalinī, the slumbering serpent power. The Kuṇḍalinī rises in her madness. But Mantrāghāta alone cannot produce the desired result unless the Yogi fulfils the other two conditions, *i.e.* Mantra-dīpinī and Mantra-caitanya.

Mantra-dīpinī stands for the inner and outer purification of mind. This purification known as morality can be achieved by the observation of Yama and Niyama Sādhanā. Adherence to the moral norms of life is essential for spiritual aspirants. And though morality is not the goal of spiritual life, yet it is a stepping stone to reach the culminating point of the spiritual march. It brings mental harmony which provides the congenial psychic climate necessary for spiritual Sādhanā. The Kuṇḍālinī has been called Śivātmā.[7] According to *Śāradā Tilaka* the Kuṇḍālinī has been identified with Antarātmā. She is the soul of the soul. She is infinitely gracious and beauteous. She is the Transcendental Power (Śiva Sāmarasya).

Mūlādhāra has been universally said to be the abode of the Kuṇḍalinī. *Śāradā Tilaka* describes the Kuṇḍālinī as the Serpent Power. She is the queen of spiritual kingdom, of which Śiva is the Supreme Lord. She leaves her abode and goes up through the path of Suṣumṇā and drinks the divine nectar continuously secreted by the thousand-petalled Lotus called the pineal gland. 'The Kuṇḍalinī which is like a serpent and which is the queen of the Divine kingdom, leaves Mūlādhāra when she is awakened. She rises up through the path of Suṣumṇā. She is like lightning. She goes up after piercing the different *cakras* or the mystic knots. After reaching the destination, her spiritual goal, she embraces Śiva, who is the Lord of Sahasrāra Cakra (pineal gland) which remains submerged in divine nectar. After attaining the spiritual unification with Śiva, she returns to her native home and starts for Sahasrāra again and again.'[8]

The Kuṇḍalinī is neither a biological nor a psychic principle. It is a spiritual concept. There is no objective proof of her existence. But she can be *seen* intuitively. She has the brilliancy of millions of suns.[9] The sole objective of the Kuṇḍalinī-Yoga is to make pilgrimage to the kingdom of Lord Śiva, *i.e.* Sahasrāra, which is the place of Infinite Bliss. She is the creative matrix. She is the bewitching power of the world. She is eternal, infinite, non-causal and the creative principle of the world.

The discovery of the Kuṇḍalinī and the esoteric process of awakening it is prehistoric achievement of human ingenuity. It is one of the priceless treasure of Indian culture. Kuṇḍalinī Sādhanā was popularised and practised in pre-historic India when its civilization was in full bloom and Indians were in the hey-day of spiritual culture. When a spiritual seeker is initiated into Kuṇḍalinī Sādhanā, he becomes Bhairava.

The piercing of the Kuṇḍalinī cuts asunder the psychic knot (Hṛdaya-granthi) that rivets all involvements and attachments in the many strands of nature. With the awakening of the Kuṇḍalinī, all the metaphysical doubts are shorn off and all *karmas* dwindle away.

Tāntric Sādhanā is directed to awaken the dormant Kuṇḍalinī. According to Tāntric belief, there is a thousand petal Lotus at the pineal gland. The Parā-Bindu which is well concealed, is the main force of liberation. It is concealed by Amā Kalā and Nirvāṇa Kalā. Amā Kalā is full of divine nectar. The drinking of this divine nectar by the Kuṇḍalinī brings God-intoxication and spiritual ecstasy.

'Well concealed, and attainable only by great effort, is that subtle Bindu (Śūnya) which is the chief root of Liberation and which manifests the pure Nirvāṇa Kalā with Amā Kalā. Here is Deva who is known to all as Parama Śiva. He is the Brahman and the Ātmā of all beings. In Him are united both Rasa and Virasa and He is the Sun which destroys the darkness of nescience and delusion.'[10]

Thus, Parā-Bindu is Parama Śiva. The whole universe has emanated from this transcendental point. All the pencils of waves have originated from it. It is a supreme controller. It has sub-centres in all beings. It is said He is the soul of the soul. The mind is the doer. Jīvātmā is the knower. Parā Bindu is the witnessing counterpart of Jīvātmā. Thus, Jīvātmās are many but Antarātmā is a singular entity. Parā-Bindu is called Antarātmā because He is both the *seer* and the *knower* of all the Jīvātmās. The realization of Parā-Bindu is called the attainment of Parama-Pada.

The realization of Parā-Bindu is possible only after the awakening of the Kuṇḍalinī. When the Kuṇḍalinī reaches Sahasrāra, it drinks the divine nectar contained in Amā Kalā. Parā-Bindu can be realized when in a mystic state. In this state of spiritual realization, mind is dissolved. The mystic realization of formless and colourless Parā-Bindu is the greatest esoteric experience. This realization comes only after the commingling of Parama-Śiva and Parā Śakti. Parā-Bindu here is Parama-Śiva and the Kuṇḍalinī Para-Śakti.

Ṣaṭcakra Nirupaṇa further gives a mystic description of Nirvāṇa Śakti. The conception of Nirvāṇa Śakti is not possible for an ordinary human being. Above the Nirvāṇa Kalā is the place of Parā-Bindu. *Ṣaṭcakra Nirupaṇa* says: 'Within it, middle space (*i.e.*, middle of the Nirvāṇa Kalā) shines the Supreme and the Primordial Nirvāṇa Śakti; she is lustrous like ten million suns, and is the mother of the three worlds. She is extremely subtle, like unto the ten-millionth part of the end of a hair. She contains within Her the constantly flowing stream of gladness, and is the life of all beings. She graciously carries the knowledge of the Truth to the mind of the sages.'[11]

This shows that Kuṇḍalinī Sādhanā is very subtle and sublime. To have the conception of Amā Kalā, Nirvāṇa Kalā and Nirvāṇa Śakti, who are as fine as the ten millionth part of the end of a hair, a Sādhaka will have to extremely keenly sharpen his mind. Thus, Kuṇḍalinī Sādhanā is not a crude process of sexual contact as is wrongly believed. It is a psycho-spiritual process for sublimating mind. With the arousal of the Kuṇḍalinī, the dark chambers of mind are lighted up. The Sādhaka makes new inroads into the deeper realm of Consciousness. The intuitive visualization of Nirvāṇa-Śakti and Parā-Bindu means the realization of the transcendental nature of Being and Self.

Metaphysically speaking, the realization of Parā-Bindu brings about the dissolution of mind. Mind cannot visualize the ten millionth part of a hair ordinarily, But with the awakening of the Kuṇḍalinī mind becomes subtler and it acquires the spiritual power of visualization. Thus, the process of Kuṇḍalinī Sādhanā is a process of spiritualization of mind or, in other words, it is a technique of transforming mind into Self. It is a process of elevation of human consciousness.

The awakening of the Kuṇḍalinī is a great event in the life of a Sādhaka, Adherence to the principles of Yama and Niyama is a precondition. Tantra Sādhanā is not a mechanical process. It is the highest form of spirituality. The esoteric process of awakening the Kuṇḍalinī has been laid down in Tantra alone. *Ṣaṭcakra Nirupaṇa* says: 'The Sādhaka, whose mind is purified by the practice of Yama and Niyama and other forms of intuitional Sādhanā, learns from his Guru the way to the discovery of the great liberation. He rouses the Kuṇḍalinī by Hūṁ-kāra, pierces the centre of the Svayambhū Liṅga, the mouth of which is closed, and is, therefore, invisible and by means of the air and fire places her within the Brahmadvāra.'[12]

It states the method for rousing the Kuṇḍalinī from its dormant stage. The

Kundalinī can be awakened by uttering its *bīja-mantra, Hūṁ.* The utterance of *Hūṁ* creates an acoustic vibration in the psychic body which strikes the sleeping Kuṇḍalinī and awakens her. The creation of this acoustic vibration with the utterance of Hūṁ-kāra is referred to in the verse as 'air' and 'fire'. *Gorakṣa-Vacana-Saṁgraha* deals with the esoteric science of the awakening of the Kuṇḍalinī. The Nātha cult is analogous to Tāntric Sādhanā of the non-dualistic ideology of both Hindu and Buddhist Āgamic spiritual culture. Nāthaism represents all esoteric aspect of the Hindu culture. It emphasizes the awakening of the Kuṇḍalinī for the highest consummation of spiritual oneness. 'The Kuṇḍalinī, is in a dormant state lying above the Kāṇḍa. She is the giver of liberation to a yogi and is the cause of bondage for the ignorant. One who knows the Kuṇḍalinī alone is yogi.'[13]

The Kuṇḍalinī is the cause of both bondage and liberation. The awakening of the Kuṇḍalinī brings the realization of occult power. The Sādhaka whose mind is not rendered quiet and is not free from lust and attachment becomes baffled at the sudden possession of occult power. This brings degeneration in inferior minds. It clouds the spiritual vision and man engages in black magic. This sort of wanton misuse of occult power for the satisfaction of senses and ego is known as Avidyā Tantra.

Gorakṣa-Vacana-Saṁgraha speaks about the mode of arousing the Kuṇḍalinī. It says: 'The Kuṇḍalinī should be aroused by force by catching her by the tail. The moment she awakes, she starts moving upward.'[14]

Here it gives a mystic account of the esoteric process of arousing the Kuṇḍalinī. This is the most secret part of Tantra Sādhanā. It does not give the whole process of the mode of awakening the Kuṇḍalinī. It just gives an idea of the Tāntric mysticism. It is true that the Kuṇḍalinī moves with her tail upward. This is because the tail is subtler than the mouth and it widens the Suṣumṇā canal and makes possible for her to pierce the different *cakras.* After reaching Sahasrāra she starts drinking the divine nectar of Amā Kalā. At Sahasrāra she stands on her tail like a cobra.

A Misconception

This process of arousing the Kuṇḍalinī by force by catching her by the tail is sometimes mistaken as a process of Haṭha-Yoga. It is not. Before forcing the Kuṇḍalinī to move upward, a Sādhaka recites the Dhyāna mantra of the Kuṇḍalinī. Without this the Kuṇḍalinī can never be awakened. The incantation of Dhyāna mantra creates an acoustic vibration which cultivates an esoteric climate for the arousal of the Kuṇḍalinī. And after Dhyāna mantra, the Sādhaka recites Hūṁ-kāra and forces the Kuṇḍalinī to move upward. One should not practise this process more than thrice at a time. It can be practised for a maximum of four times on the eve of four Sandhyās.

This mode of arousing the Kuṇḍalinī should be performed only by those who have been initiated by a Guru. This verse, referred to above, also speaks of the importance of Yama and Niyama Sādhanā. The practice of *yama* and *niyama* brings, about a moral change and revolution in a Sādhaka. It cleanses the mind. But *yama* and *niyama* are not sufficient to destroy such baser inclinations like lust, anger, sex and the like which disturb the mental equilibrium of a Sādhaka. Adherence to the principles of morality is necessary for learning the art of arousing the Kuṇḍalinī. But Yama and Niyama Sādhanā is not sufficient to cultivate that spiritual climate which is necessary for the awakening of the Kuṇḍalinī. Along with the practice of *yama* and *niyama*, the other aspects of intuitional Sādhanā are also to be strictly followed. A wavering mind cannot perform spiritual Sādhanā. To arrest the cruder propensities of mind and to eliminate the baser passions of being, morality plus Kuṇḍalinī Sādhanā is required.

The esoteric process of uttering Hūṁ-kāra is a scientific process of arousing the Kuṇḍalinī. The utterance of Hūṁ-kāra opens the gateway to Śiva. It opens the door of Svayambhū Liṅga; and the Kuṇḍalinī rises through the Nāḍī-citrāṇī.

There is some confusion about the process of arousing the Kuṇḍalinī. There are some schools of yoga like Haṭha-Yoga which believe in the physical culture of yoġa and put more emphasis on the physical technique like the contracting of the anus and the practice of Khecarī-Mūdrā. *Haṭha-Yoga-Pradīpikā* deals mostly with the physical culture of yoga.

Āgama-Kalpa-Druma speaks about the mode of arousing the Kuṇḍalinī in the following words: 'Having seated oneself in the Padmāsana posture, the two hands should be placed in the lap. Thereafter, having mentally recited the Haṁsa Mantra, the anus should be gently contracted. One should then repeatedly raise the air by the same way, and having raised it let him pierce the *cakra.* I now speak of its process. In the Mūlādhāra lotus is a very beautiful triangle. Inside it is *kāma-pīṭha* like ten million young suns; above it (*kāma-pīṭha*) and recoiling Svayambhū Liṅga is Kuṇḍalinī Śakti.'[15] But as the Kuṇḍalinī is not a physical organ or principle, it cannot be awakened by the physical process of contracting the anus or the practice of Khechari-Mudrā. The process of awakening the Kuṇḍalinī is a mystic one. Researches[16] have confirmed that there is no proof for the physical existence of the Kuṇḍalinī. However, the other description about the Kuṇḍalinī is correct. The incantation of Haṁsa-Mantra is always fruitful. But the recitation of the *mantra* without proper initiation does not bring the desired result. Moreover, Haṁsa is not the only Īṣta Mantra. There are other *Siddha-Īṣṭa-Mantras.* It is necessary that a seeker should learn them from a proper Guru.

Āgama-Kalpa-Druma further says: 'As the result of excitation by the *Kāmāgni* and the action of the Kūrca-mantra on the Kuṇḍalinī, she is seized with the desire for Parā-Haṁsa.'[17] Here *Āgama-Kalpa-Druma* extols the Kūrca-mantra as the necessary means to awaken the Kuṇḍalinī. Kūrca- mantra means the *bīja-mantra* of Devī, which is *Hūṁ.* The Kuṇḍalinī is aroused by Hūṁ-kāra, and not by contracting the anus, since it is a crude process, whereas the Kuṇḍalinī is a spiritual principle. There cannot be any logical relation between the two. Thus, the utterance of Hūṁ-kāra is an esoteric process of Tantra Sādhanā to arouse the Kuṇḍalinī and take her to Sahasrāra, which is the abode of Lord Śiva.

Here *Kāmāgni* does not mean lust for sex indulgence. It means longing for the spiritual unification of the Kuṇḍalinī with Parama Śiva, Devī with Mahādeva or Rādhā with Kṛṣṇa. The word Rādhā has been derived from Rādh-dhātu which means the force (Śakti) that performs the act of worship, *i.e.* Kuṇḍalinī-Śakti. Kṛṣṇa here stands for the Parā-Bindu, which is the supreme controller of all beings and existence. The strong desire for the unification of the Kuṇḍalinī with Parama Śiva is created by the utterance of Hūṁ-kāra. Like a maiden whose heart bleeds for union with her lover, the Kuṇḍalinī becomes restless to embrace Parama Śiva. This mystic excitation of the Kuṇḍalinī has been described here as *Kāmāgni.*

The mystic union of the Kuṇḍalinī with Parama Śiva produces the divine bliss of salvation. The non-qualified liberation can be attained only by the Kuṇḍalinī Yoga. The Kuṇḍalinī has to open the three *granthis* (mystic knots) of Rudra, Brahmā and Viṣṇu. These *granthis* are called liṅgas. *Ṣaṭcakra Nirupaṇa* says: 'The Devī who is a Śudha-Sattva pierces the three *Liṅgas,* and, having reached all the lotuses, shines therein in the fullness of her lustre. Thereafter in her subtle state, lustrous like lightning and fine like lotus fibre, she goes to the gleaming flame like Śiva, the Supreme Bliss and all of a sudden produces the bliss of liberation.'[18]

The Kuṇḍalinī pierces all the six *cakras* and then reaches Sahasrāra. Of them, three Maṇipūra, Anāhata and Ājñā are the greatest stumbling blocks for the Kuṇḍalinī. These three are also known as Rudra, Brahmā and Viṣṇu *granthis.* They are described as liṅgas. Arthur Avalon describes Mūlādhāra, Anāhata and Ājñā as Svayambhū, Bāṇa and Itara *liṅgas* like the three *liṅgas* referred to in the above verse. But the Mūlādhāra where the Kuṇḍalinī resides is a minor obstacle for an individual's spiritual awakening. As the Mūlādhāra is the lowest and the first *cakra* the Kuṇḍalinī has no difficulty in piercing it. Mūlādhāra, Svādhiṣṭhāna and Viśudha Cakras offer the least resistance.

Arthur Avalon has erroneously identified Brahma-Nādī with Citrāṇī. The Suṣumṇā, the Citrāṇī and the Brahmāṇī are three independent Nāḍīs. Neither the Suṣumṇā nor the Citrāṇī is the mystic path of the Kuṇḍalinī. It is the Brahmāṇī, which is the spiritual passage of the Kuṇḍalinī. The Brahmaṇī is inside the Citrāṇī and the Citrāṇī is inside the Suṣumṇā. This mystic Suṣumṇā is inside the vertebral column. The Brahmāṇī is the most subtle and shining Nādī. When the Kuṇḍalinī reaches different *cakras,* which are in the form of a lotus, she swallows up all the different instincts (*vṛttis*) of the respective *cakras.* Thus, when she pierces Ājñā Cakra she eats up all the fifty human instincts and the Sādhaka becomes completely divinized. He has the realization of Saguṇa Śiva. He attains Savikalpa-Samādhi. When the Kuṇḍalinī approaches Śiva, who is in the form of Parā-Bindu in the pericarp of Sahasrāra Cakra, she brings to the Sādhaka the eternal bliss of salvation. The Sādhaka attains Nirvikalpa Samādhi.

'The Kuṇḍalinī Śakti, which has the brilliance of lightning and is composed of three *guṇas*, after piercing the unmanifest, lustrous abode of Śiva, which is in the form of Bindu and which is situated in the midst of eternal bliss and divine nectar, having the brilliance of a million moons and suns, returns to her resting place Mūlādhāra. One should meditate this form of the Kuṇḍalinī.'[19]

There is a universal belief that the divine nectar is being ever secreted from the pineal gland. When the Kuṇḍalinī embraces the Śambhu Liṅga, the Sādhaka experiences the spiritual ecstasy and goes into a mystic trance. The intensity of joy and happiness that issues from this esoteric union of the Kuṇḍalinī and the Parā-Bindu beggars description. One is lost in meditation and becomes one with Parama Śiva. The realization of Parama Śiva is the chief objective of Tantra Sādhanā. Tantra prescribes the esoteric discipline for the realization of Parama Śiva, who is the Absolute of Tantra philosophy. The Absolute of Tantra is Parā-Bindu. Parā-Bindu is situated in the Nirvāṇa Śakti, which is pregnant with the divine nectar. The realization of Parā-Bindu is the quintessence of Kuṇḍalinī-Yoga.

'The beautiful Kuṇḍalinī drinks the excellent red nectar issuing from Parama Śiva, and returns from there where shines Eternal and Transcendental Bliss in all its glory along the path of Kula and again enters the Mūlādhāra. The Yogi who has gained steadiness of mind makes offerings to the Īṣṭa Devatā and to the devatās in the six centres. The Ḍākini and others, with that stream of the celestial nectar which is in the vessel of Brahmāṇḍa, the knowledge whereof he has gained through the tradition of the Gurus.'[20]

The pineal gland is known as the mystery gland in modern psychology. The hormonal secretion of this gland has some mystic influence on both mind and body. This is the most precious of all the hormones. The different glands are different mental sub-stations. The higher gland controls the lower. The pineal gland controls all the subsidiary glands of the human structure.

The *ojas* of Swami Vivekananda was nothing but the effect of the pineal nectar. The pineal gland normally secretes three drops of hormones in twenty-four hours. These pineal hormones come to the pituitary gland or the Ājñā Cakra which is the controller of the conscious mind. Thus, if the mind is filled with filthy thoughts and ideas, the pineal hormones are burnt up. But when the mind is pure and engrossed in cosmic ideation, it drenches in the pineal hormones which brings about spiritual ecstasy to man. It is, therefore, a moral and psychic necessity to keep the mind free from the filth and dirt of mundane thoughts. The dry intellectual jargon and the ostensible desire for crude enjoyment bring about degeneration of the mind. That is why adherence to Yama and Niyama Sādhanā is the precondition for the elevation and evolution of human consciousness.

When the mind takes the ideation of Parama Śiva, it becomes pure and divinized. The hormonal secretion of the pineal gland brings about mental dilation. Swami Vivekananda calls it the effect of *ojas* which is nothing else than the working of the pineal nectar. He writes: 'The Yogis claim that of all the energies that are in the human body the highest is what they call "*ojas*". Now this *ojas* is stored up in the brain, and the more *ojas* is in a man's head the more powerful he is, the more intellectual, the more spiritually strong.'[21] The glandular system plays an important role in the making of man.

A good number of *vṛttis* are controlled by the different glands. The number of *vṛttis* varies according to the complexities of the physical structure. The developed one possesses more *vṛttis* than the undeveloped being. There are one thousand expressions of inter- and intra-ectoplasmic occupations of the mind. The seeds of all the thousand *vṛttis* or expressed sentiments are present in the brain. The pineal lotus is called Sahasrāra Cakra because it controls all the thousand expressed sentiments of the human mind. The six *cakras* are associated with certain *vṛttis.* The Mūlādhāra Cakra is associated with four *vṛttis,* i.e. *Artha, Dharma, Kāma* and *Mokṣa.* The Ājñā or the pituitary gland controls Parā (knowledge of Brahman) and Aparā (knowledge of the physical world). The pineal controls all the thousand *vṛttis* taken internally or externally by all the ten *indriyas.* Thus, if we work out these *vṛttis* they come to one thousand, *i.e.* 50 × 2 × 10=1000.

The piercing of the different *cakras* by the Kuṇḍalinī means control of the mind over the *vṛttis* associated with those *cakras.* The piercing of the Sahasrāra by the Kuṇḍalinī signifies the liberation of mind from all the *vṛttis.* It results in one's unification with Śiva. In other words the control over the pineal gland by a Sādhaka means the exhaustion of all the Saṁskāras as the different *vṛttis* are the repositories of good and bad dispositions.

The arousal of the Kuṇḍalinī leads to spiritual illumination. It illumines the different spheres of mind. Kāmamaya Koṣa is converted into Manomaya Koṣa (subtle mind), Manomaya is transformed into Atimānasa Koṣa (supramental sphere), and again Atimānasa is transmuted into Vijñānamaya Koṣa. Vijñānamaya Koṣa is transformed into Hiraṇyamaya Koṣa. This last vestige of mind is ultimately transformed into Self. The Śruti says: 'Beyond the sphere of Hiraṇyamaya Koṣa is the transcendental Brahman.'[22]

The purpose of Tantra Sādhanā is the realization of Parama Śiva. This can be achieved only by the transformation of Crude Mind into Subtle Mind and of Subtle Mind into Causal Mind and lastly of Causal Mind into Parama Śiva.

Blaze of Illumination

With the piercing of the different nerve plexuses, the process of transformation of different spheres of mind begins. There cannot be any other means, to achieve this spiritual goal. Kuṇḍalinī Sādhanā is the only process of spiritualization. The realization of Parama Śiva is achieved by Kuṇḍalinī Yoga. Swami Vivekananda says: 'Now, if this coiled up energy be roused and made active, and then consciously made to travel up the Suṣumṇā canal, as it acts on centre after centre, a tremendous reaction will set in. When a minute portion of energy travels along a nerve fibre and causes reaction from centres, the perception is either dream or imagination. But when by the power of long internal meditation the vast mass of energy is stored up and travels along the Suṣumṇā, and strikes the centres, the reaction is tremendous, immensely superior to the reaction of dream or imagination, immensely more intense than the reaction of sense perception. It is a super sensuous perception. And when it reaches the brain, metropolis of all sensations, the brain, as it were, reacts, and the result is full blaze of illumination, perception of the Self. As this Kuṇḍalinī force travels from centre to centre, layer after layer of the mind, as it were, opens up, and this universe is perceived by the Yogis in its fine or causal form.'[23]

The arousal of the Kuṇḍalinī is the quintessence of the Tāntric cult. It needs a constant practice. A Sādhaka will have to remain mentally vigilant and physically alert. With the arousal of the Kuṇḍalinī the process of spiritual transformation begins. Those who start Sādhanā with determination, the Kuṇḍalinī is aroused, and the whole nature of the Sādhaka begins to change. The awakening of the Kuṇḍalinī opens the divine wisdom and the Sādhaka gets entrance into the Divine Realm. He does not need to go through the books for knowledge, as he becomes all-knowing. He becomes conscious about the infinite knowledge of Self. This realization of perfection and purity can be attained only by Kuṇḍalinī Sādhanā — the mystic process of going beyond the senses and mind.

Saundaryalaharī, a poem in Sanskrit, is the canonical literature of the Tāntric Śrīvidyā cult and deals with the esoteric science of Kuṇḍalinī Yoga. Tantra scripture state the use and importance of seed-syllable (*bījākṣara*), Mystic Diagram (Yantra) and Kuṇḍalinī Sādhanā. W. Norman Brown says: 'Certain practices of Śrī Vidyā associated with the *Saundaryalaharī* all over India today find no overt support in the teaching of the text itself. These are the assignments to each stanza of a seed-syllable (*bījākṣara*) as its essence and the use in connection with each stanza of a special mystic diagram (*yantra*).'[24] In order to maintain the secret nature of Tantra, they have always used a language of symbolism which only the 'initiates' can understand. To understand the deeper and esoteric significance of the Tāntric symbolism, one will have to undergo the rigours of Tāntric Sādhanā. *Saundaryalaharī* puts emphasis on Kuṇḍalinī Sādhanā. It says: 'With streams of nectar flowing from between your feet sprinkling the universe (recreating) through the power of reciting the secret texts that produce the six [*cakras* which had been dissolved when Devī regressed to the Sahasrāra by the *kula* path], again you reach your own abode and into the form of a serpent in three and a half coils. You convert yourself and sleep in the *kula kuṇḍa* hollow.'[25]

Saundaryalaharī describes elaborately the piercing of the Kuṇḍalinī. The Kuṇḍalinī after piercing the Mūlādhāra, Maṇipūra, Svādhiṣṭhāna and other *cakras* reaches the thousand-petalled lotus where she sports in secret with Lord Śiva. The most significant thing is that the Kuṇḍalinī has to pierce earth, water, fire, air, ether and the mind between the eyebrows in order to embrace Parama Śiva which resides in the thousand-petalled lotus. The esoteric importance of the piercing of all the six *cakras* is great. The Sādhaka whose Kuṇḍalinī is aroused and reaches Sahasrāra attains control over all the five fundamental factors and the mind. A Tāntric acquires great occult power by Kuṇḍalinī-Yoga. Without the awakening of the Kuṇḍalinī one cannot acquire occult power. But the acquisition of occult power is not the goal of Tantra Sādhanā; it only necessarily comes while on the spiritual march. The sole objective of Tantra Sādhanā is to enrich life with the spiritual force which grants salvation from the cobweb of ignorance and mundane attachments. It stands for self-fulfilment which can be attained by Kuṇḍalinī-Yoga. W. Norman Brown says: 'This is by arousing the individual's Kuṇḍalinī power of Śakti. The notion is a part of the teaching concerning the *cakras,* centres of energy, situated in human body, and pierced by a path called the *kula* path, leading from the lowest of the *cakras* through the topmost to the place at the top of the skull which the Tantras call the Sahasrāra (thousand petalled lotus). The *cakras* vary in number according to different schools of Tāntric teaching, but the usual number is six. In the lowest *cakra* the Kuṇḍalinī power lies asleep as a serpent in three and a half coils. The devotee endeavours to awaken it, generally by employing Haṭha-Yoga. As he becomes adept he causes it to ascend until finally he causes it to go the whole way to the Sahasrāra. This constitutes self fulfilment.'[26]

Brown has tried to give an objective view of Tantra Sādhanā while editing *Saundaryalaharī.* Kuṇḍalinī-Yoga constitutes the main trunk of the Tantra cult. The Vedic philosophy takes us to the doors of the Divine, but it cannot let us in; for that intuitional realisation is necessary, which can be attained only by Kuṇḍalinī Yoga. It throws light on the true nature of Being and liberates us from the enthralment of the mundaneness. It grants freedom from the phenomenal existence in which condition man lives. It brings the realization of Parama Śiva, which every man is, in his essential existence. The Tantra Sādhaka can be compared with a lotus unsullied by the mire in which it originates. The concept of the Kuṇḍalinī has a philosophical basis. Tantra believes in the theory of Samarasa of Śiva and Śakti. The concept of Samarasa means homogeneity. A thing or being which appears different from another thing or being but in reality is the same is to be called Samarasa with the first. This concept of Samarasa forms the basis of the metaphysics of the Bhedābheda theory of reality and appearance. A drop of water is in appearance different from a sheet of water but the fact remains that a drop of water in reality is not different from the bulk of water. Śiva, which is the fundamental principle, manifests himself in many forms without losing his transcendental existence. Śiva is the ultimate reality and the fountain-head of all power. He does not exhibit himself except through his different manifestations. Surendranath Das Gupta writes: 'So, the all-powerful Śiva, though it is the source of all power, behaves as if it were without any power. This power, therefore, remains in the body as the ever-awakening Kuṇḍalinī or the serpentine force, and also as manifesting in different ways. The consideration of the body as indestructible is called *kāya-siddhi.*'[27]

The concept of the Kuṇḍalinī is a landmark in the history of Indian culture and tradition. It created a mystic stir in the minds of spiritual aspirants and paved the path for Tāntric mysticism. It subordinates reason to intuition. Reason is not the ultimate category of universe. The awakening of the Kuṇḍalinī opens the gates of Super-Consciousness, and then the Sādhaka has the vision of Parama Śiva, which involves a purer illumination and a wider compass. Life cannot be comprehended in its fullness by mere philosophical speculation. Hence, arises the need for an intuitional science to bring spiritual unification of *jīva* with Śiva. It helps in reaching the higher level of consciousness, through the process of transformation of psyche, which enables a spiritual aspirant to go beyond the limits of general human experience.

When the Kuṇḍalinī is awakened in man, his longing for the Supreme becomes intense and his psychic power becomes kinetic and strives to rise above through the Suṣumṇā Canal. The psychic impulses and baser propensities which are normally diverted towards outward and downward manifestations come under the supreme control of the higher mind. Internal conflicts and confusions are obliterated. External obstacles are easily conquered. Man sets out for the mystic pilgrimage of Lord Śiva. A.K. Banerjee while explaining the philosophy and esoteric practice of Nāthaism writes: 'This is often described as the sacred Yātrā (journey) of awakened Kuṇḍalinī-Śakti for the most blissful union with her eternal Beloved Śiva, in the highest region of spiritual experience, Sahasrāra Cakra. In the course of this gradual ascent of the psycho-vital energy along the path of Suṣumṇā, Yogis meet with a number of subtle *cakras,* at particular stages and particular centres, in which they are required to perform particular forms of meditation for particular yogic achievements and which they have to pierce through in order to reach the highest plane of transcendental spiritual experience.'[28]

REFERENCES

1. जीव: शिव: शिवो जीव: स जीव: केवल: शिव:।
   पाशबद्ध: स्मृतो जीव: पाशमुक्त: सदाशिव।। 42।। *Kulārṇava Tantra*, p. 241
2. कुण्डलिनी सा मूलीभूता ऋणात्मिका 4/8 *Ānanda Sūtram*, p. 40
3. परैव सूक्ष्मा कुण्डलिनी शक्ति:। *Tantrāloka*, II, p. 77
4. *Bhāratiya Saṁskṛti aur Sādhanā*, pp. 303-4.
5. *The Mysterious Kuṇḍalinī,* (9th ed.), p. 43, D.B. Taraporevala Sons & Co. Private Ltd., Bombay, 1960.
6. ध्यायेत् कुण्डलिनी देवी स्वयंभूलिङ्गवेष्टिनीम्।
   हंसेन मनुना देवी सहस्त्रारं समानयेत्।।
   सदाशिवो महादेवो यत्रास्ते परमेश्वरि।

देवी रूपवतीं कामसमुल्लास विहारिणीम्।।
मुखारविन्दगन्धेन मोदिदं परमं शिवम्।
प्रबोध्य परमेशानि तत्रैवोपविशेत् प्रिय।।
शिवस्य मुख पद्मं हि चुम्बे कुण्डली शिवे।
सताक्षिवेन देवेशि क्षणमात्रं रमेत प्रिय।।
अमृतं जायेत देवी तत्क्षणात् परमेश्वरि।
तदुद्भवामृतं देवी लाक्षारस समायुतम्।।
तेनामृतेन देवेशि तर्पयेत् परदेवताम्।
षटचक्र देवतास्तम संतर्प्यामृतधारया।। *Ṣaṭcakra Nirupaṇa*, p. 86

7. पिण्ड भवेत्कुण्डलिनी शिवात्मा पद तु हंसः सकलान्तरात्मा।
रूपं भवेद्बिन्दूरनन्तकान्तिरतीतरूपं शिवसारस्यम्।।63।। *Śāradā Tilaka*, p. 547

8. मूलोम्निद्रभुजङ्ग राजमहिषीभान्ती सुषुम्नान्तरम्।
भित्वाधारसमूहमाथु विलत्सौदामिनीसन्निभास।।
व्योमाम्भोजगतेन्दुमण्डलगहिव्यामृतौधालुताम्।
सम्भाव्य स्वगृहं गतां पुनरिमां सञ्चितर्यत्कुण्डलीम्।।65।। *Śāradā Tilaka*, p. 548

9. *Ibid.*

10. सुगुप्तं तद्यन्तादतिशयपरमा मोद संतान राशेः।
परं कन्दं सूक्ष्मं सकलशशिकलाशुद्धरूपप्रकाशम्।।
इह स्थाने देवः परमशिवसमाख्यानसिद्धः प्रसिद्ध।
स्वरूपी सर्वात्मा रस विरसमितोऽज्ञानमोहान्ध हंस।।42।।
Ṣaṭcakra Nirupaṇa, ver. 42, p. 62

11. एतस्या मध्यदेशे विलसति परमापूर्वनिर्वाणशक्तिः
कोट्या दिव्यप्रकाशात्रिभुवन जननीकोटिभौगकरूपा
केशाग्रस्थातिसूक्ष्मा निरवधि विगलत्प्रेमधारा धरा सा
सर्वेषां जीवभूता मुनिमनसि मुद्रा तत्त्वबोध बहन्ती।।48।। — Ver. 48, p. 73

12. हूंकारेणैव देवी यमनियमसमभ्यासशीलः सुशीलो
ज्ञात्वा श्रीनाथवक्यात्यच्ममति च महामोक्षवर्त्मप्रकाशम्
ब्रह्मद्वारस्य मध्ये विरचयति सा ता शुद्ध बुद्धि स्वभावो
भित्वा तल्लिङ्गरूपं पवनदहनयोराक्रमेणैव गुप्तम्।।50।। — Ver. 50, p. 79

13. कन्दोर्ध्वं कुण्डलीशक्तिः सुप्ता मोक्षाय योगिनाम्
बन्धनाय च मूढ़ानाम त्रस्तां वेत्ति स योगवित्।।107।। *Gorakṣa-Vacana-Saṁgraha*

14. पुच्छे प्रगृह्य भुजगीं सुप्तामुद्बोधयेच्चताम्।
निद्रां विहाय सा शक्ति ऊर्ध्वमुत्तिष्ठते इठात्।।111।।

15. पद्मासने निवेश्याङ्के ततः पाणिद्वयं न्यसेत्।
ततो हंसमुपस्मृत्य शनैः संकोचयेदगुदम्।।
वायुमुत्तोलयेत्तेन वर्त्मना स पुनः पुनः।
उत्तोल्य भेदयेच्चकं तस्यानुष्ठानमुच्यते।।
मूलाधारसरोजे तु त्रिकोणमतिसुन्दरम्।
कामो भवति तन्मध्ये वालार्ककोटिसंनिभम्।
तदूर्ध्वे कुण्डलीशक्तिं स्वयंभूलिङ्गवेष्टिनीम्।। *Ṣaṭcakra Nirupaṇa*, p. 81

16. Yoga Research Centre, All India Institute of Medical Sciences, New Delhi.

17. *Ṣaṭcakra Nirupaṇa.*

I8, भित्वालिङ्गत्रयं तत्परमरसशिवे सूक्ष्मधाम्नि प्रदीपे

सा देवी शुद्ध सत्त्वा तडिदिव विलसत्तन्तुरूपस्वरूपा।
ब्रह्माख्याया: सिराया: सकलसरसिजं प्राप्य देदीप्यतेत्
न्मोक्षाख्यानन्दरूपं घटयति सहसा सूक्ष्मतालक्षणेन।। 51।। Ver. 51.

19. अव्यक्तं परबिन्दुमञ्चितरुचिं नीत्वा शिवस्यालयम्।
शक्ति: कुण्डलिनी गुणत्रयवपुर्विद्युल्लतासन्निभा।।
आनन्दामृतमध्यगं पुरभिदं चन्द्रार्ककोटिप्रभम्।
सं वीव्य स्वपुरगता भगवतो ध्येयाडनवद्या गुणै:।। 67।। *Śāradā Tilaka.* Ver. 67, p. 548.

20. लाक्षात्रं परमामृत परशिवात्वीत्वा पुन: कुण्डली
नित्यानन्दमहोदयात्कुलपपान्मूले विशेत्सुन्दरी।
तद्दिव्यामृतधारया स्थिरमति: सेतर्पयचदैवतं
योगी योगपरंपराव्रिदितया ब्रह्माण्डभाण्डस्थितम्।। 53।। *Ṣaṭcakra Nirupaṇa,* Ver. 53.

21. *Rāja-Yoga,* pp. 72-73.
22. *Subhāṣita Saṁgraha.*
23. *Rāja-Yoga* (12th Impression), p. 64, Advaita Ashram, 5 Entally Road, Calcutta-14, 1962.
24. *Saundaryalaharī,* p. 18.
25. सुधाधारसारैश्चरण्ययुगलान्तर्विगलितै:
प्रपञ्चं सिञ्चन्ती पुनरपिरसामम्नायमहसा।
अवाप्य स्वां भूमिं भुजगनिभमध्युष्टवलयं
स्वमात्मनं कृत्वा स्वपिषि कुलकुण्डे कुहरिणि।। 10।। *Ibid.,* p. 53.

26. *Saundaryalaharī,* p. 18.
27. *History of Indian Philosophy,* vol. V, p. 59.
28. *Philosophy of Gorakhnath,* p. 172. Mahant Digvijay Nath Trust, Gorakhnath Temple, Gorakhpur.

1. Proto-Śiva (Seal)
Mohenjodāro c 2500 B.C.

National Museum, New Delhi

2. Śrī Yantra
(Painting on Cloth)
Gujarat, 17th Century A.D.

National Museum, New Delhi

National Museum, New Delhi

3. Aradhanāriśvara (Stone) Bengal 12th Century A.D.

National Museum, New Delhi

4. Śiva and Śakti, Kangra School 18th Century A.D.

National Museum, New Delhi

5. Rati Kriyā (Stone) Rajasthan, 16th Century A.D.

National Museum, New Delhi

6. Ṣatacakra (Painting) Kangra School, 18th Century A.D.

7. Bhuvaneśwarī Yantra (Copper) South India, Early 18th Century A.D.

National Museum, New Delhi

8. Bhairavī Yantra (Copper) Vārāṅāsī, 18th Century A.D.

National Museum, New Delhi

National Museum, New Delhi

9. Ardhanārīśvara (Painting) Calcutta, 18th Century A.D.

10. Śrī Yantra (Copper Plate) South India 17th Century A.D.

National Museum, New Delhi

National Museum, New Delhi

11. Yantra (Silver) Rajasthan 18th Century

National Museum, New Delhi

12. Couple Seated in Maithuna (Painting)

13. Consort of Śiva, 10th Century A.D, Chamba, Himachal Pradesh

National Museum, New Delhi

National Museum, New Delhi

14. Kuṇḍalinī (Painting) Rajasthan, 18th Century A.D.

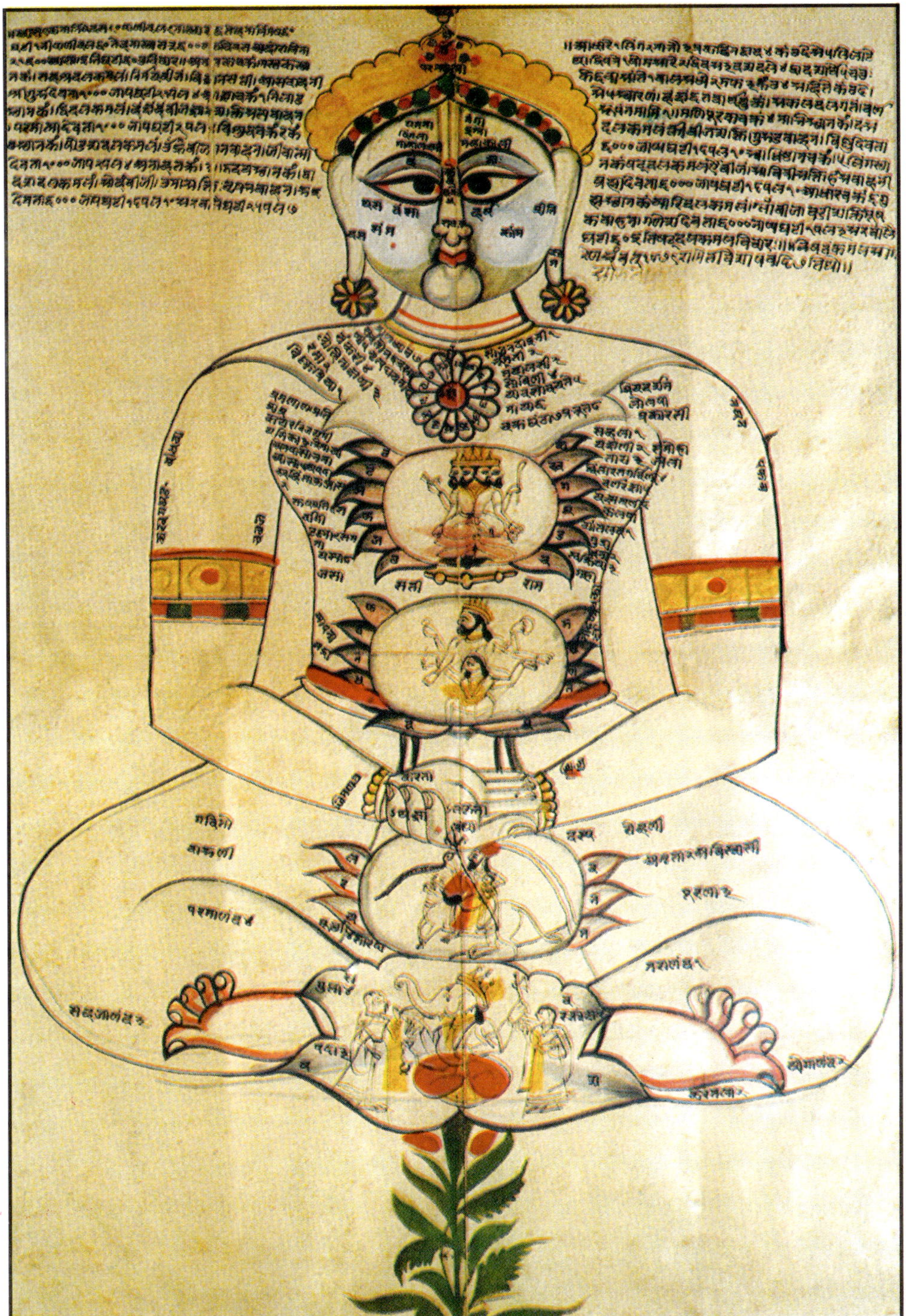

National Museum, New Delhi

15. Ṣatacakra (Painting) Rajasthan 18th Century A.D.

16. Ram Yantra (Copper)
South India 17th Century A.D.

National Museum, New Delhi

17. Rādhikā Yantra (Brass)
Rajasthan, 18th Century

National Museum, New Delhi

National Museum, New Delhi

18. Śiva and Kāli, Kangra School 18th Century A.D.

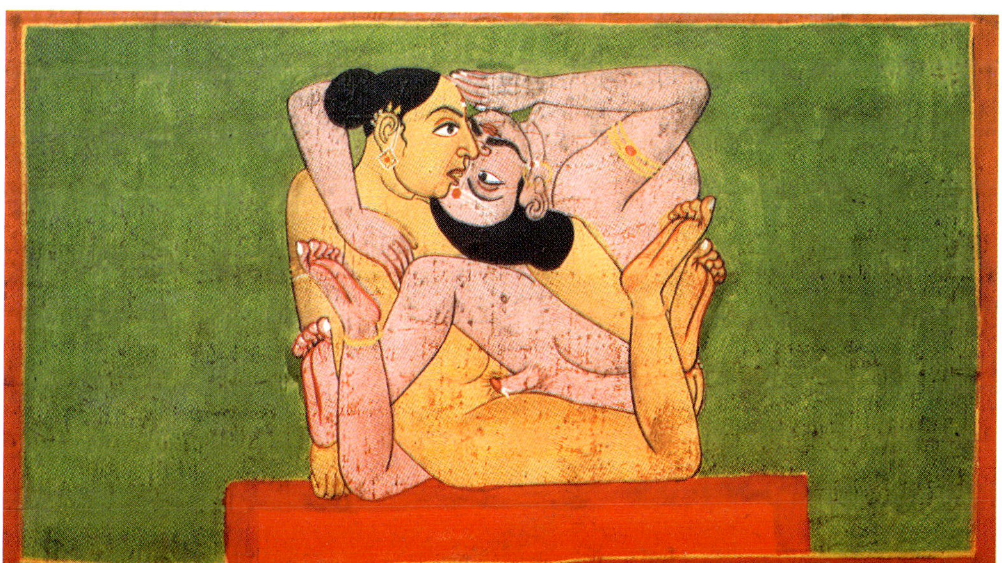

National Museum, New Delhi

19. Tantra Āsana (Painting) Rajasthan 18th Century A.D.

20. Yoni Yantra (Copper)
South India
18th Century

National Museum, New Delhi

21. Yantra (Copper)
Rajasthan
17th Century A.D.

National Museum, New Delhi

National Museum, New Delhi

22. Lalitā Seated on Śiva, Rajasthan, 18th Century A.D.

National Museum, New Delhi

23. Dancing Chamuṇḍā, Pratihāra, Rajasthan, 11th Century A.D.

6 Mantra

Mantra is the first principle of Tāntric esotericism. It is the most potent weapon to cut asunder the trammels of Māyā. But Mantra Sādhanā is erroneously identified with Japa Sādhanā which is an intellectual process of recitation of different Vedic hymns. The Vedic hymns are not *mantrās.* They are merely sublime poems. The chanting of the Vedic hymns does not create that acoustic vibration which is necessary for the awakening of the Kulakuṇḍalinī. The Vedic hymns may create a psychological climate for Mantra Sādhanā. The process of incantation of *mantra* is called Praṇidhāna and not Japa. Praṇidhāna means taking shelter in divinity by establishing oneness with Cosmic Ideation. With the help of *mantra* a Sādhaka atunes his individual existence with Cosmic vibration and gets drenched in the divine effulgence. He becomes one with the Divine Being. He does not remain an individual. He becomes Parama Śiva. The realization of the non-dualistic existence is the main aim of Mantra Sādhanā. Rāghava Bhaṭṭa defines *mantra* as a mystic formula. 'The incantation of which brings the realization of Cosmic Consciousness (Visva-vijñānam) and rids one of the bondage of worldliness is verily the *mantra.*'[1] The realization of Cosmic Consciousness means Parā-jñāna, the knowledge of the Absolute. A Sādhaka attains the Supreme when he succeeds in establishing a parallelism between the rhythms of incantation, the rhythms of ideation and the rhythms of pulsation. With the help of constant ideation of the Supreme and incantation of *mantra,* mind becomes pure and impeccant. Mantra Sādhanā is a constant mystic effort to restore equilibrium. In that condition, a man goes beyond himself. He gives up the consideration of both virtue and vice. He has neither the frivolity of sex and hunger, nor the self-gratifying sense of sublimity. He becomes one with Parama Śiva. He loses his own individuality.

Mantra-Sādhanā is the main theme of Tantra. It is the life-force of Tantra cult. According to Tantra, *mantrās* are scientific formulas which are to be practised according to a strict psycho-spiritual discipline to attain the desired goal, whether it is of mundane or supramundane import. Each and every letter from *a* (अ) to *kṣa* (क्ष) of Mātṛkā Varṇa is living energy. They are the acoustic root of the different waves and vibrations of the cosmos. These letters are the representative sonoric manifestations of the universe. When these letters are arranged after the Tāntric precepts, a living force is generated which creates para-psychological wonders. It is not only a fact but a living reality. To understand the full significance and psychic import of *mantra,* a discussion and knowledge of sound (*śabda*) is imperative.

Sound is the first manifestation of Parama Śiva. That is why effect Brahman is known as Śabda-Brahman. Sound (*śabda*) in its primary stage is a psychic wave. The very existence of sound (*śabda*) entails the presence of *spanda* or movement. There cannot be sound without any motion. Movement (*spanda*) is the property of qualified Brahman (Saguṇa Brahman). That is why Nirguṇa Brahman, where Śakti remains dormant, is called *aśabda* (without sound) and *niṣpanda* (without motion).

The very first aphorism of *Śāradā Tilaka* explains the significance and hidden meaning of Śabda-Brahman.[2] The whole universe is a mess of different waves and vibrations. Where there is action, there is vibration. The relative transposition of any object is called action. The nature of any action is judged by the waves it creates. These waves are known as vibrations. Action is of many varieties, so is vibration. Vibrations of two actions are not the same. No two vibrations are alike. Every vibration has sound and colour. The world is the thought-projection of Saguṇa Śiva. The creative ideation has vibration. Every vibration is associated with sound. Man cannot catch the supramental vibration due to lack of spiritual development. The first and subtlest vibration is *śabda* (sound). Sound being the first expression of the Supreme, effect Brahman (Kārya-Brahman) is known as Śabda-Brahman.[3]

Parāsaṁvita is beyond the reach of Śabda-Brahman. Parāsaṁvita (Parama Śiva), the witnessing counterpart of Śabda-Brahman, remains undefined. He is also called Parāvāk (the supreme word). He is transcendental (स्वसंवेद्य). But when the Infinite Self is transformed into finite beings, the first expression is that of sound. But the crude sound, devoid of divine effulgence of Bindu, is not Śabda-Brahman. Śabda-Brahman is the composite form of Brahman-hood and acoustics. The acoustic aspect of Śabda-Brahman is sound and the spiritual part of it is Brahmanhood.[4]

The unmanifest sound was created due to the division of the Supreme Bindu.[5] This causal sound is unmanifested, undifferent. Śabda-Brahman is the cause of the manifest sound, meaning and *mantra.* It is the composite form of Bindu and Nāda. He is devoid of all particularities.

Śāradā Tilaka refutes the theory that Śabda-Brahman is Śabda and others Śabdārtha, because both are crude manifestations whereas Śabda-Brahman is the Consciousness in all beings.[6] Śabda cannot be identified with Śabda-Brahman because the former is rhythmic in nature, whereas the latter is unrhythmic.

Rāghava Bhaṭṭa has quoted Vāmakeśvara Tantra in support of his argument. According to this Tantra the unmanifest Śabda-Brahman is the cause of all beings.[7] Śabda-Brahman is effect Brahman because it is the first manifestation of cosmic creation. The difference between causal Brahman (Kāraṇa-Brahman) and effect Brahman (Kārya-Brahman) is very subtle. All the expressions of causal Brahman are personal and subjective, whereas the manifestations of effect Brahman are inpersonal and objective. This is the basic difference between the two. Being the personal and subjective expression, all the manifestations of causal Brahman are devoid of consonants. They are elementary expressions. Hence, no compound or addition (योग) can be made out of them. There is a vast difference between the scientific and the Tāntric concept of sound. According to Tantra, sound at its initial stage was in the form of a pscyhic wave. It was in the form of an idea. Anandamurti says : 'Before coming to the physical form, sound was in the realm of idea and the first point of sound in the realm of idea is called Parā-Śakti. But sound does not get the scope of its expression in the state of Parā-Śakti in spite of its all possibility without a medium. It gets the scope of expression only when a medium is available. Thus, the vibrational expression is sound, *i.e.*, where there is internal clash in the medium, we hear internal and external sound. This is what we call sound.'[8]

The Saṁskṛta alphabets are of Tāntric origin. They are not called simply 'alphabet' but Varṇamālā. Its fifty letters, from *a* to *kṣa,* are the fifty basic vibrations of the Cosmos. Each letter is bīja-mantra of fifty human instincts. Here bīja-mantra means the acoustic root of different psychic expressions. It is said that the divine nectar that secretes from the pineal gland (Sahasrāra) takes different forms of letters in six different *cakras* or Padams. These six *cakras* are : Mūlādhāra, Svādhiṣṭhāna, Maṇipūra, Anāhata, Viśudha and Ājñā. They are called Padmas (Lotuses) because they are in the form of a lotus with a distinct colour and petals. The different petals of the respective *cakras* represent the different basic human longings and instincts.

There is a great controversy regarding the colour of the different letters. Dr. Shiva Shankar Awasthi says : 'The colours of vowels (स्वरवर्ण) are smoky. From *ka* to *ta* are of pinkish colour.[9] From *da* (द) to *pha* (फ) are of yellow colour (गौरवर्ण). The five *ba,* etc., are of light reddish (अरुणवर्ण) and *la's* are of golden colour. *Ha* and *kṣa* are of the colour of lightning (तड़ितवर्ण). This is the view of Sanata Kumar's *Saṁhitā.*[10] But some others hold different views. Saubhagyabhaskara says : 'All letters are of different colours.'[11] Dr. Shiva Shankar Awasthi has given a detailed description of all the fifty letters.[12] His metaphysical exposition of different letters with different colours, forms and deities cannot be accepted to be true. All the letters do not have the same colour. The view of Sanata Kumar's *Saṁhitā* is nearer to the truth. Those who are adept in Tantra Sādhanā know the different colours of the group of letters and their presiding deities. Meditation of different letters and their presiding deities is of great mystic significance. As we have already said the different letters are the acoustic roots (*bīja-mantras*) of psychic manifestations of individual and cosmic minds. Man is a cosmic being but due to the bondage of Māyā or mala, he has identified himself with a lower manifestation. The bondage of Māyā is in the form of different propensities of mind. Both the baser and the benign propensities are the causes of bondage; one is a chain of iron and the other of gold but both are chains which keep man in bondage. Mantra Sādhanā frees man from enthralment. One has to conquer one's desire. Mantra Sādhanā sublimates our desires. Meditation of different letters and their deities brings sublimation. Each *cakra* has a different number of petals. Each petal represents one letter and one psychic conation. As for example, Maṇipūra Cakra controls ten instincts. One of the instincts it controls is peevishness (कषाय). A man who suffers from a stomach disease develops the psychology of peevishness due to the abnormal hormonal secretion from Maṇipūra Cakra or the pancreatic gland. With the physical pressure by yogic exercise (*āsanas*) and psychic meditation of different *cakras* with their petals and presiding deities a Sādhaka achieves absolute control over his senses and desires. The Sādhanā of Mātṛkā (letters) is of profound importance. 'There is nothing beyond the science of Mātṛkā (letters).'[13]

Mātṛkā Varṇa means mother of colours. There are innumerable waves and vibrations. Tāntric seers have divided them into fifty categories. The division is based on intuitive realization. These are fifty controlling sounds. The fifty letters of the Sanskrit alphabet, from *a* (अ) to *kṣa* (क्ष), are the resultant sounds. They are the controlling sounds (*bīja-mantras*) of the fifty categories. *A* (अ) is the *bīja-mantra* of creation. अ of Sanskrit, *a* of Latin, *alpha* of Greek and *aliph* of Persian are the first letters of their respective alphabet because they represent the creative manifestation. The fifty letters are the embodiments of fifty gross sounds. Mātṛkā Varṇa is a causal matrix.

Tāntric deity Bhadra Kālī means creative matrix. She is the supreme creativity. Kālī means, the timeless principle (कालजयी शक्ति). In the garland of Kālī there are fifty heads of human skulls. They represent the fifty letters. Kālī is the Supreme Controller of the seed of creation.

The Mute or Internal Sound of causal Brahman is 'vowel letters' and the Manifest Sound of effect Brahman is 'consonant letters', according to Tantra Śāstra.

All the letters are divided into two groups, vowels and consonants. Vowels are called *bīja*, consonants are called *yoni*. Vowels are called *bīja* because no compound can be made out of them. Consonants are called *yoni* because they are productive letters. Consonants have the potentiality of making compound and addition (यौगिक). The cosmic creation is a consonantal expression of effect Brahman. Vowels are known as Śiva-form and consonants as Śakti-form.[14] *A* (अ) is the first letter of the vowels because it is the acoustic root of creation. That is why when Brahma (ब्रह्म) is with *a*, *i.e.*, Brahmā (ब्रह्मा), He is said to be the creator of the universe. *Ka* is the first letter of the consonants. The mystic idea behind is that when causal Brahman is overpowered by the desire of creation it is transformed into effect Brahman. Causal Brahman is mystically represented by a vertical line (|) and effect Brahman is symbolically represented by a horizontal line (—). When both are combined they take the form of cross (+). In the ancient Brahmi script *ka* (क) was written as a cross (𑀓), and subsequently for the convenience of writing *ka* without break it took the present form of Bengali (ক) and Nāgari (क).

Puṇyānanda in his commentary on *Kāma-kalā-Vilāsa* has referred to *Śrī Tantra-Sadbhāva* according to which all *mantras* consist of letters. *Śrī Tantra-Sadbhāva* says : 'All *mantras* consist of letters (Varṇātmaka). They again, O beloved, are at base Śakti. Śakti again is *mātṛkā* and she is Śivātmikā. She, the *mātṛkā*, who in the world appears possessed of the energy and brilliance of the Supreme, pervades all his universe beginning from Brahma and ending with Bhuvana.'[15]

According to *Mālinī Vijoyattara Tantram* the different parts of human body are represented by different letters. However, the arrangement of the alphabet, according to *Mālinī*, is different. Here the alphabet begins with *na* (न) and ends with *pha* (फ).[16] The arrangement of letters, according to *Mālinī*, is as follows: न ऋ ॠ लृ ॡ थ च ध ई ण उ ऊ ब क ख ग घ ङ इ अ व भ य ड़ ढ़ ठ झ ञ ज र ट प छ ल आ स अः ह ष क्ष म श अं त ए ऐ ओ औ द फ.

The above arrangement is not according to the order of metaphysical manifestations of different vowels and consonants. Probably it is according to some esoteric practice. Pandit Madhusudan Kaul, editor of *Mālinī Vijoyottara Tantram*, says: '*Mālinī* is of the greatest utility in infusing the divine life into the body of practicers and all the Tāntrists are enjoined to have recourse to it for the attainment of desired objects in all the cases in which particular details and instructions could not be punctiliously observed regarding *nyāsa*. Different parts of the human body represent the different letters of the *Malinī*. While giving the three kinds of *mantra* called *parā*, *aparā* and *parā-parā*, instances are furnished as to how a particular incantation can be made out from particular technical terms such as head, eyes, etc.'[17]

Except *Mātṛkā cakra vivecana*[18], there is general agreement on fifty letters. *Tantrāloka, Svacchanda Tantram, Mālinī Vijoyottara Tantram* are in agreement regarding the total number of letters. Tāntrik Texts refer to *Niruttara Tantra* which says. 'She is adorned with a garland of beads representing the 50 letters.' *Kāmadhenu Tantra* says: 'In my throat is the wonderful Bīja of 50 letters. Again, "I worship the Mother, the source of the universe, Śabdabrahman itself, blissful". Viśvasāra says: "Blissful Brahman is adorned with Śabdabrahman and within the body is represented by all Mantras".[19]

Tāntric Origin

The Sanskrit alphabet are of Tāntric origin. They represent the different acoustic vibrations of the Cosmos. The fifty letters are the fifty basic vibrations. which constitute the entire universe. They are the *bījākṣara* of Tāntric esotericism. The word '*mantra*' has been made from *man+trai* (*dhātu*) +*i* (suffix) = *mantra*, and means the incantation of which brings liberation from the trifarious bondage—physical, mental and spiritual. It creates an acoustic vibration in the psychic body of Sādhaka, which awakens the Kuṇḍalinī Śakti. All *mantras* are words, but all words are not *mantras*. All words have originated from Parā, but only few words which have been originated from Parā are *mantras*.

Parā-Bindu is present both in individual self and Cosmic Self. All the sounds have their origin in Parā-Bindu both in the individual and the Cosmos. 'Śakti has originated from Śabdabrahmayī-Kuṇḍalinī. From Śakti has emerged primordial Sound, from primordial Sound Nāda, from Nāda Nirodhikā, from Nirodhikā Ardhendu and again Bindu, and from Bindu Parā, Paśyanti, Madhyamā and Baikhari

Sound have been originated.'[20] *Śāradā Tilaka* expounds the theory of the origin of sound. It deals with the causal form of Cosmic Sound. Madhavācārya says in *Tatparyadīpikā* that the primordial form of *mātṛkā* is of Bindu and Nāda character which is beyond Parā and Paśyanti.[21]

In the individual life, Mūlādhāra Cakra is the origin of Parā. Parā is the first point of origin. It is in the form of a point. It may be called the causal form of the sound. Mūlādhāra is the lowest *cakra.* It is the residing place of Kulakuṇḍalinī. The Kuṇḍalinī is the origin of Śakti, Nāda, Bindu and Sound. That is why Mūlādhāra has been called the birthplace of all sounds.[22]

Paśyanti is the mental vision of the sound. For instance, Mr. Ram would like to utter the sound, 'I am going to New Delhi'. He will visualize New Delhi in his psychic plate before uttering the actual sound, This psychic visualization of the sound *New Delhi* is called Paśyanti. Svādhiṣṭhāna Cakra is the birthplace of Paśyanti.

Madhyamā is the mental sound. In this state of Madhyamā, the psychic vision is transformed into the psychic sound. Madhyamā is the junction of vision and form. Being the mental vision, it is said to be the subtle form of sound, and Parā and Paśyanti are astral and subliminal forms of sound.[23] The Madhyamā (sound) comes from Anāhat Cakra.

Baikharī is not the physical form of sound. It is a state of mute language. The psychic form is transformed into natural language or mother tongue. In the state of Baikharī, the sound takes the form of natural language, but it may not be expressed in its natural form. For example, Mr. Shyam is talking to Mr. John! If Mr. Shyam happens to be the resident of Delhi and his mother tongue is Hindi and if he wants to say, 'Well, Mr. John! If you want to know Indian philosophy, you will have to learn Saṁskṛta', in that case 'Well, Mr. John! If you want to know Indian philosophy, you will have to learn Saṁskṛta'. In the state of Baikharī the real form of the sound will be in its last state of linguistic form. The English translation of the mother tongue is called Śrutigocarā. The spoken language or sound is called Śrutigocarā and not Baikharī. The source of Baikharī is Viśudhya Cakra and the plane of Śrutigocarā is between the throat and the lips.

There is no difference of any language till the state of Madhyamā. All languages are at the same level. At a lower stage of Baikharī the psychic vision is transformed into different mother tongues.

The other salient feature of Baikharī is its universal character. The acoustic roots of different vibrations of Baikhari and Śrutigocarā are similar to one another. The acoustiç root of the vibrations of 'I go' and 'अहम् गच्छामि' is the same. That is why a man of spiritual attainment knows and reads the minds of others, though he may not be knowing the language they spoke. A person of higher spiritual achievements reads the thoughts of others in their initial state. He can dive deep into the human consciousness and scan the process of an idea even at the stage of Parā.

Bhaskara Rai says: 'The seed form of Śabda-Brahman is Parā, the budding state is Paśyanti, the unmanifest blooming state is Madhyamā and the expressed state is Baikharī.'[24]

There is a great difference between the metaphysical conception of Śabda (sound) and the scientific concept of sound. Sound of physics is really the shadow of the real sound. All empirical knowledge is inferential. What is knowledge? According to empiricists or objective thinkers, knowledge is nothing but subjectivization of external objectivities. What we subjectivize is not the real object but the different waves and vibrations that the objects emanate. There are five kinds, of vibrations. They are known as Tanmātrās or Sensible or Ultrasensible Inferences or Essences. These five Tanmātrās are: sound, touch, form, taste and smell. We subjectivize them with the help of our sensory organs. It is all vibrational play. These vibrations emanate from things and beings, and acts. They are the characteristic essence of an act or thing. Among the vibrational manifestations or Parama Śiva sound is the first and the subtlest. Sonic Tanmātrā is the first stage of crudification. The musical notes of Beethoven are a superb and sublime form of music. They are preserved in the mute lines of a gramophone record. The sweet music is there, but one hears it only when the mute vibrational lines are transformed into sound waves. We hear different sounds only when the sonic Tanmātrā or wave, are carried to the gates of our ears by ethereal or aerial vibrations. Then again sympathetic vibrations are created in the auditory nerves. They transmute these vibrations into the objective mind that takes the form of sonic vibrations and the subjective mind goes through the act of hearing. What we hear is not 'sound as it is' but the shadow of the same. Physics deals with this 'shadow of sound' and not the original sound.

Swami Pratyagātmānanda says: 'The real sound or the sound as it is can be heard only by an absolute ear. "The sound as it is" is the original sound. The sound which you, I, scientists and yogis hear is the distortion of the original form.'[25] However, he has used the word 'Tanmātrā' in the Sāṁkhyian sense. According to Sāṁkhya, Tanmātrā is beyond the reach of an ordinary person. Only a Yogi can have the perception of Tanmātrā. But we differ from this Sāṁkhyian concept of Tanmātrā. Tanmātrā means the 'minutest form of that (objective)'. We receive and transmit Tanmātrā according to our capabilities. The difference between our concept of Tanmātrā and that of Sāṁkhya is conceptual. 'The sonic Tanmātrā can be heard by an absolute ear, subtle sound can be heard by a Yogic ear and the physical sound can be heard by the physical ear.'[26] Here by sonic Tanmātrā, Swami Pratyagātmānanda means the Sonic Consciousness or Śabda-Brahman and not the sonic vibration.

The Oṁkāra

Śabda-Brahman is Oṁkāra. Oṁkāra is the first supersonic manifestation of Parama Śiva. That is why it is called Śabda Brahman. Oṁkāra is the seed of all sounds. It is the collective form of all sonic expressions. It may be called the sum total of all cosmic vibrations. It is the primordial sound (Parā-Vāk). Dr. Gopinath Kaviraj says:

'According to the Scriptures though Brahman is one and eternal, it is known as Supreme Consciousness (Parā-Brahman) and Sonic Consciousness (Śabda-Brahman). The proper knowledge and understanding of Sonic Consciousness leads to the attainment of Supreme Consciousness (शब्दब्रह्मणि निष्णातः परं ब्रह्माधिगच्छति).

'To know the real nature of Śabda-Brahman and having known it to go beyond it is verily the sole purpose of a Sādhaka. Without transcending Śabda-Brahman, the Pure and Supreme Consciousness is unattainable.'[27]

Praṇava is the synonym of Oṁkāra. It is the life of all lives. It is the substratum of all existence and beings.[28] Praṇava has been derived from Pra-nu+al (प्र-नु + अल्). It means the proper form of devotion. 'Oṁkāra controls and regulates all the twelve Kalās, *i.e.* Akāra, Ukāra, Makāra, Bindu, Artha Candra, Rodhinī, Nāda, Nadānta, Śakti, Vyāpinī, Samanā and Unamnā. It illumines every thing from the crudest matter to Śiva.'[29]

According to Kashmir Śaivism, Unmanā is the supreme state of consciousness. It is Parama Pada. The attainment of this state of Unmanā or Supreme Consciousness is the *summum bonum* of life. One will have to tread the path of *mala* to attain the supreme state of Bliss and Consciousness. The trammels of *mala* create the snares of subjective illusion.

Oṁ is composed of three letters — A, U, M. *A* (अ) is the acoustic root (*bīja-mantra*) of Creation, *U* (उ) is the acoustic root of Preservation and *M* (म) is the acoustic root of Destruction. Creation, maintenance and destruction are the three functional activities of Śiva. Brahmā, Viṣṇu and Rudra represent the three functional forms of Parama Śiva. Gods of the Trinity of Hindu mythology are not different. They are the immanent aspects of the Absolute.

Tantra is a monistic philosophy. It believes in one God. To make it more clear let us think about a person named Mr. Ram. He is a university professor. He has one son. Now, Mr. Ram is professor in relation to students. He is father in the eyes of his son. He is husband for Mrs. Ram. Professor Ram, Father Ram and Husband Ram are one and the same person. Similarly, the Hindu Trinity does not represent three different entities. Woodroffe says: 'These three powers are A, U, M or the Devatās Brahmā, Viṣṇu, Rudra. These are not 'Gods'. There is only one God. Scientifically, they stand for the three functions of vital substance. It is incorrect to suppose that God in His aspect as Brahmā created the world some millions of years ago and has since done nothing or that He in His form as Rudra has as yet had no opportunity of displaying His power of dissolution. Brahmā is always creating and recreating the elements of manifested substances which Rudra is ever breaking down. Throughout Nature there are these twin forces upbuilding and destroying forms, integrating and disintegrating, anabolism and catabolism tending to change and conserve tissues and so on. The three aspects — A, U, M — of the Primordial Power (Nāda bindu) are always operating.'[30]

Oṁ represents Śiva. The entire universe is the thought projection of Śiva. He is the Creator, Maintainer and Destroyer of the universe. All things and being, live, move and exist in the cosmic ideation of Śiva. Over the *Oṁ* (ॐ) is written the sign of Candra-bindu, shown as a crescent with a dot or point over it. The bindu or dot represents Parama Śiva. The crescent sign is the line of demarcation between Śiva and Parama Śiva.

The *Muṇḍakopaniṣad* says: *"Oṁ* the Sonic Consciousness is the bow, the Self is the arrow and the Brahman is the target. One should hit that mark with an undistracted mind, and like the arrow become one with it."[31]

Oṁ is not the final goal of spiritual pursuits. The attainment of Parama Śiva is the objective behind Spiritual Sādhanā. As *Oṁ* is the bow, it will be left behind in the soul's journey towards the Supreme. One should endeavour to reach that divine province whence Oṁkāra has emerged.

The other great confusion regarding *Oṁ* is about its recitation. A large section of the educated attach great significance to the chanting of *Oṁ*. Oṁkāra is not to be recited but listened to in deep meditation. When the Kulakuṇḍalinī awakens in an individual divine self, the latter listens different sounds. When the Kuṇḍalinī leave Mūlādhāra, one hears the sound of cricket (झींगुर), when she crosses Svādhiṣṭhāna, the sound of an anklet (नूपुर) is heard, in the Maṇipūra one hears the sound of a bell (घंटा), at the Anāhata one hears the musical symphony of flute and finally when the Kuṇḍalinī crosses Viśudha, the Sādhaka hears Oṁkāra. Beyond Ājñā there is no sound.

Oṁkāra is the *bīja-mantra* of all Mātṛkā Varṇa. Oṁkāra is the unified form of all sounds. There is sound wherever there is vibration. Every action is vibrational. Cosmic thought projection is also an action. It has vibrations and sounds. We cannot hear this supramundane sound with our physical ears. But if we can tune our mind with the help of the intuitional scientific process, we can apprehend that eternal sound Oṁkāra. This Oṁkāra is the sum total of all cosmic vibrations. All other sounds are different manifestations of this Cosmic Sound. It may appear gibberish to the ignorant but it has great mystic significance. To make it more clear let us take the example of the village market place. From a distance one feels as if people there are only gibbering; it is only din and noise. But as one goes near it all makes sense and the nonsensical sounds become meaningful words like, 'Give me one kilo of peas', 'What is the price of cauliflower', etc. Yet these very utterances, collectively, were meaningless syllables from a distance. 'Just as all the sounds of the market place have been unified into one howl carrying sound wave, just as all have blended their respective thought waves into one howl, similarly all the sounds of the universe are implanted in one Oṁkāra. Oṁkāra is the unified form of all sounds.'[32]

The Yogi proceeds from the path of Oṁkāra to Parama Śiva. He awakens his dormant divinity by Mantra Sādhanā and becomes one with the Supreme Self. Sādhanā of Oṁkāra. or Śabda-Brahman rids him of an untold suffering. It leads one and all from the transitory world of Time and Space to the Eternal Kingdom of

God. The Śruti says: 'All Vedas sing the song of *Oṁ*. It is accepted by all. All the spiritual pursuits are done for its attainment. The great Sādhaka ideates and meditates and observes Brahmacarya in the hope of attaining that Pada which is known as *Oṁ*.'[33]

Mantra is an esoteric formula to awaken the dormant Kuṇḍalinī. It is an acoustic science which brings the realization of the inner psychic potentialities of man. Incantation of the mantric formula creates an acoustic vibration which awakens the sleeping Kuṇḍalinī. This is the most secret science of Tantra. The sole objective of *mantra* is to attain liberation from the mundane, supramundane and spiritual bondage. That alone is *mantra* which brings liberation.[34] Incantation of *mantra* brings about the attainment of the fourfold objective of life, *viz. Dharma* (righteousness), *Artha* (wealth), *Kāma* (mundane happiness) and *Mokṣa* (liberation).[35]

Kulārṇava Tantra deals with Mantra-Sādhanā. According to it Siddha-Mantra alone can bring the desired result. One who has attained mastery over the inner power or potency of one *mantra* can achieve mastery over other mantras as well because the inner power of consciousness of all *mantras* is one and the same.[36]

Mantras are innumerable. But only Siddha-Mantras are to be meditated. Siddha-Mantra when received from a Guru is sure to bear the spiritual fruit.

What is Siddha-Mantra? All *mantras* are acoustic. The acoustic vibrations of *mantras* are flowing without any feeling both in the Cosmos and in the unity body. When through the esoteric process of mantric incantation, one establishes parallelism between his unity ectoplasmic vibration and cosmic vibration, it is called Mantra-Siddhi. The Siddha-Mantra is pregnant with divine consciousness and force. It comes from a perfect being or the Guru. It is a perfect *mantra*. Tantra warns, against the practice of *mantra* heard by chance, seen by deceit and taken from some printed books; these bring inevitable disaster.[37]

Mantra works when it is duly received from a Guru who has attained perfections in Mantra Sādhanā. Success in Mantra Sādhanā depends upon the purity and dedication of the Sādhaka, the inner potency of the Siddha Mantra and the grace of the Guru. If any of the three is wanting, it will be sheer waste of time. But when practised correctly and truthfully, it is sure to bring esoteric results.

Śiva is the originator of Mantra-Śāstra. There are three kinds of *mantras*. They come from Śiva.[38] Every *mantra* is associated with a deity (Devatā).[39] Śiva is associated with every *mantra*. According to some the objective behind Mantra Sādhanā is the realization of the Devatā. T. M. P. Mahadevan writes: 'Mantra Sādhanā is an essential part of spiritual discipline. The most potent way of realizing a *devatā* is with the help of *bīja-mantra*.'[40] Every *mantra* has a presiding deity. Mantra-Siddhi is attained when the Sādhaka becomes one with the deity. After this the Sādhaka is rewarded with the wealth of esoteric power of the deity. The mystic and the scientific basis of the realization of the deity is the emanation of mantric vibrations appropriate to the deity invoked. Incantation of *mantra* creates a spiritual environment and acoustic vibrations which awaken the presiding deity and make him visible in intuition and mystic experience. Is deity a supernatural being'? No. He is not. He is the psychic projection of the Sāḍhaka. Every *jīva* is a dormant Śiva. To awaken the dormant divinity is the purpose behind Mantra Sādhanā. Psychologically, mind can be divided into three: Crude Mind, Subtle Mind and Causal Mind. The Crude Mind controls the physical hunger of man. It deals with the external physicality It is known as Kāmamaya Koṣa. The Subtle Mind deals with the intellectual process of recollection and contemplation. It is called Manomaya Koṣa. The rest is called Causal Mind or Kāraṇamanaḥ. It is the collective name of the three Koṣas, *i.e.* Atimānasa (supramental sphere), Vijñānamaya Koṣa (subliminal sphere) and Hiraṇyamaya Koṣa (astral mind). Sometimes they are loosely called Conscious, Subconscious and Unconscious mind. The concept of Unconscious of Freud and Jung is quite different from the Tāntric concept of Causal Mind. According to Freud the Unconscious is the storehouse of suppressed and repressed desires, whereas, according to Tantra, the Causal Mind is all-knowing. There is virtually no difference between the Cosmic Causal Mind, which is the origin of the Cosmos, and the individual Causal Mind. When with the help of mantric Sādhanā an individual acquires control over his Causal Mind, he becomes timeless, all-knowing and all-powerful. The intuitive experience of the Causal Mind is the realization of deities. The realization of deities (मन्त्रेश्वर) is nothing but the knowledge of one's own psychic power.

There are seven crore *mantras.*[41] These are Śiva-Śakti-Maya.[42] They are very powerful and fulfil the desires of the worshipper. These *mantras,* associated with Śiva and Śakti, have originated from Śudha-Vidyā.

Parā which resides in Mūlādhāra Cakra represents Śiva-tattva. It is also called Bindu-tattva. Paśyanti lives in Svādhiṣṭhāna Cakra. It represents Śakti-tattva. It is called Nāda-tattva. There are some who believe that Parā is Nāda-tattva and Paśyanti is Bindu-tattva.[43] But we differ from their stand. We view that Parā being the first point of origin of Śabda, it cannot be Nāda-tattva. Nāda means the expressed sound. Tribindu or Kāmakalā is the root of all *mantras.* It is derived from the wedlock of Bindu and Nāda-tattva. The three Bindus are the White (Sīta), the Red (Sona) and the Mixed (Miśra). They stand for Icchā, Jñāna and Kriyā, and represent Prakāśa (effulgence), Vimarśa (distinction) and Prakāśa-Vimarśa (combination of both aspects of Parama Śiva). Thus the *mantra* is called Śiva-Śakti-Maya and Jñāna-Kriyātmikā because it is the science of Nāda and Bindu. Mantra is the acoustic formula which, when practised according to the strict spiritual discipline, produces, vibrations of the same length as is of the vibrations of the deity and brings about an identification of Self with the presiding deity.

Śrī-Tantra-Sadbhāva says: 'All Mantras consist of letters (*varṇātmaka*). They again, O beloved, are at base Śakti. Śakti again is Mātṛkā and She again is Śivātmikā. She, the Mātṛkā who in the world appears possessed of the energy and brilliance of the Supreme (Paratejaḥ-Samanvita) pervades all this universe beginning from Brahma and ending with Bhuvana.'[44]

Netra Tantram expounds the philosophy and the nature of *mantra*. The dialogues of Devī and Parmeśvara throw light on the mystic and metaphysical problem of *mantra*. According to *Netra Tantram*, *mantra* is composed of three factors (Tritattvātmaka) and creates bliss through the medium of vibration of consciousness (Ātman).[45] Thus, the two Bindus, white and red, are Śiva and Śakti. They are the causes of Word (*Vāk*) and Meaning (*Artha*). Śiva is Pure Consciousness; He requires the association of some active principle for creation. Śiva cannot create without Śakti. He is devoid of force, power and creativity. Metaphysically speaking Śakti is the perfect mirror in which Śiva experiences Himself.

Śiva and Śakti play together in mutual enjoyment out of which Word (*Vāk*) and Meaning (*Artha*) have been created. Word (*Vāk*) stands for Parā, Paśyanti, Madhyamā and Vaikharī sounds. *Artha* represents the thirty-six Tattvas of Tantra metaphysics. *Kāma-Kalā-Vilāsa* says: 'By Vacaḥ is meant all the sounds — Parā, Paśyanti and so forth; and by *Artha* is meant the thirty-six Tattvas beginning with Śiva and ending with Kṣiti. The creation of these is the creation of the world (*Jagat*) of six Adhvas.'[46]

The two Bindus, white and red, are inseparable and indistinguishable.[47] They represent Śiva and Śakti, who are eternally inseparable. Similarly, Vidyā and Devatā are also inseparable. Lord Mahādeva says: 'Mantras are Tritattvajā. The three Tattvas stand for Śiva, Śakti and Ātman. Mantras have three characteristics. Mantras are bestowers of all desires (*sarvadā*), are all pervasive (sarvagā) and are of all forms (*sarvarūpiṇī*). Mantras are all powerful.'[48]

If *mantra* is formless it cannot bestow any power. If it has form, it can have only limited power. If *mantra* is Śivātmaka, it is all pervasive and ultimately it becomes void. Mantra bereft of material and efficient cause is passive and non-creative. If it is formless it is immutable, static and devoid of creative force. Action warrants individuation. On the other hand if *mantra* is recognized as a principle of individuation then it becomes the subject of bondage. Hence, one who is himself under the spell of bondage cannot grant liberation to others. Mantra being the liberating principle, it cannot be without any force.

On the other hand if Śakti be recognized as the life-force of mantra than the question arises whose Śakti it is?[49] The idea of Śakti without the one who possesses it (Śaktimān) is not possible. Lord Śiva says to Devī that there is nothing in the world which is not composed of the three factors of Śiva, Śakti and Āṇava (individual).[50] Mantra has of these three principles. Mantra is essentially Prakṛti in nature.[51]

The confusion arises only due to the dualistic or pluralistic approach to the problem. Sometimes we overlook the fact that Śiva and Śakti are not two entities. They are only two facets of the Reality. When we experience the monism of Śiva and Śakti, the ignorance of duality disappears. As Śiva is also the material cause of the universe, He is the originator of Mantra Śāstra. Śakti is the immanent principle of Śiva and as such, She is the *force* of *mantra*. But Śiva being the Lord, He is the originator and exponent of Mantra-Śāstra.

Śrī Mṛgendra Tantram makes a passing reference to *mantra*. It says that the deity of *mantra* is full of consciousness.[52]

Śāradā Tilaka deals in detail with the different kinds of *mantra*. According to it there are three kinds of *mantras*, *i.e.* Masculine, Feminine and Neuter.[53] Masculine Mantras are those whose presiding deities are male gods. These *mantras* are called Jñeya. Those *mantras* which are presided over by female deities are known as Female Mantras. These are called Vidyā.

According to acoustic considerations those *mantras* which end with *Hūṁ* and *Phūṭ* are Masculine Mantras and those which end with double *Tha* are Feminine Mantras. Neuter Mantras are those which end with *Namaḥ*.[54]

Śāradā Tilaka further says: 'There are ten kinds of mantric Saṁskāras. They are Janana, Jivan, Tāram, Bodhan, Abhiṣeka, Vimalikaraṇa, Apyāthan, Tarpaṇa, Dīpan and Gupti.'[55]

Mantra Sādhanā offers the mystic and scientific process for the realization of the non-dual state of Śiva and Śakti. The realization of the unity of the two is experienced in one's condition of salvation. The purpose of Mantra Sādhanā is to neutralize the positive effect of Māyā by arousing the force of fundamental negativity or Kulakuṇḍalinī and bring about the realization or Self as Transcendental Being. This non-qualified liberation can be attained only by Mantra Sādhanā.

The efficacy of *mantra* has been accepted by all Tāntric systems. Mantra Sādhanā is directed for the attainment of Śivahood. Śivahood is the supreme unification of Self with Parama Śiva. *Śiva Sūtra* emphasizes the practice of *mantra* for the attainment of liberation. The efficacy and potency of *mantra* can be experienced only by its incantation. 'By the constant intuitional research of Mahahṛda, one can have the realization of the spiritual power of mantra.'[56] Mahahṛda means Parama Śiva.

The second chapter of *Śiva Sūtra* deals with the importance and great significance of Mantra Sādhanā. *Śiva Sūtra Vārttika* expounds the nature and potency of *mantra* for the attainment of Śivahood.[57] Mantra is employed for the liberation of Soul from Māyā. A man can attain the state of perfection and purity (पूर्णहन्ता) only by freeing himself from the feeling of individuation (*āṇava-mala*). Mantra Sādhanā is the most efficacious weapon to cut asunder the trammels of *āṇava-mala*. Mantra is a force of consciousness. *Śiva Sūtra* says: 'Mantra is Citta.'[58] Citta means here Cosmic Consciousness. Citta here stands for Supreme Subjectivity (Pramātman). Citt has not been used here in the sense of objectivated consciousness as described in *Pratyabhijñāhṛdayam*.[59] Citta means Śiva. Bhaskara, the great commentator of *Śiva Sūtra* and author of *Śiva Sūtra Vārttika* says: 'Mantra is that which is of the nature of bringing intuitive realization of Self.'[60] The nature of *mantra* is consciousness.[61] The mantric power is not a mechanical force but a spiritual principle which awakens the dormant divinity. Tantra enjoins upon every man and woman to awaken *mantra*. Mantric Consciousness is the supreme state of evolution. It is a mystic technique for accelerating the process of evolution.

The consciousness is the sole repository of *mantra*. Without the force of consciousness mantra is dead and useless. Mantra *caitanya* is the *elan vita* of Mantra Sādhanā. It is an esoteric principle for unifying the internal ectoplasmic vibration with the cosmological vibration and lead one to the realm of spiritual sublimity. The adjustment between the individual ectoplasmic vibration and the cosmic vibration is the science and metaphysic of Mantra-Śāstra.

Existence is a mass of waves. Destiny is nailed with multilateral miseries. The *summum bonum* of human life is the attainment of Parama Śiva — the one singular unrhythmic entity. The moment an individual unites his own Parā-Śakti with Parama Śiva, his *mantra* begins to vibrate with life and consciousness. Mantra becomes *caitanya.* Mantra without conscious-force is of no consequence. Mantras which are alive with their life-force give all success.[62] Bereft of this conscious-power *mantras* are combinations of mere letters. They do not fructify. 'Mantras whose potency is asleep do not give any result. In the absence of the consciousness-force *mantras* become mere letters; even millions of incantations of such lifeless *mantras* do not give any fruit.'[63]

Mantra-Caitanya and Siddha-Mantras are the giver of the fourfold object of life, *viz., Dharma, Artha, Kāma* and *Mokṣa.*

With the incantation of mantra mind becomes detached from the world and attains the condition of Pure Consciousness. This is called the awakening of mantra.[64] *Śiva-Sūtra Vārttika* says: 'The secret of mantra lies in Vidyā Śarīra (psychic body).'[65] The acoustic vibration which is created in the psychic body illumines Self. The divine state of Pure Consciousness is Vidyā. It is the psychic body of *mantra* (मान्त्रिक शरीरसत्ता). The mantric incantation vibrates the psychic body and awakens divinity. It detaches mind from mundane enjoyments.

Mantra incantation should be associated with the ideation of Parama Śiva. The ideational part of Mantra Sādhanā should not be ignored. It is a necessary part of Mantra Sādhanā. Gopinath Kaviraj says: 'According to the directive of Maharṣi Patañjali, in *mantra* incantation, the ideation of *mantra* is essential. Incantation and ideation are inseparable.'[66]

The ideation of *mantra* is a psychic process of superimposition of Cosmic Consciousness. It is of two kinds, *i.e.,* auto-suggestion and outer-suggestion. Both are psychic parts of Mantra Sādhanā. It is of great importance and of scientific nature. With the constant ideation or superimposition of Cosmic Consciousness, psyche (mind) is transformed into Self (Ātman). This transformation, of *psychic* into Self, is the central objective of Tantra Sādhanā.

The process of transformation of mind into spirit is scientific and logical. Self or Cosmic Consciousness is pure and transcendental. In the scientific language we can say that the wave of Cosmic Consciousness travels in a straight line. It means the wavelength of Consciousness is infinite or zero. Mind being an ever-changing relative and functional organism, it is not an absolute entity. Being a relative entity mind is represented by a curvature. With the constant ideation of

Parama Śiva during *mantra* incantation, the wavelength of mind gets gradually straightened. And at the auspicious moment of spiritual advent, mind attains the wavelength of Self which results in the merger of mind into Parama Śiva. Mind becomes Self. The realization of the *advaita* (non-dual) state of Spiritual Sublimity is not possible in the state of *dvaita* (dualism). Jīva is Śiva and Śiva is *jīva.* The realization of this identity is the purpose behind Tantra Sādhanā. 'When the Supreme Self is under bondage, he is jīva, when he is without bondage, he is Sadā-Śiva.[67] Mantra Sādhanā leads to the attainment of enjoyment and salvation. Mantra is a liberating force. It wipes away all the blemishes and makes a man pure.

Mantra Sādhanā should be performed under a strict esoteric discipline. Adherence to the principles of morality is a pre-condition of Mantra Sādhanā. Negligence of the esoteric discipline and disobedience to moral principles obnubilate the Soul.

Kinds of Incantation

There are three kinds of *mantra*-incantation: Vācanic, Upanṣu and Mānasika. Vācanic Japa is the loud incantation of *mantra.* It is the lowest form of *mantra*-incantation. When *japa* is done in the lowest tone, in other words, when only the movement of lips is observed by others, it is called Upanṣu Japa. The best form of *mantra*-incantation is mental. 'The *mantra* which are incanted loudly are no *mantras* at all.'[68] Tantra rules out loud *mantra*-incantation. This is one of the points of disagreement between Tantra and the Veda. The Vedic hymns are chanted loudly; they are devoid of consciousness and force. The chanting of the Vedic hymns does not awaken the dormant divinity because it does not create that psychic and esoteric vibration in the psychic body which is the pre-condition for the arousal of the Kulakuṇḍalinī.

Japasūtram discusses in detail the importance of Japa in Tantra Sādhanā. According to it there should be complete harmony and collaboration between Vāk, Manaḥ and Prāṇa before starting *mantra*-incantation of *Iṣṭa-mantra.*[69] Collaboration between the three factors creates an approriate field for successful *mantra*-incantation. Collaboration of Śudhi, Ṛdhi and Budhi creates a psychic field for *mantra* evolution. Vidyā does not mean theoretical knowledge. It is the right understanding and disposition of things. *Japasūtram* outlines the mantric requirements (see diagram on p. 149).

Tantrarāja Tantra puts emphasis on *mantra*-incantation. According to it *mantras* are all-pervading. It expounds the doctrine of oneness of Mātṛkās with sixteen Nityās. The proper and mystic practice of Mantra Sādhanā removes the worldly attachment and brings the realization of the Eternal and Pure Consciousness (Śiva).[70]

The greatness of *mantra* has been accepted by all schools of Tantra. Mantra is an inevitable part of Tantra Sādhanā. Different *mantras* are employed for different deities and for various objectives.

REFERENCES

1. मननं विश्वविज्ञानं त्राणं संसारबन्धनात्।
यतः करोति संसिद्धो मंत्र इत्युच्यते ततः। *Śāradā Tilakam*, p. 126
2. *Śāradā Tilakam,* ver. 1, p. 2.
3. शब्द ब्रह्म यतू चिरे सुकृतिनश्चैतन्यमन्त्र्गतम्
तद्वोऽव्यादनिशं शशाङ्कसदनं वाचामधीशं महः।।1।। *Ibid.*
4. शब्दब्रह्मापि यत्प्रोक्त तदुद्देश्यः प्रवर्त्यते
अतः परमवाच्यं हि स्वसंवेद्यस्वरूपतः।।61।।
शब्दब्रह्मेति शब्दवगम्यमर्थं विदुर्बुधाः।
स्वतोऽथानवबोधत्वात् प्रोक्तो नैतादृशोखः।।11।। *Prapañcasāra Tantra.*
5. भिद्यआनात्यराद्विदोख्यन्कात्मा खोऽभवत्।।11।। *Śāradā Tilaka*, p. 11.
6. चैतन्यं सर्वभूतानां शब्दब्रह्मेति मेमतिः।।13।। *Ibid.*, p. 11.
7. *Ibid.*, p. 13.
8. Mantra Caitanya, *Prout* (Hindi), Feb. 6, 1968, published from New Delhi.
9. अकाराद्याः स्वरा धूम्राः सिन्दूराभास्तुकादयः। तानि च सनत्कुमारसंहितायां
Mantra aur Mātṛkāyon kā Rahasya, p. 114. Chowkhamba Sanskrit Series, Varanasi, 1966.
10. *Ibid.*, pp. 114-115.
11. अकारं सर्वदेवव्यं रक्तं सर्ववशङ्करम् — *Saubhāgyabhāskara,* p. 125.
12. *Mantra aur Mātṛkāyon kā Rahasya,* pp. 115-39.
13. न विद्या मातृकापरा। *Svacchanda Tantra, paṭal* 11, ver. 199.
14. बीजयोन्यात्मकाद् भेदात् द्विधा बीजं स्वरा मताः।।10।।
कादिभिश्च स्मृता योनिनवधावर्ग-भेदतः।
प्रतिवर्णविभेदेन शतार्धकिरणोज्ज्वला
बीजमंत्र शिवः शक्तिर्योनिरिव्यभिधीयते।
Mālinī Vijyottara Tantram, ch. III, vv. 10, 11, 12, p. 15.
15. सर्वे वर्णात्मका मन्त्रा ते च शक्त्यात्मकाः प्रिय।
शक्तितस्तु मातृका ज्ञेया सा च ज्ञेया शिवात्मिका।।
या सा तु मातृकालोके परतेजः समन्विता।
तया व्याप्तमिदं सर्वमाब्रह्मभुवनात्मकम्।।
Kāma-Kalā-Vilāsa (3rd ed.), p. 30, Ganesh & Co., Madras, 1961, No. 37/1922.
16. *Mālinī Vijoyottara Tantram,* vv. 37-41, p. 18.
Kashmir Sanskrit Series, Srinagar, no. 37, 1922.
17. *Mālinī Vijoyottara Tantram.*
18. श्लिष्ट पुरः स्फुरित सद्वयकोटिलक्षरूपं परस्परगतं च समं कूटम्।
19. *Tantrik Texts,* p. 43 Agamanusandhara Samiti Sanskrit Press Depository, 30 Cornwallis Street, Calcutta, 1922. Luzac & Co., 46 Great Russell Street, London, 1922.
20. सा प्रसूते कुण्डलिनी शब्द ब्रह्ममयी विभुः।
शक्ति ततो ध्वनिस्तस्मान्नादस्तस्मान्निरोधिका।।111।।
ततोद्धन्र्दुस्ततो बिन्दुस्तस्मादासीत् परा ततः
पश्यन्ति मध्यमा वाचि वैखरी शब्दजन्मभूः।।112।। *Śāradā Tilaka,* ch. 1, pp. 34-35.
21. परापश्यन्त्याद्यावस्थातः प्राक् बिन्दुनादाद्यात्मकं यन्मातृकायाः सूक्ष्मरूपम्। *Yagyabaibhava.*
22. देहेऽपि मूलाधारेऽस्मिन् समुदेति समीरण।

विवक्षोरिच्छयोत्थेन प्रत्यनेन सुसंस्कृतः।।
स व्यञ्जयति तत्रैव शब्दब्रह्मापि सर्वगम्।। *Saubhāgyabhāskara.*

23. मध्यमा सूक्ष्मा मातृका मध्यमाधिकारिणः पूजोपकरणम्।
कारणकार्यबिन्द्वात्मिका परापश्यन्तिरूपा सूक्ष्मतरा मातृकोत्तमाधिकारिणः। *Tatparyadīpikā Anandasharama,* p. 54.

24. तत्र शब्दब्रह्मरूपस्य बीजस्योच्छूनतावस्था परा स्फुटितावस्था पश्यन्ती मुकुलिताव्यक्तं दलद्वयं मध्यमा। सम्यग् त्रिकासेन प्रसृतं मिथः संसृष्टमूलं दलद्वयं वैखरी।
Saubhāgyabhāskara.

25. *Japasūtram* (Ist ed.), p. 17, Bharatiya Vidya Prakashan, Varanasi, 1966.
26. *Ibid.*, p. 18.
27. *Bharatiya Saṁskṛti and Sādhanā,* vol. 1, p. 414.
28. प्रणवः प्राणिना प्राणो जीवनं सम्प्रतिष्ठितम्।
गृह्णाति प्रणवः सर्व कलाभिः कलयेच्छिवम्।। *Netra Tantra,* ver. 129.

29. अकारश्च उकारश्च मकारो बिन्दुरेव च
अर्द्धचन्द्रो निरोधी च नादो नादान्त एव च।। 225।।
कौण्डिली व्यापिनी शक्तिः समनैकादशी स्मृता।
उन्मनाच ततोऽतीता तदतीतं निरामयम्।। 226।। *Svacchanda Tantra, Paṭala* 4.

30. *The Garland of Letters,* p. 209.
31. प्रणवो धनुः शरोह्यात्मा ब्रह्मतल्लक्ष्यमुच्यते
अप्रमत्तेन वेद्वच्यं शरवत् तन्मयो भवेत्। — ch. 11, ver. 4.

32. *Subhāṣtia Saṁgraha,* part III (eng.), pp. 59-60.
33. सर्वे वेदा यदपद्यामनन्ति तपांसि सर्वाणि च यद्वदन्ति।
यदिच्छन्तोब्रह्म चरं चरन्ति तत्तेपदं संग्रहेण ब्रवीभ्योमित्येतद्। *Yajura-Veda*

34. मनना तारयेत यस्तु स मन्त्र परिकीर्तितः। *Netra Tantra,* p. 257.

35. शृणु देवि प्रवक्ष्यामि यन्मां त्वं परिपृच्छसि।
तस्य श्रवणमात्रेण मन्त्रतत्त्वं प्रकाशते।।
जपयज्ञात परो यज्ञो नापरोऽस्तीह कश्चन।
तस्माज्जपेन धर्मार्थकाममोक्षांश्च साधयेत्।।
Kulārṇava Tantra, Ullāsa, 15. vv. 2-3, p. 320. Ganesh & Co., Madras, 1965.

36. *Ibid.*
37. *Ibid.*, p. 15.
38. मन्त्राणां कोटयस्तिस्रः सार्धाः शिवनियोजिताः। *Mālinī Vijoyottara Tantra,* ch. I, ver. 41, p. 5.

39. मन्त्रमन्त्रेश्वरेशत्वे संनियोज्यं ततः पुनः।
Ibid., ver. 21, p. 3

40. *The Garland of Letters,* p. viii.
41. सप्तकोटीस्तु मन्त्राणां सृजते ज्ञानक्रियात्मिकाः
Svacchanda Tantrum, vol. VI, p. 40. Kashmir Series of Texts and Studies, no. LVI. Srinagar, 1935.
मन्त्राणामसृजत्तद्वन्सप्त कोटीः समण्डलाः।। 21।। *Mālinī Vijoyottara Tantra,* p. 3.

42. शिवः शक्तिः सविद्येसा मन्त्रा मन्त्रेश्वराण्व
उपादेयमिति प्रोक्तमेतत्सटकं फलार्थिनहम्।। 15।। *Ibid.*, p. 2.

43. *The Garland of Letters,* p. vi.
44. जयति स्वपरिस्पन्दानन्दान्दोलनलीलया।
मन्त्र तत्त्वं त्रितत्वात्म तन्त्रयन्त्रेत्रमैश्वरम्।।

Netra Tantram, vol. II, p. 248. Kashmir Series of Texts and Studies, no. LXI, Srinagar, 1939.
45. *Ibid.*
46. *Kāma-Kalā-Vilāsa* (3rd ed.), p. 15. Ganesh & Co., Madras, 1961.
47. *Ibid.*, ver. 11, p. 26.
48. एवमुक्तेन विधिना मन्त्राः सर्वे त्रितत्वजा।
शिवाख्याः शक्तिरूपाश्च तथैवात्मस्वरूपकाः।। 57 ।।
त्रिस्वभावाः समुदृष्टा सर्वत्र बलशालिनः।
भवन्ति सर्वदाः सर्वेसर्वगाः सर्वरूपिणः।। 58 ।। *Netra Tantram*, p. 248
49. *Ibid.*, p. 252.
50. तत्वत्रयं विना वस्तु मन्त्रो वक्तुं न युज्यते।। 16 ।। *Ibid.*, p. 157.
51. प्रकृतो मंत्र वर्गः।
52. मन्त्रेशेशचिदाविष्टरूद्रव्यूहाष्टकानुगः।
Śrī Mṛgendra Tantram, p. 332. Kashmir Series of Texts and Studies, no. L, Srinagar, 1930.
53. मन्त्राः पुंदेवता ज्ञेया विद्याः स्त्रीदेवताः स्मृताः।। 58 ।।
पुस्त्रीनपुंसकात्मानो मन्त्रा सर्त्रे समीरिताः।। ch. II, p. 46.
54. पुं मन्त्रा हुम्फऽन्ताः स्युर्द्धिठान्ताश्चस्त्रियो मताः।
नपुंसका नमोऽता स्युरिव्युक्ता मनवस्त्रिधा।। 59 ।। *Ibid.*
55. मन्त्राणां दशसंस्कारा कश्यन्ते सिद्धिदायिनीः।
जननं जीवनं पश्चात् ताडनं बोधनं तथा।। 112 ।।
अथाभिषेको विमलीकरणाष्यापने पुनः।
दर्पणं दीपनं गुप्तिदेशैता मन्त्रसंस्क्रिया।। 113 ।। *Ibid.*
56. महाह्रदानुसंधानान्मन्त्रवीर्यानुभव।। 23 ।।
Śiva Sūtra Vārttika, ch. I, ver. 23, p.26. Kashmir Series of Texts, and Studies, Srinagar, 1916.
57. *Ibid.*, p. 29.
58. चित्तं मन्त्रं।। 1 ।। *Ibid.*, ch. II, ver. 1, p. 29.
59. चितिरेव चेतनपदादवरूढ़ा चेत्थसङ्कोचिनी चित्तम्।। 5 ।। *Pratyabhijñāhṛdayam.*
60. स्वात्मानुभवंधंर्भित्वात्स मन्त्र इति गीयते। *Śiva Sūtra Vārttika*, p. 30
61. *Ibid.*, p. 31.
62. मन्त्राचैतन्यसहिताः सर्वसिद्धि कराः स्मृताः।
Kulārṇava Tantra, ch. 15, ver. 60, p. 326.
63. चैतन्यरहिता मंत्राः प्रोक्ता वर्णास्तु केवलम्।
फलं नैव प्रयच्छन्ति लक्षकोटिजपादपि।। *Ibid.*, ver. 61.
64. *Ibid.*, p. 32.
65. विद्याशरीरसत्ता मन्त्ररहस्यम्।। 3 ।। *Ibid.*, p. 31.
66. *Tāntrika Vāṅgamaya Me Śāktadṛṣṭikoṇa*, p. 286.
67. *Kulārṇava-Tantra,* p. 241.
68. उच्चार्यमाणा ये मन्त्रा न मन्त्राँश्चापि तद्बिदुः।
Śiva-Sūtra-Vimarśini, p. 48.
69. *Japasūtram*, p. 106.
70. *Tantrarāja* (second impression), p. 81. Ganesh & Co., Madras, 1964.

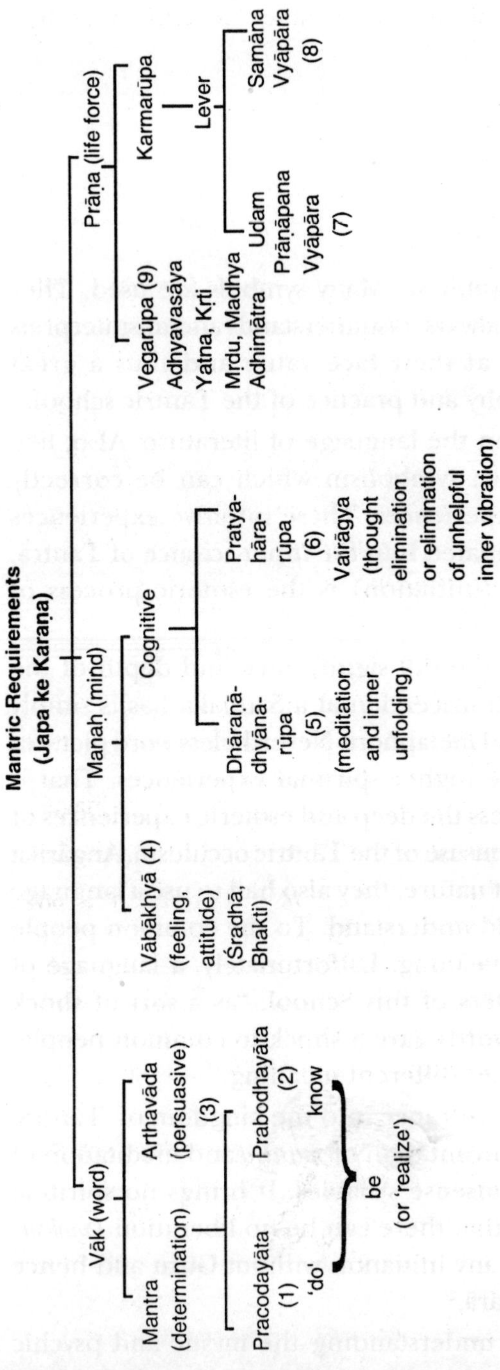
Mantric Requirements
(Japa ke Karaṇa)
Vāk (word)
Mantra
(determination)
Arthavāda
(persuasive)
(3)
Pracodayāta
(1)
'do'
Prabodhayāta
(2)
know
be
(or 'realize')
Vābākhyā (4)
(feeling,
attitude)
(Śradhā,
Bhakti)
Manaḥ (mind)
Cognitive
Dhāraṇā-
dhyāna-
rūpa
(5)
(meditation
and inner
unfolding)
Pratya-
hāra-
rūpa
(6)
Vairāgya
(thought
elimination
or elimination
of unhelpful
inner vibration)
Prāṇa (life force)
Vegarūpa (9)
Adhyavasāya
Yatna, Kṛti
Mṛdu, Madhya
Adhimātra
Karmarūpa
Lever
Udam
Prāṇāpana
Vyāpāra
(7)
Samāna
Vyāpāra
(8)

7 Dīkṣā and Yantra

Tāntric scriptures are written in Sandhyābhāṣā. Many symbols are used. They have great esoteric significance. But a layman always misunderstands and misinterprets them. He takes them and the scriptures at their face value and thus a great misunderstanding arises about the philosophy and practice of the Tāntric school.

The language of Tantra is different from the language of literature. Also, like every branch of science Tantra has its own symbolism which can be correctly understood only in the light of intuitive experiences. These intuitive experiences can be had only by those who have been initiated into the inner science of Tantra, who practise Tantra Sādhanā. And Dīkṣā (initiation) is the esoteric process of imparting secret of Tantra Sādhanā.

The ordinary language cannot express the full significance and depth of the mystic experience. The experience of the transcendental a Sādhaka has is simply inexplicable. It may be described in similes and metaphors. Nevertheless word pictures cannot correctly and adequately convey the higher spiritual experiences. That is why Tantra adopts varied symbolism to express the deep and esoteric experiences of the intuitional science. It protects it from the misuse of the Tāntric occultism. Angārika Govind writes: 'In order to preserve its secret nature, they also had to use a language of symbolism which only the 'initiates' could understand. To the common people the words carried an altogether different meaning. Unfortunately, a language of double interpretation was used by the writers of this School, "as a sort of shock therapy". The apparent meaning of these words gave a shock to common people, but to the 'initiates' they carried an altogether different meaning.'[1]

The initiation is a mystic passport to get entrance into the kingdom of Tāntric esotericism. Without proper initiation, the incantation of *mantra* and meditation of God become an intellectual exercise of nonsense syllables. It brings no spiritual advancement. 'It is laid down by Lord Śiva that there can be no liberation (*mokṣa*) without initiation (*dīkṣā*). There cannot be any initiation without Guru and hence he comes down to the line of Guru-paramparā.[2]

The initiation is a scientific process of understanding the mystic and psychic association of *mantra* with Self. The conceptual understanding of *mantra* is the most vital part of mantric incantation. The ideational realization and vision of *mantra* is the most important aspect of Tantra Sādhanā. The conceptual understanding of *mantra* is known as Mantra Caitanya. After initiation, *mantra* become conscious (*caitanya*) and brings the desired result of spiritual awakening. *Śāradā Tilaka* says: 'Now, I explain the meaning of initiation (*dīkṣā*) without which no result of *mantra* can be achieved.'[3]

Along with Mantra-caitanya, Mantra-dīpinī is also essential. These two constitute the process of initiation. Mantra-dīpinī is like a beacon light. It throws light on the dark chamber of the Tāntric mysticism. Without it a Sādhaka cannot see properly the priceless treasures of esotericism. With this, a Sādhaka becomes conscious of the spiritual wealth of Self and strives for its acquisition. The initiation brings the visualization of *mantra*. Mantra-dīpinī enables one to make full use of the mantric potentialities. The effects of *mantra* can be tested only after proper initiation.

Śāradā Tilaka defines initiation in the following words: 'That which gives spiritual knowledge (Divya-jñāna) and brings the annihilation of baser propensities (Pāpa) is verily the Initiation according to all Tantrās.'[4]

Attainment of spiritual realization is possible only after proper initiation. With the help of Mantra-caitanya and Mantra-dīpinī, the Kuṇḍalinī is aroused; the awakening of the Kuṇḍalinī brings spiritual realization. The Sādhaka becomes conscious of the transcendental nature of Self. He becomes one with Parama Śiva. The attainment of this supreme unification of *jīva* with Śiva is called spiritual realization (Divya-jñāna).

Initiation brings annihilation of Saṁskāra. Good or bad Saṁskāra is a binding principle. Liberation means total obliteration of Saṁskāra. Initiation accelerate the process of consummation. With the initiation, suddenly either happiness increases or suffering multiplies. It simply means that a man is heading towards the total annihilation of Saṁskāra. That is why *Śāradā Tilaka* says that initiation brings the annihilation of baser propensities of Saṁskāra. It burns the very seed of Saṁskāra.

What is Saṁskāra? Reaction in its potentiality is called Saṁskāra. It is said that every action has an equal and opposite reaction. But this is not wholly correct. The reaction of any action would be equal only if there was no lapse of time between the two, which is impossible. Thus, the reaction is never equal. It is either more or less. The reaction in its potential form is always less or more. A man will have to reap the harvest of his past actions either less or more. Whatever the harvest, bad or good, it is by nature binding. Saṁskāra by nature is Tāmsika. Good Saṁskāra is like a chain of gold whereas bad Saṁskāra is like a chain of steel, but both are the causes of bondage. Therefore, without the annihilation of Saṁskāra, liberation is not possible.

Śāradā Tilaka explains the process of initiation as the giver of spiritual knowledge and a means to annihilation of Saṁskāra. The initiation is an esoteric process of unfolding the mysteries of Mantra-Śāstra. It directs the Sādhaka to make proper use of *mantra* for awakening the Kuṇḍalinī. Abhinavagupta, the chief exponent of Kashmir Śaivism, speaks very highly of initiation. He says : 'The initiation is a process of purification of Tattvas and a means to attain Śivahood.'[5] According to him there are thirty-six *tattvas.* Attainment of liberation is possible only after the purification of these *tattvas.* Parama Śiva is above the categories of these *tattvas.* He is Absolute. Due to these thirty-six *tattvas,* the soul which is Parama Śiva in its essential nature comes within the bondage of individuation. It is known as Āṇava Mala. This Āṇava Mala cannot be annihilated by intellectual knowledge. It is the primordial cause of the bondage of Ātmanā. Āṇava Mala is not the illusion, but the cause of the illusion. Therefore, it cannot be conquered by knowledge but by the spiritual unification of *jīva* with Parama Śiva. This state of spiritual unification is possible only after the purification of all *tattvas.* Initiation is thus the process of purification. Liberation from the bondage of Mala when achieved obliterates the last traces of illusion which is the by-product of Mala.

The purpose of initiation is to bring elimination of the principle of obscuration (Pāśa) and to expose what it veils and thus enable the Sādhaka to attain self-recognition (*pratyabhijñā*). The bondage of Pāśa creates three kinds of impurities, *i.e.* Āṇava Mala, Kārma Mala and Māyīka Mala. It conceals the real nature of Self. It creates the bondage of individuation which is the cause of Āṇava Mala. Due to the feeling of individuation man forgets the real nature of Self. He becomes conscious of the supposed imperfection and limitation and as a result becomes the *Doer* and forgets that he is the *Knower* (Sākṣī-cetā). This feeling of doer *I* is the cause of Kārma Mālā. His action is not God-dependent (Brahmāśrayī). He becomes the victim of the innate illusion of Māyā. He moves with the wheel of rebirth till he gets initiation and achieves perfection.

Abhinavagupta defines Dīkṣā as 'a process of imparting Real Knowledge (*jñāna*) and a preceptorial instruction which removes the bondage of Pāśa. Such kind of benediction and benevolent act is known as Dīkṣā.'[6]

Elevation to divinity and elimination of animality is the aim of Sādhanā. Dissolution of Pāśa and identification of the individual with the Universal Self is the sole purpose of initiation. *Kulārṇava Tantra* admits the importance of initiation which, it holds, transforms *jīva* into Śiva. It says: 'As the touch of the purified and processed mercury changes iron into gold so does the soul struck by Dīkṣā become Śiva.'[7]

Transformation of *jīva* into Śiva is the goal of Tantra Sādhanā. Jīva is Śiva He is in the state of bondage. This bondage is due to Saṁskāra. Exhaustion of the past Saṁskāra and total stoppage of further increase of Saṁskāra is essential for the attainment of Śivahood. When a Sādhaka takes initiation he comes to know the art of stopping further increase of Saṁskāra. This art is known as Madhu Vidyā. It is a spiritual process of superimposing cosmic ideation before doing any action. He takes the world not as a collection of different physical atoms and molecules, but as the manifestation of Parama Śiva. The practice of Madhu Vidyā enables one to put a total halt to further addition of Saṁskāra. It burns the very seed of Saṁskāra and paves the path for liberation. 'Dīkṣā burns out all Karma. It severs the bond of Māyā and brings the attainment of spiritual knowledge (Parā-jñāna). The Sādhaka becomes seedless (*Dagdhabīja*) and attains Śivahood.'[8]

Initiation has been considered to be the secret part of Tantra Sādhanā. The Tāntric mysteries are revealed only to the *initiates.* In *Mahānirvāṇa Tantra* on the behest of Devī, Lord Śiva while describing initiation says: 'In the three Ages this rite was a great secret; men then used to perform it in all secrecy, and thus attain Liberation.'[9]

Initiation erodes animalism and wears out Saṁskāra. It is an esoteric process. Through initiation the Guru imparts the practical lesson to make use of *mantra* and *yantra.* Mantra is imparted during initiation. Mantra which has not been received from a Guru bears no fruit. That is why Tantra forbids the use of *mantra* without proper initiation.

Kinds of Initiation

Dīkṣā is correlated with the *adhikāra* of the Sādhaka. The Guru confers only that initiation (*dīkṣā*) on a Sādhaka which he deserves. The specific entitlement of the conferee decides the type of initiation he receives. There are different kinds of Sādhakas, so are *dīkṣās.* Abhinavagupta says: 'The Sādhakas have different objectives, there is predominance of some Adhvas and the rest remain subdued in them. Due to these differences in Sādhakas, there are infinite forms of initiation.'[10]

Kulārṇava Tantra presents a detailed analysis of different categories of initiation. At the outset, it says that there are three kinds of *dīkṣā.* They are: Sparśa Dīkṣā (initiation by touch), Dṛka Dīkṣā (initiation by sight) and Manasā Dīkṣā (initiation by thought). Only a realized soul with an outstanding spiritual power can initiate into the intuitional science of Tantra Sādhanā. Parama Śiva alone is the Guru. In the form of initiation He showers blessings on the parched up soul of human beings. He removes the dust of Mālā from the Self and paves the path for Self recognition. He bestows benediction by touch, by sight or by thought and cleanses the dirt of Māyā.

Sparśa Dīkṣā

The Guru divinizes the Sādhaka by his mystic touch. He causes the Kuṇḍalinī to awaken and forces her to pierce the different *cakras.* The Sādhaka vibrates and starts shivering and shedding copious tears. The burning example of such initiation is Vivekananda. Ramakrishna Paramahansa one fine morning put his feet on the chest of Narendra and as a result of that mystic touch he lost body-mind consciousness. The mystic touch of the Guru transformed the sceptic Narendra into God-intoxicated Vivekananda.

The relation between Guru and disciple (*śiṣya*) is like that between father and son. The Guru gives the affection of mother to his disciple. By spiritual touch, the Guru destroys the soul's attachment. The mystic touch of the Guru is a spiritual nourishment for the disciple. The disciple learns to use the spiritual force of *mantra* only after getting initiation. *Kulārṇava Tantra* describes Sparśa Dīkṣā as a 'form of nourishing of the young by the bird with the warmth of its wings.'[11]

Dṛka Dīkṣā

Dṛka Dīkṣā is a subtle form of initiation. It is a process of transmission of Śakti by sight. The Guru transmits spiritual power to his disciple by mere seeing. An ordinary Guru cannot perform this form of initiation. In meditation the disciple is instructed to gaze constantly on the Guru. The spiritual seeing of the Guru awakens the dormant divinity. Raman Maharṣi used to impart initiation by sight to his disciples at Arunachalam in South India. Dṛka Dīkṣā provides spiritual feeding for the psychic growth of man. It strengthens the supramental and enables one to live up to the ideals of Tantra. 'O! Supreme Goddess! Dṛka Dīkṣā is like nourishing of the young by the fish through its seeing alone.'[12]

Manasā Dīkṣā

This is the subtler form of initiation. Only the highly developed soul is entitled for such initiation. Parama Śiva directly imparts this initiation to the blessed one. It is said that Maharṣi Janaka received such initiation by Brahman Himself. It is imparted in dream also. Lord Śiva imparts Manasā Dīkṣā to those elevated soul, who have done Sādhanā in their previous lives and had attained spiritual sublimity of a high degree. *Kulārṇava Tantra* defines Manasā Dīkṣā as nourishing of the young by the tortoise by only thinking of them.[13] At times Lord Śiva reveals the secret of Tantra Sādhanā by taking human form also, and after initiating the disciple He disappears. Swami Yogananda has given a detailed account of the mysterious Babajee who appeared before Lahiri Mahasaya at Ranikhet (U.P.) and created a Golden Palace in which Babajee gave initiation to Lahiri Mahaśaya.[14] The said Babajee is no other than Lord Śiva himself. This is also a case of Manasā Dīkṣā.

Kulārṇava Tantra speaks about various kinds of *dīkṣā*. According to one consideration, there are seven, namely, Anuṣṭhāna Dīkṣā, Varṇamayī Dīkṣā, Kalā Dīkṣā, Sparśa Dīkṣā, Vāk Dīkṣā, Dṛka Dīkṣā and Manasā Dīkṣā.[15]

Anuṣṭhāna Dīkṣā

This is a lowest form of initiation. This sort of initiation imparted to the laity. The observation of ritual is necessary for a man of Paśu Saṁskāra. This initiation has become an instrument of exploitation. In ancient India, it was customary to take

Anuṣṭhāna Dīkṣā before entering into the deeper and more sublime form of spiritual Sādhanā. It was like a preparatory class. This sort of initiation was known as Vaedikī Dīkṣā. Before taking Tāntric Dīkṣā, it was customary to go through the Vedic rites and rituals. In the absence of a competent Guru, who could initiate and guide a person in the deeper science of Sādhanā, the Vedic Dīkṣā became very popular amongst the ordinary run of men and the Tāntric Dīkṣā was confined only to a fortunate few. Gradually, the common man was completely cut off from Tāntric tradition and Anusthāna Dīkṣā became the guideline of religious life in India.

Varṇamayī Dīkṣā

There are fifty instincts in a human being. They are represented by fifty letters. These fifty letters are represented by different petals of different lotuses. The lotuses are known as *cakras.* Each petal represents one instinct (*vṛtti*). The different letters are placed in the different cakras of the disciple. The different letters are swallowed by the Kuṇḍalinī as it ascends, freeing the Sādhaka from those *vṛttis.* When all the letters are swallowed up, the Sādhaka attains the state of Eternal Blessedness. This is called Samādhi. It means all the *vṛttis* are extinguished. According to Patañjali, Yoga means extinction of all the *vṛttis.*[16]

The man who is initiated in this kind of Dīkṣā attains the state of godhood. Varṇamayī Dīkṣā removes all bonds and brings the realization of supreme godhood and a state of eternal bliss.[17] It liberates man from the bondage of Pāśa. Man becomes free and attains liberation.

Kalā Dīkṣā

The different expressions of Śiva are known as Kalā. The crude manifestation of Śiva is in the form of waves and vibrations. Bindu, Nāda and Kalā are the three stages of cosmic evolution. In the state of Bindu and Nāda, the bondage of Śakti is theoretical. Parama Śiva undergoes transformation due to the activation of Śakti but in the state of Bindu and Nāda, there is no objective manifestation of Parama Śiva. Gradually due to the predominance of the static principle (Tamo Guṇa) Parama Śiva is transformed into the phenomenal world. This is the state of Kalā. Kalā is nothing but the physical waves and vibrations of the cosmological order. Kalā constitutes the cosmos. Amongst the six *adhvas,* Kalā is the primordial. To our mind the other five *adhvas,* namely, *bhuvana, tattva, varṇa, pada* and *mantra,* are the different aspects of *Kālādhva.* Dr. Gopinath Kaviraj also holds the same view.[18]

According to Tantra the whole universe is Śiva-Maya. Every being is transcendental. But due to these six *adhvas,* the world becomes Śiva-Śakti-Māyā. Due to Māyā, the being, who in reality is transcendental in nature, does not have the realization of his perfection. The being thinks he is an imperfect creature, which he is not. To the ignorant, world is Pāśa-Māyā and for the liberated soul the 'whole universe is Śiva-Maya'.

In initiation there are two elements. Firstly, it brings the extinction of Pāśa (Pāśa-Kṣapaṇa). Secondly, it is a mystic arrangement of Śiva (Śiva-Yojana). Kalā Dīkṣā destroys the cimmerian darkness of the soul. 'Man attains divinity. He becomes Śiva. This is Kalā Dīkṣā which destroys the bonds of *pāśa*.'[19]

There are three kinds of Kalā Dīkṣā, namely, Āṇavi, Śakti and Śāmbhavī. When, with the help of Mantra Sādhanā, a man becomes free from the bondage of Māyā, it is called Āṇavi.

The Guru transmits Śakti to his disciples to conquer Māyā. This sort of initiation is called Śakti-Pāta. It is not a separate device to cut asunder the trammels of Māyā. The very objective of initiation is to transmit spiritual power (Śakti) to the initiate.

The Śāmbhavī initiation is the highest form of Tāntric tradition. By mere touch of the Guru, a disciple goes into temporary Samādhi. This is called Śāmbhavī Dīkṣā. 'When by the mere look or speech or touch of the Guru, a disciple attains instantaneously Knowledge of the Supreme, that is Śāmbhavī Dīkṣā.'[20]

To our mind Āṇavi, Śakti and Śāmbhavi Dīkṣā are not different from each other. They are the different methods which the Guru employs to awaken the Kuṇḍalinī of his disciple. Śakti pāta (the Grace of Śiva) is the very essence of initiation. Though every *jīva* is a Śiva, he has no realization of the Śivahood because he is under the bondage of the cosmic causal matrix. Māyā which binds his Śivahood is the cause of separation. For an embodied soul, it is impossible to overpower the influence of Māyā and attain liberation on his own. Here comes both the metaphysical and esoteric necessity on the part of *jīva* to invoke Śiva. Śiva alone is the Guru. The Guru (spiritual teacher) transmits Śakti through mantra or through touch and divinizes *jīva*. Jīva becomes conscious of his hitherto lost treasures of his illuminated Self and casts off the veil of Māyā. He becomes Śiva. Śakti-pāta is the most secret part of Tantra Sādhanā. Utpaladeva, one of the chief exponents of Śaivism, says: 'Oh God! Thou never maketh any discrimination between Pātra and Apātra at the time of Śakti-pāta? What have I done that there is delay in bestowing that blessing of self-illumination on me.'[21]

One receives the grace of Śiva according to one's capacity. Initiation only helps the transmission of Śakti to the Sādhaka. One cannot attain salvation with Śakti-pāta. 'The disciple receives the Grace according to the impact of Śakti-pāta; where there is no impact of Śakti, there is no Siddhi.'[22] Without Śakti-pāta no one can attain salvation. Dīkṣā is in itself the Grace of God. Dīkṣā is, in a sense, a synonym of Śakti-pāta.

Mano Dīkṣā

We have discussed about Manasā Dīkṣā. It is the most sublime form of initiation. There are two types of Manasā Dīkṣā, namely, Tīvra and Tīvratarā.[23] This sort of initiation provides an esoteric art of piercing the different *cakras*. The piercing of the different *cakras* is known as Vedhakriyā. With the application of Vedhakriyā the Sādhaka becomes free from bondage. One attains Perfection. This is called Tivra Dīkṣā which brings liberation.

Meditation of the Guru on the part of the disciple, who is proficient in Vedhakriyā, severs all his sin. He becomes pure and divinized. It is called Tīvratarā Dīkṣā. He attains self illumination. He becomes God-intoxicated. The godly state of omniscience arises in him. He attains oneness with Parama Śiva. The impact of Śakti-pāta is so intense that the Sādhaka falls on the ground. He just cannot bear the impact of divine effulgence. The Śāstra has described many characteristics of such an impact. According to *Kulārṇava Tantra*[24] there are six, namely, joy, tremor, new birth, reeling, sleep and swoon. These six characteristics are seen at the time of the impact of Śakti-pāta during Dīkṣā. Whenever a Sādhaka feels such an impact he is liberated. He attains the Śivahood and freedom from rebirth. 'Struck by such an impact one verily becomes Śiva. He has no more birth. Tīvratarā Dīkṣā is that which liberates one from the bondage of birth, and yields the very state of Śiva.'[25]

Only Mahākaula can initiate a person in Tīvratarā Dīkṣā. It is very difficult to get such a Guru and an able disciple. Tantra says that this sort of initiation should not be given to anybody and everybody. Ādhāra Śuddhi is the pre-condition for such initiation. Ādhāra Śuddhi means the purification of the psycho-physical body. If the mind is not purified and the body is not fit for such initiation, the Śāstra says that in no circumstances should Tīvratarā Dīkṣā be imparted.[26] The impact of Śakti-pāta is so great in Tīvratarā Dīkṣā that any want of proper Ādhāra Śuddhi may cause insanity and even death to the disciple.

Tīvratara Dīkṣā is the same as what is known as Ekatattva Dīkṣā. According to *Tantrāloka* initiation is a process of purification of thirty-six *tattvas*. There are different kinds of Tattva Dīkṣā, namely, Chattisa-tattva Dīkṣā, Nava-tattva Dīkṣā, Pañca-tattva Dīkṣā, Tri-tattva Dīkṣā and Eka-tattva Dīkṣā. The last is most subtle.

Kriyā Dīkṣā and Vedha Dīkṣā

Kriyā Dīkṣā is an external process of purification of body and mind. It is ritualistic in character. According to Gopinath Kaviraj, Kriyā-Dīkṣā includes Kalā-Dīkṣā, Tattva-Dīkṣā, Pada-Dīkṣā, Varṇa Dīkṣā, Mantra Dīkṣā and Bhuvan Dīkṣā.[27] However, Kriyā and Vedha are two aspects of Dīkṣā. They are not two separate methods of spiritual attainment. They are complementary to each other.

The rituals which are observed in Kriyā Dīkṣā are not like the dead rites of the Veda. The external use of yantra, mālā, etc., are not ritualistic in character. It has some esoteric importance. The worship of yantra and the use of *mālā* are aids to make Vedha-Kriyā (the piercing of the *cakras*) of the Kuṇḍalinī smooth and certain. The purpose of Tāntric initiation is to provide to the Sādhaka the mystic technique of arousing the Kuṇḍalinī. The Kuṇḍalinī cannot be made to move upwards without the purification of body and mind. Kriyā and Vedha are two categories of Dīkṣā. 'There are two forms of Dīkṣā, Bāhya (external) and Antara (internal); the external is Kriyā-Dīkṣā and the internal is Vedha-Dīkṣā. There are two kinds of purifications, inner and outer. The inner is purified by the appropriate ritual and the outer is sanctified by Dīkṣā.'[28]

Pandit Ramadatta Shukla[29] deals with the problem of Dīkṣā. But he has mixed up the whole issue. He has tried to bring some sort of reconciliation between the Vedic and Tāntric Sādhanās which are poles apart. He mentions articles like ghee, *puṣpa, akṣata, kuṣāgre, tīla,* etc., used in Vedic Yajña as the necessary requirements for Dīkṣā. Tāntric Sādhanā has nothing to do with these articles. Tantra is against lifeless rituals and dead dogmas which blind the vision of the soul.

Mantra Mahārṇava mentions over two hundred forms of initiation. Tāntric Dīkṣā is a giver of spiritual knowledge and destroyer of sin. As one lamp is lit from the flame of another so is the divine Śakti, consisting of *mantra,* transferred from the Guru to his disciple. Without Dīkṣā, *mantra-japa, pūjā* and other rituals are entirely useless.[30] Dīkṣā is a pre-condition for the Sādhaka who wants to perform intuitional practice.

There are different kinds of Dīkṣā according to the objectives of Sādhanā. Tantra is an intuitional science. It brings the realization of both inner spiritual wealth and occult power. Those who want to perform Sādhanā only to attain some occult power for the gratification of ego and have no higher objective get Avidyā Dīkṣā. But Avidyā Dīkṣā becomes the cause of degeneration of the Sādhaka, who having acquired some occult power uses it for the gratification of his lower self. This brings about the Sādhakā's nervous breakdown. But it is a fact that Avidyā Dīkṣā provides a technique to acquire some supernatural power.

Vidyā Dīkṣā

This is the real Tāntric initiation which stands for self-realization. The sole objective of Vidyā Dīkṣā is to provide the Sādhaka with the esoteric knowledge of arousing the Kuṇḍalinī from Mūlādhāra Cakra and to take it to Sahasrāra which is the abode of Parama Śiva. When Śakti is united with Śiva in the spiritual wedlock, *jīva* becomes Śiva. He attains supreme bliss and immortality.

There are two kinds of Vidyā Dīkṣā, namely, Yoga Dīkṣā and Kāpālika Dīkṣā. Yoga Dīkṣā can be imparted to any man who has a strong longing for salvation There is no danger in imparting Yoga Dīkṣā. It is performed in the house or in some lonely place. But Mantra Sādhanā is an essential part of it. (There is no Dīkṣā without Mantra Sādhanā.) The second and rather risky and perilous kind is Kāpālika Dīkṣā. It is the most difficult part of Tantra Sādhanā. Here is a question of Adhikāri of both

Guru and disciple. Any Guru cannot initiate one into Kāpālika Sādhanā. Only those who have attained salvation and are well versed in the Āgama Śāstra are entitled to impart Kāpālika Dīkṣā. The recipient of Kāpālika Dīkṣā must be a devout soul. He must be physically strong, mentally pure and spiritually developed. Kāpālika Dīkṣā is sublime but dangerous form of initiation.

Tāntric Dīkṣā and Vedic Saṁskāra

Vedic Saṁskāra and Tāntric Dīkṣā are not one and the same thing. Vedic Saṁskāra stands for the observance of the Vedic rituals as laid down in the *Brāhmaṇas.* Observance of the Vedic rituals is restricted to Brahmans and Kṣatriyas. Only they are entitled to Vedic abhiṣeka. Śūdras and Vaiśyas are not allowed to recite Vedic hymns. The orthodox section of the Hindu community does not allow, by an injunction, the womenfolk also. Women are not allowed to go through Vedic Saṁskāra. But Tantra is universal. It has no such inhibitions. It does not believe in any distinction on the basis of sex, caste, creed, colour and religion. It despises parochial and religious chauvinism. It believes in one humanity and one human society. Everybody is entitled to Tāntric Dīkṣā. If a so-called Śūdra is versed in the Āgama Śāstra, he is superior to one who is a Brahman only by birth. 'A *caṇḍāla* versed in the knowledge of the Kaulika doctrine (Tantra Śāstra) excels a Brahman, and a Brahman who is wanting in this is below even a *caṇḍāla.*'[31]

Only merit counts in Tantra Sādhanā. If a so-called Śūdra enters into Tantra Sādhanā prior to a Brahman, he (Śūdra) will be senior to the Brahman in every respect. 'If a Brahman is initiated later and a low born is initiated earlier, then the Brahman is junior and the low born is senior; this is the mandate of the Śāstra.'[32]

Vedic Saṁskāra is ritualistic. Tantra Dīkṣā is spiritualistic. Vedic Saṁskāra is done by religious parasites; Tāntric Dīkṣā is imparted only by the Guru who is well versed in the Āgama Śāstra. Vedic Saṁskāra can be performed on behalf of others but there is no place for proxy in Tāntric initiation. In Vedic Saṁskāra mantra is not essential but in Tantra Dīkṣā a person is initiated into the use of *yantra* (*maṇḍala*) and along with it a *mantra* is invariably conferred.

Necessity of Dīkṣā

There is a strong condemnation of Dīkṣā today. A section of the intelligentsia are against any spiritual discipline. They decry initiation as a dogmatic approach to the attaining of salvation. They say Dīkṣā is a useless spiritual tradition thrust upon the present enlightened generation by the blind religious past. They are not only apathetic to it but have developed some obsession for it. In their scathing attack they argue that Dīkṣā is a cunning device to keep alive the dogmatic tradition of Gurudom. It is an evil cabal to perpetuate religious exploitation. In an age of science, they argue, mystic approach to any problem has no logical justification.

Viewed dispassionately all the charges against Dīkṣā will be seen to have sprung only from spiritual ignorance and lack of proper understanding and appreciation of Tāntric esotericism. Tantra is an intuitional science. Dīkṣā is a spiritual enrolment to carry on scientific research with the Self. It is not a religious anointment but an esoteric discipline. It is not a faith but an inner conviction. It is not a religious ceremony but a spiritual beginning. It is not ritualistic ostentation but a mystic necessity.

Yantra

Yantra is a mystic diagram. Yantra worship is a marked feature of Tantra Sādhanā. It symbolizes the higher mystic power. When a Sādhaka attains a higher degree of spiritual progress, he is initiated into *yantra* worship. Yantra means an apparatus by which anything is accomplished.

Yantra Sādhanā is a higher form of spiritual life. It is an esoteric method to fix the mind on the Supreme Reality. It subdues the *fetters.* Yantra is invariably used in higher Vīrācāra Sādhanā.

Yantra is of various kinds, depending on the mode of worship. Different deities (Devatās) have different *yantras.* Different *mantras* are used for different deities. Only an appropriate *mantra* and *yantra* can bring *siddhi* (success) in Sādhanā. The selection of *mantra* and *yantra* is a very difficult problem. The Guru alone can help and guide in this intricate problem of mysticism. The symbolism of *yantra* is pregnant with mysticism. Śrī Cakra symbolizes the Cosmos and its divine cause. There are in it two sets of triangles, one composed of four male or Śiva triangles and the other of five females or Śakti. According to *Kāmikāgama,* the Śakti triangles denote the five *dhātus,* namely, skin (*tvac*), blood (*asṛj*), flesh (*māṁsa*), fat (*medas*) and bone (*asthi*), and the Śiva triangles stand for bone marrow (*majjā*), vital fluid (*śukra*), life force (*prāṇa*) and *jīva.* This division has been made from the microcosmic point of view. From the macrocosmic point of view, the Śakti triangles stand for the five vital functions, the five senses of knowledge, the five senses of action, the five subtle and five gross forms of matter and the mind. The Śiva triangles represent the four higher *tattvas, viz.* Māyā, Śudhavidyā, Maheśvara and Sadāśiva.

In the centre of Śrī Cakra, which is represented by a point (*bindu*), resides Śiva (Kāmeśvara) and Śakti (*Lalitā*) in an undifferentiated (*abheda*) union. Enclosing the *bindu* is an inverted triangle which symbolizes will (*icchā*), action (*kriyā*) and knowledge (*jñāna*) aspects of Śakti. The three guṇas and the deities preside over them. The other *cakras* are the Aṣṭakoṇa (eight triangles), Daśāra-yugma (two *cakras,* each of ten triangles), Manvasra (fourteen triangles), Aṣṭadala (eight lotus petals), Ṣoḍaśadala (sixteen lotus petals), Vṛttatraya (three circles and three squares). These nine *cakras* are ruled over by Yoginis (divinities) presiding over forms of minds, sense and matter. Yoginis are called Āvaraṇa Devatas (veiling deities), because they veil the Pure Consciousness (Cit) and create the appearance of the world of mind, sense and matter. The whole and undifferentiated entity (*pūrṇa*) appears limited and differentiated (apurṇa) Śrī Cakra is the mansion of Devī.[33] The realization of Devī (Śakti) and consequent bliss for the Yogi come from Her *mantra* which is the Śrī Vidyā.[34] The prescription for this *mantra* is given, and it is considered to be the most important esoteric item in Śaktism.

Yantra is one of the cardinal principles of Tantrism. There is a close relation between Devatā and Yantra. Yantra is the body and Devatā the Soul. John Woodroffe writes: '*Kaulavaliya Tantra* says that the distinction between Yantra and Devatā is like that between the body and the Self. Mantra is Devatā and Yantra is Mantra in that it is the body of the Devatā who is Mantra.'[35] 'Yantra is ensouled by Mantra. The deity is in the form of Mantra. The deity is immediately pleased if he is worshipped in the Yantra.'[36] Yantra occupies a very important place in Tantra Sādhanā. It regulates and subdues (*niyantrana*) all misery arising from sex, anger and other failings. It is imbedded in mysticism. As body is to the *jīva* and oil is to the lamp, yantra is to the deities.[37] Yantra is the mystic seat of all deities.

Yantra Sādhanā is not important to everybody. After getting initiation into Yantra Sādhanā, the Sādhaka draws Yantra and meditates upon its esoteric form. Yantra Sādhanā is done with great care and restraint. Each deity has his own *yantra*, and he must be installed in his proper *yantra*. If the Sādhaka is absent minded and installs another deity and invokes him, he is cursed by both the deities.

Yantra worship is the essential part of Kāpālika and Śava Sādhanā. Any mistake on the part of the Sādhaka lands him in great trouble. Sometimes, negligence of the esoteric rituals may lead to lunacy and even death. Here is the importance of *Adhikārī*. This Sādhanā is imparted to its rightful claimant. The Guru also must be a realized soul. One should not learn this Sādhanā from any Guru. One should be very careful in the selection of a Guru.

Yantra and Mantra are the body and the soul of the Tantra Śāstra. Every deity has his own *mantra*. After the drawing up of the *yantra* the deity is invoked with his proper *mantra*. The inner life force is aroused to its full potential and is dedicated to the deity through the mystic process of its awakening. John Woodroffe says: 'The Yantra is an essential part of the Kaul worship and without proper Yantra the Deity is not pleased to be present. And where worship is offered according to the scripture, the Lord himself with the Devī is present.'[38]

Mahānirvāṇa Tantra deals in detail with the formation and significance of Bhairavī Cakra and Tattva Cakra.[39] The formation of Cakra is an essential part of Sādhanā. Mantras 'Kliṅg' and 'Phaṭ' (Kāma and Astra Bīja) are used by the Kulācārya in the formation and purification of Cakra. Īṣṭa Devatā is installed in the Bhairavī Cakra. The Sādhaka is locked in the mystic unification with the Kuṇḍalinī Śakti. 'Pārvatī in Bhairavī Cakra and Tattva Cakra the excellent worshipper should be wedded to his Śakti according to the laws prescribed by Śiva.'[40]

Yantra worship is a mystic process of awakening the Kuṇḍalinī Śakti. The use of *mālā* (rosary) and other articles is made to purify *yantra* and to awaken the life force of *mantra.* The beads of the rosary represent different letters of Mātṛkā Varṇa. 'The *mālā* (rosary) prescribed consists of the letters of the alphabet, strung on the Kuṇḍalinī as the thread.'[41] The beads of the rosary represent the different expressions of the cosmological order. They also represent the different *vṛttis.* The Kuṇḍalinī is the string. It means the different *vṛttis* are associated with the Kuṇḍalinī Śakti. With the mystic unification of the Kuṇḍalinī with Parama Śiva, the Yogi becomes free from all *vṛttis.* It is the state of spiritual trance.

Yantra worship is employed for mundane gains also. Yantra Sādhanā grants the fourfold (*Dharma, Artha, Kāma* and *Mokṣa*) aim of human existence.[42] Yantra-rāja has been described thus: 'Draw a triangle with the Māyā-Bīja within it and around it two concentric circles (one outside the other). In the space between the two circumferences of the circles draw in pairs the sixteen filaments, and outside these the eight petals of the lotus, and outside them the Bhū-pūra, which should be made of straight lines with four entrances and should be of pleasing appearance.[43]

Śāradā Tilaka[44] discusses in detail the formation and esoteric significance of different *yantras.* According to it *yantras* are innumerable. Different *yantras* are employed for different objectives. Rakṣā Yantra, Gāyatri Yantra, Vaśyakṛde Yantra, Mṛtuñjaya Yantra, Sarpaghna Yantra, Māraṇa Yantra are some of the *yantras* which have been dealt with in this chapter. According to it, *yantra* is that which fulfils all the desires of the Sādhaka.[45] According to the Saṁhitā,[46] in the etymological sense, *yantra* satisfies all the longings of man. It subdues and liberates man from the long sufferings arising out of sex, anger, etc. Yantra worship is a mystic process of awakening the divine power. The mantric incantation is associated with Yantra Sādhanā. However, Yantra Sādhanā is not a complete process in itself. It is always associated with other esoteric disciplines.

REFERENCES

1. *2500 Years of Buddhism* (Second Reprint), p. 313. Publication Division, Government of India, New Delhi, 1964.
2. विना दीक्षं न मोक्षः स्यात्तदुक्तं शिवाशासने।
   सा च न स्यादिनाचार्यामित्याचार्य परम्परा।।3।। *Kulārṇava Tantra*, p. 308.
3. अथ दीक्षा प्रवक्ष्यामि मन्त्राणं हित काम्यया।
   विना यया न लभ्यते सर्वमन्त्रफलं यतः।।1।। *Śāradā Tilaka*, p. 125.
4. दिव्य ज्ञानं यतो दद्यात्कुर्यात्पापस्य संक्षयः।
   तस्माद्दीक्षेति संप्रोक्ता देशिकैस्तन्त्र वेदिभिः।।2।। *Ibid.*, p. 126
5. ..... तत्त्वशुद्धि शिवयोजनारूपाया दीक्षाया इति।
   Tantrasāra, p. 13. Kashmir Series of Texts and Studies, Srinagar, No. XVII, 1918.
6. दीयते ज्ञानसद्भावः क्षीयते पशुवासना।
   दानक्षपणसंयुक्ता दीक्षा तेनेह कीर्तिता।।
   Tantrāloka, vol. I, p. 80, Kashmir Series of Texts and Studies, Srinagar, 1918.
7. रसेन्द्रेण यथा विद्धमयः सुवर्णतां व्रजेत्।
   दीक्षाविद्धस्तथा ह्यात्मा शिवत्वं लभते प्रिये।।89।। *Kulārṇava Tantra*, p. 317.

8. दीक्षाग्निदग्धकर्मासौ मायाविच्छिन्नबन्धनः
गतः परां ज्ञानकाष्ठां निर्बीजस्तु शिवो भवेत्।।90।। *Ibid.*
9. *The Great Liberation*, p. 324.
10. यत्र यत्र हि भोगच्छातत्प्राधान्योपयोगतः।
अन्यान्तर्भावनातश्च दीक्षानन्तविभेदभाक्।। *Tantralok.*
11. यथा पक्षी स्वपक्षाभ्यां शिशुनसंवर्द्धयेच्छने।
स्पर्श दीक्षोपदेशच्च तादृशः कथित प्रिये।।35।। p. 311.
12. स्वापत्यानि यथा मत्स्यो वीक्षणेनैन पोषयेत्।
दृग्भ्यां दीक्षोपदेशश्च तादृशः परमेश्वरि।।36।। *Kulārṇava Tantra*, p. 311.
13. *Ibid.*, p. 312.
14. *Autobiography of a Yogi.*
15. *Kulārṇava Tantra*, ver. 39, p. 312.
16. चित्तवृत्ति निरोधस्य योगः। *Patañjali Yoga Sūtra.*
17. जायते देवताभावः परानन्दमयः शिशोः।
एषा वर्णमयी प्रोक्ता दीक्षा पाशहरा प्रिये।।45।।
Kulārṇava Tantra, ver. 45, p. 312.
18. *Bhāratiya Saṁskṛti āur Sādhanā*, p. 284.
19. जायते देवताभावो योगिनी बीरमेलनम्।
कला दीक्षा समुद्विष्टा पशुपाशापहारिणी। *Kulārṇava Tantra*, p. 313.
20. जायते देवताभावो योगिनी बीरमेलनम्।
कला दीक्षा समुद्विष्टा पशुपाशापहारिणी। *Kulārṇava Tantra*, p. 313.
21. शक्तिपातसमये विचारणं प्राप्तमीश न करोषि कर्हिचित्।
अद्य मां प्रति किमागतं यतः स्वप्रकाशनविधौ विलम्बसे।।
Bhāratiya Saṁskṛti aur Sādhanā.
22. शक्तिपातानुसोरषा शिष्योऽनुग्रहमर्हति
यत्र शर्क्तिन पतति तत्र सिर्द्धि न जायते। *Kulārṇava Tantra*, p. 312.
23. *Ibid.*, p. 314.
24. आनन्दश्चैव कम्पश्चोद्भवो धूर्णा कुलश्वरि
निद्रा मूर्च्छा च वेधस्य षड्वस्था प्रकीर्त्तिता। p. 315.
25. एषा तीव्रतरा दीक्षा भवबन्ध विमोचनी।
शिवभावप्रदा साक्षात त्वां शपे कुलनायिके।। *Kulārṇava Tantra*, p. 314.
26. *Ibid.*, ver. 66, p. 315.
27. *Bhāratiya Saṁskṛti aur Sādhanā*, p. 282.
28. *Kulārṇava Tantra*, p. 316.
29. *Hindi Tantrasāra*, Kalyan Mandir, Prayag.
30. *Ibid.*
31. *Mahānirvāṇa Tantra*, p. 73.
32. द्विजो यो दीक्षितः पश्चादन्त्यजः पूर्वदीक्षितः।
द्विजः कनिष्ठः स ज्येष्ठ इति शास्यनिर्णयः।। *Kulārṇava Tantra*, p. 318.
33. चतुर्भिः श्रीकण्ठेः शिवयुतिभिः पञ्चभिरपि
प्रभिन्नामिः शभेनिवरिति मूलप्रकृतिभिः।
त्रयश्चत्वारिशद्वसुदलकलाश्रत्रिवलय–
त्रिरेखामिः सार्ध तव चरणकोणाः परिणताः।। *Saundaryalaharī*, p. 52.

34. *Ibid.*, p. 9.
35. यंत्रं मंत्रं यम प्रोक्तं मंत्रामा देवतैव हि।
    देहात्मनोर यथा वेदो यंत्रदेवतयोसतया। *Śakti and Śākta*, p. 548.
36. यन्त्रं मन्त्रमयं प्रोक्तं देवता मन्त्ररूपिणी।
    यन्त्रे सा पूजिता देवि सहसैव प्रसीदति।। 85 ।। *Kulārṇava Tantra*, p. 208.
37. शरीरमिव जीवस्य दीपस्य स्नेहवत प्रिय।
    सर्वेषामषि देवानां तथा यन्त्रं प्रतिष्ठितम्।। 87 ।। *Ibid.*
38. *Kulārṇava Tantra*, p. 74
39. *Mahānirvāṇa Tantra*, p. 233.
40. *Ibid.*, p. 237.
41. *Ibid.*, p. 124.
42. *Ibid.*, p. 129.
43. *Ibid.*, p. 130.
44. *Śāradā Tilaka*, ch. XXIV.
45. अथ वक्ष्यामि यन्त्राणां भेदांस्तन्त्रेषु गोपिताम्।
    ये साधयन्ति सनतं मन्त्रिणोनिजवाञ्छितम्।। *Śāradā Tilaka*, p. 519.
46. यन्त्रशब्दव्युत्पत्तिरूक्ता संहितायाम् "मनोरथाक्षरारख्यम् नियन्त्यन्त
    तपोघनाः। कामक्रोधादिदोषान्वा दीर्घदुःखनियन्त्रणात् यन्त्रमित्याहुरिति" *Ibid.*

8 Schools of Tantra

Tantra is a way of life. It is not merely philosophical system engaged in systematization of different concepts and theories. It is a science of religion, and different from and opposed to the religion of doctrine. The schools of Tantra are either monotheistic or monistic. The different forms of Tantra Sādhanā do not make any difference to a man so long as he is truly devoted to the realisation of the vast and incomprehensible Śiva Absolute. The mysticism of Tantra combines science and speculation, knowledge and realization, fact and ideal, physico-psychic experience and intuitive vision. The intuitive experience of Śiva-Absolute cannot be achieved through repression and asceticism but through unitive consciousness. With unitive consciousness and oneness of Śiva and Śakti, *jīva* becomes Śiva, with the realization of one's identity with the Absolute.

Tantra covers the whole gamut of life. It is a vast and varied form of spiritual Sādhanā. It is a quest for both mystic experience and material ends. It is a law of socio-spiritual living.

Tantra can be divided into different schools according to the different deities worshipped, esoteric procedures followed and their ends. *Śatisaṅgamatantra*[1] refers to the sects of Vaiṣṇavas, Gāṇapatyas, Śaivas, Svāyambhuvas, Candras, Pāśupatas. Cīnas, Jainas, Kālamukhas and Vaidikas. A close and scientific study of Tantra delivers us from the erroneous knowledge of the different sects and sub-sects. Tantra is an integral science, with different branches complementing one another.

Śākta, Vaiṣṇava and Śaiva are the metaphysical schools of Tantra. Avidyā, Upa-Vidyā and Vidyā are the esoteric divisions of Tantra. Dakṣiṇācāra, Vāmācāra and Madhyamācāra are the Psychological Schools of Tantra. The Metaphysical Schools of Tantra form the central core of the different sects of Tantra Sādhanā. We now propose to dwell upon the different schools of Tantra and their further sub-divisions.

METAPHYSICAL SCHOOLS OF TANTRA

Śākta Tantra

The genetic idea of Śākta Tantra is that Sakti is the force of the cosmological order. Parama Śiva, the eternal, inconceivable Supreme-Absolute, is a passive force whereas Śakti, the immanent principle, is all activity. Śiva and Śakti have been anthropomorphically described as husband and wife. Śakti is the creation and recreation of the universe. She is the *magna mater*. She is more important than Śiva. Śiva is a corpse without Śakti.[2] W. Norman Brown writes: 'The feminine principle, or Śakti (power), personified as the Goddess Devī, is the first and supreme principle of the universe. It includes both the spiritual and material principles and hence may be understood to comprise both Soul (Puruṣa) and Nature (Prakṛti) of the Sāṁkhya system. As such it is equivalent to the neuter Brahman of the Advaita thought.'[3] Śakti is the creative aspect of the Reality. The Absolute in Tantra is represented by Bindu (the personified form of Devī and Śiva). The feminine principle in conjunction with the masculine principle creates the cosmos. However, the masculine principle or Śiva-tattva is always secondary in the creative manifestation of the universe. The material universe has evolved from the great feminine principle, the spouse of Śiva, which is called Mahāmāyā.[4] However, Śakti cannot be identified with Nirguṇa Brahman of the Advaita Vedānta. In our opinion Parama Śiva is the same as Nirguṇa Brahman of the Advaita school. But they differ in the spiritual and metaphysical import.

Nāda Bindu and Kalā are the stages of creation of the world. Tantra believes in the mystic and the metaphysical power of sound waves. Everything is vibrational. Every letter of the Mātṛkā Varṇa is imbued with the divine power of Śakti. Mantras, the mystic syllables framed from these letters according to esoteric formulae, become potent weapons to cut asunder the trammels of Māyā. Thus, in Śākta Sādhanā, *mantra* plays a very important part in liberating the Sādhaka from the bondage of nescience.

In Śākta Tantra we find a scientific approach to spirituality. Corresponding to Bindu, Nāda and Kalā there are Bindu, Nāda and Kalā Yogas to neutralize the fundamental positivity of the creative process. Sādhanā plays an important part in Śākta Tantra. Yoga means esoteric unification of Śiva and Śakti.

Śakti is Kuṇḍalinī. Śiva is Bindu. Śakti is personified as Devī. Mūlādhāra is the dwelling place of Śakti and Sahasrāra is the abode of Śiva. According to the Śākta system cosmos has been conceived as the body of Devī[5] which has been evolved in six stages. The six stages have been described as six *cakras*. One of these, Sahasrāra Cakra, is the pineal gland. Here, in Sahasrāra Cakra or the thousand petalled lotus, both the feminine and masculine principles co-exist before the creation of the cosmos. Śakti dwells with Śiva in her mansion described as Śrī Cakra.[6] The highest goal of Śākta Sādhanā is to get merged into Devī, that is, to become one with the Absolute. The esoteric identification with Devī can be attained through the grace of Devī and by the use of Mantra Sādhanā.

There is an anecdote in *Tripurā-Rahasya* which establishes the superiority of Devī over all the gods. In an assembly of gods and saints a philosophical question was raised as to the nature of the transcendental reality which could not be answered even by saints and gods like Bhṛgu, Aṅgirā, Praceta, Nārada, Vāmadeva, Viśvāmitra and Brahmā. They approached Mahādeva, the god of all gods. Mahādeva meditated upon the goddess of knowledge, Vidyā-Devī along with other saints and gods. The goddess answered all their questions. She says: 'My transcendental form is evident to all, it being that which makes the world appear reflected as in a mirror and that which sustains and dissolves the world. Those who do not know the Self find me in the form of the world. My true form is that which the Yogis realize it their pure awareness as absolute peace, tranquillity and fathomlessness of the ocean.'[7] *Tripurā-Rahasya* is a Śākti literature of the post-Vedic period. It establishes the superiority of Śakti worship over the Vedic ritual. The transcendental form of Reality cannot be realized through Vedic rituals. It can be attained only through Śakti Sādhanā. Devī says: 'Knowledge of non-dual reality is really knowledge proper. How can one attain Myself as Great Knowledge — Mahāvidyā — without propitiating me as the Goddess Śrī Vidyā?'[8] The highest form of non-dual knowledge can be attained only through the esoteric practice of Śākta discipline. Śakti destroys the darkness of ignorance. She is Tripura Sundarī. She liberates man from the ocean of mundane existence.[9] She is the fountain of bliss. Tripura, is Parā-Vidyā. After having known Her, a man becomes the master of all the *Siddhis.*

According to Śākta Tantra, *siddhi* can be attained only through the divine grace of Devī. Devī has been described here as the transcendental Self. Tripurā means three cities, *i.e.* Crude Mind (Conscious), Subtle Mind (Sub-conscious) and Causal Mind (Unconscious). Devī is called Tripura-Sundarī or only Tripurā as she lives in these three cities. She is the supreme subjectivity (Self), the subjective counterpart of the conscious, the sub-conscious and the unconscious mind. With the help of Kuṇḍalinī Yoga, a man acquires absolute control over all the three mental spheres. All the occult powers lie within the mind. It is simply an esoteric display of mental potentialities. Śākta Tantra has laid down certain mystic disciplines to acquire those occult powers. That is why Śakti has been identified as Parā-Vidyā (Divine Science).[10] Śakti is Viśvamayī. She is Mūla-Vidyā, the root of all knowledge.[11]

The whole universe has been created by Śakti. Śakti is the creative matrix (Sṛṣtirūpā).[12] All the nine *cakras* have been created by Śakti, *i.e.*, Nāda, Bindu, Kalā, Jyeṣṭhā, Raudrī, Vāmā, Viṣāghnī, Dutarī and Sarvānandā. Śakti resides in all nine *cakras.*[13]

Every *jīva* (self) is a transcendental being. But due to Māyā, he forgets his real nature and being. Cosmic Consciousness (Parama Śiva) is not different from individual self or *jīva,* but the identification of pure intelligence with ego or pure Iness leads one to error. One forgets one's identity with Cosmic Consciousness or the real Self. This is split within, which creates the other. Consciousness is one whole, cosmic and universal. But it becomes divided and split into finite and limited consciousness. This takes place because one identifies oneself with the lower objects, ideas or ideals. The division of the Infinite Consciousness into the finite and limited one is projected as outside. To achieve the unification of the disintegrated Consciousness into the one whole is the aim of Tantra Sādhanā. Psychic unification cannot be attained by any objective methods. One has to look within. Through the subjective approach alone can one gain the lost unity. The different mental tendencies (*vṛttis*) are the splitting force. One will have to overcome the weaknesses of different tendencies. One will have to sublimate (*nirodha*) all the mental tendencies and temperaments. Śākta Sādhanā is the spiritual process for transforming the finite consciousness into the Infinite Consciousness. The Supreme Goddess is variously addressed as Tripurā, Sundarī, Lalitā, Ṣoḍaśī, Śrī Vidyā and Kāmeśvarī. She is called Tripurā because she consists of three Śaktis, *i.e.* Brāhmī, Vaiṣṇavī and Raudrī.[14] She is the Eternal and Supreme Truth beyond all the relative factors of time and space. She is called Lalitā due to her transcendental nature. Lalitā takes the form of Kṛṣṇa or Puruṣa.[15] She is called Sundarī. Sundarī is one of the ten Mahāvidyās.[16] The collective name of all the ten Vidyās is Mahāvidyā but Ṣoḍaśī is Mahāvidyā by herself. Mahā-Tripura-Sundarī is called by the name of Pañcamī with five-faced Śiva as Her Bhairava.[17] The Śakti Saṅgama scripture differs and makes Laliteśvara as Her Bhairava.[18]

In our view Śākta Tantra is also monotheistic. This system is named as Śākta because of its identification with Kuṇḍalinī Śakti. The Kuṇḍalinī is the Parā-Śakti. The esoteric awakening of the Kuṇḍalinī through Mantra and Yantra Sādhanā is the central theme of this school. Most of the occult powers are acquired in the state of esoteric dualism of the Śākta Sādhanā. It is the most difficult stage of a Sādhaka. Śākta Sādhanā is like walking on a razor's edge. It is full of esoteric allurements to which there is every possibility of the Sādhaka falling a victim, and degenerating. The Sādhaka, therefore, takes refuge in Śakti worship, to gain enough strength to overcome the allurements, and egoism. But, on the other hand, Śakti worship is the surest and most scientific way of achieving monistic oneness with the Supreme Reality. It is a definite process though dangerous.

The main aim of Śākta Sādhanā is to enable one to overcome the infatuation with the worldly objects, and show him that there is a higher or greater and intenser enjoyment and bliss in one's spiritual realization.

Śākta Sādhanā stands for the ceaseless struggle to restore equilibrium. Every instinct or tendency has both the dark and the bright side. It can work on both sides. Śakti as a liberating force represents the bright side of the Reality. Śakti as a binding principle (Avidyā Māyā) is the cause of suffering. A Tāntric Sādhaka struggles against Avidyā Māyā with the help of Vidyā Māyā, the objective being to loosen the bondage of Māyā and become one with the Supreme Consciousness (Śiva-Śakti). Śākta Sādhanā is a struggle against Eight Bondages (Aṣṭa Pāśas) and Six Enemies (Ṣaḍ Ripu).[19]

Śākta Tantra deals with the mystic process and methods of worship for propitiating Goddess Śakti. *Tripurā-Rahasya* says that Śakti is one, eternal and perfect entity.[20] She is the queen of the Three Cities. She is omni-active omniscience and Omnipotent.

Vaiṣṇava Tantra

The Pāñcarātra or Bhāgavata school belongs to Tāntric Vaiṣṇavism. *Pāñcaratrāgama* is the basis of Vaiṣṇavite Tantrism. The system is known as Pāñcarātra because it expounds five kinds of knowledge.[21] The Pāñcarātra system is associated with Śiva, Devī, Gaṇeśa, Brahman and Mahākāla.[22] This system is a devotional school of Tāntric tradition. According to R.G. Bhandarkar, the Pāñcarātra system has shown no organic connection with the monotheistic religion promulgated by the *Bhagavad-Gītā* though devotion is common to both the systems.[23] He says that this system must have developed in the third century B.C.[24] Whatever may be the date of its development, Vaiṣṇava Tantra is a very ancient devotional cult. It is as old as Tantra itself. Without devotion one will not be able to tread the spiritual path. With the grace of the Guru alone can one reach the destination. Swami Ramakrishna attained salvation through the practice of Tantra. A remarkable transformation in his life was effected by Tantra Sādhanā into which he was initiated by Bhairavī Brahmāṇī. He says: 'The Brahmāṇī put me through all the exercises mentioned in the sixty-four principal Tantra books. Most of these were extremely difficult Sādhanās. Some of them so dangerous that they cause the devotee to lose his footing and sink into moral degradation. But the infinite grace of the Mother carried me through unscathed.'[25]

Swami Ramakrishna was one of the greatest devotional figures and Tāntric Sādhakas of India at the turn of the nineteenth century. In our view he was a Tāntric Vaiṣṇavite till he received initiation into Dhyāna Yoga from Totapuri. *Ahirbudhnya Saṁhitā* of the *Pāñcarātrāgama* describes the cause of the enunciation of *Pāñcarātra Saṁhitā*. It is a canonical literature of Tāntric Vaiṣṇavism. The monograph deals with the Mantra Śāstra. It says that it dwells on many philosophies and different schools of Vidyā (esoteric science).[26] *Pāñcarātra Saṁhitā* was written in answer to the spiritual enquiries of Nārada.[27]

According to *Pāñcarātrāgama*, Śakti is the immanent principle of Viṣṇu.[28] She is the eternal coeval of Nārāyaṇa. She is known as Nārāyaṇī.[29] She is divine (*divyā*) and is acknowledged by all the schools. Śakti is free and eternal. She is the divine consort of Viṣṇu.[30]

Vaiṣṇava Tantra also accepts Śakti as the immanent principle. She is the creative matrix. The two entities are inseparable. They are like Dharma (substance) and Dharmī (attributes). Vaiṣṇava Tantra is, however, different in the form and content of Sādhanā from the devotional Vaiṣṇavism of Rāmānujācārya and others. Unlike Vaiṣṇavism of Rāmānujācārya, *Pāñcarātrāgama* describes the Tāntric occultism. With the worship of Hari, according to the principles of Tāntric Vaiṣṇavism, a man will not only attain liberation from the snares of life, but will have control over the celestial beings like Yakṣa, Gandharva, Apsarā, Gaṇa, Bhūta Piśāca, Preta, etc. These celestial beings become the tool of his hand.[31] We have already discussed that there is no objective existence of ghosts, etc. Bhūta, Piśāca, Preta denote the occult powers of Tantra Sādhanā. The occult powers displayed by the Avidyā Tāntric are known as Bhūta, Preta and Piśāca in Tantra Śāstra.

Hūṁ, Phaṭ, Svāhā, etc., are the mystic syllables. They are *bīja-mantras* and are used in awakening the different psychic powers. These *mantras* are used for creating different acoustic vibrations. The incantative rhythms of these *mantras* awaken the dormant powers. They energize the different mental powers. These *mantras* are the secret of occult powers. Vaiṣṇava Tantra describes the esoteric procedure and importance of the incantation of *bīja-mantras* Hūṁ, Phaṭ,[32] etc.

The Śrī Vidyā cult belongs to Vaiṣṇava Tantra. Many scholars have classed Śrī Vidyā as Śākta Tantra. Śrī Vidyā has been wrongly associated with Śākta Tantra. Śrī is the consort of Viṣṇu in Hindu mythology. Śrī Cakra is the abode of Viṣṇu. According to *Lalitā-Sahasranāman* between the seventeenth and the eighteenth wall of Śrī Cakra resides Viṣṇu. Śrī is the womb of the universe. She is known as Lakṣmī. Due to the eternal coexistence and association of this immanent force (Ādi Śakti), God is perfect and absolute. She has got infinite forms and modifications. The first and the immanent principle (Parā-Śakti) of Viṣṇu is known as Śrī.

Śrī Vidyā (Divine Science) and Bhakti Mārga (Path of Devotion) constitute Tāntric Vaiṣṇavism. In the state of Śrī Vidyā Sādhanā we find the predominance of devotion and lack of aggressive spiritualism which is the basis of Śaktism. After the initial stage of Śākta Sādhanā, mind becomes pure and sublime. It is the breeding ground of devotion. Tāntric Vaiṣṇavism is dualistic in nature. The dualism of Self and God exists. It is the state of spiritual enjoyment and beatitude. In the state of Vaiṣṇavism man becomes God-intoxicated. The awakening of the Kuṇḍalinī creates a tremendous spiritual vibration. The Sādhaka starts enjoying the inner pleasure of the soul. The shedding of tears, the limping of the body, continuous laughing and dancing are some of the outward manifestations of the inner pleasure. They are known as Aṣṭa-Bhāvas. We have noticed all these outward manifestations in Swami Ramakrishna and Mahaprabhu Chaitanya. When Ramakrishna got initiation in Dhyāna-Yoga from Totapuri and attained Nirvikalpa Samādhi (non-qualified liberation) he became calm and composed. He reached the destination. There was total absence of subject object, knower-known relationship. This is the state of spiritual monism or Śaivahood.

Tāntric Vaiṣṇavism is intimately connected with *yantra, mantra* and Kuṇḍalinī Sādhanā. Śrī Cakra is known as Śrī Yantra also. Uptill Ājñā Cakra is the state of Vaiṣṇavism. When the Kuṇḍalinī reaches Ājñā Cakra after piercing all the other five *cakras,* one attains qualified liberation (Savikalpa Samādhi). 'I am That', is the state of intuitive realization. One's whole being is transformed into cosmic existence. One sees himself in everything. The feeling of one in all and all in one is a Vaiṣṇavite mystic realization. It is not a theoretical articulation or dictum but a conscious mystic experience like the firm empirical feeling of 'I am Mr. X'.

The Sahajiyā cult of Bengal is a historical evidence of the development and growth of Tāntric Vaiṣṇavism as a distinct cult. The Vaiṣṇava Sahajiyā as a distinct sect was originated and developed in Bengal before Caitanya. The elements of Tāntric Vaiṣṇavism are found in abundance in the life and teachings of Caṇḍīdāsa who lived in the fourteenth century. The mystic sect of Bāul has also its origin in Tāntric Vaiṣṇavism. The elements of mysticism and esotericism are the *kernels* of Bāul songs. The mysticism of Bāul sects bespeaks of its Tāntric character.

In our view *Saundaryalaharī* is the canonical literature of Tāntric Vaiṣṇavism and not of the Samayā School of Śaktism, because it is a devotional hymn of praise Śrī Cakra belongs to Tāntric Vaiṣṇavism. *Saundaryalaharī* is Tāntric text. It dwells upon Śrī Vidyā Sādhanā. The unification of Śiva and Śakti is the sole objective of Tantra Sādhanā. Śrī Cakra is the abode of Śiva. Śakti also resides, in Śrī Cakra along with Śiva. One can have the experience of Śiva-Śakti in Śrī Cakra with the help of Bhakti Sādhanā. Devotion and *mantra* constitute the Śrī Vidyā cult of Tāntric Vaiṣṇavism.

Rāmānuja in his commentary on the *Brahma Sūtras* holds the view that Bādarāyaṇa accepts the views of Pāñcarātra. He refutes the arguments of his adversary who holds the view that Pāñcarātra is anti-Vedic and has been propounded by Śāṇḍilya as he did not find a sure basis for the welfare of man in the Vedas.[33] According to Rāmānuja the Pañcarātra system was revealed by Nārāyaṇa himself.[34] He says: 'The Śārīraka Śāstra (*i.e.* the Vedānta) does not disprove the principles assumed by the Sāṅkhyas, but merely the view of their not having Brahman for their Self; and similarly in its criticism on the Yoga and Paśupata systems, it merely refutes the view of the Lord being a mere instrumental cause, the erroneous assumptions as to the relative position of higher and lower entities, and certain practices not warranted by the Veda; but it does not reject the Yoga itself, nor again the Lord Paśupati.[35] He equates Pāñcarātra and Paśupata doctrines with Sāṅkhya, Yoga and the Vedas.[36] Rāmānuja also accepts that Pañcarātra belongs to the Tantra school. He has used the word 'Pāñcarātratantra'.[37]

On commenting on *Sūtra* (II.2.36) Rāmānuja declares the doctrines of Kāpālas, Kālamukhas, Paśupatas and Śaivas, untenable as they are, in conflict with the Vedas. He says that a Kālamukha is he who uses the human skull as a drinking bowl, smears himself with the ashes of a dead body, eats the flesh of such a body, carries a liquor jar which he uses as a platform for making offerings to gods.

Sāṅkhya, Yoga, Paśupata and Vaiṣṇava Tantra schools of Sādhanā were quite different from Trayī or Vedic religion.[38] It is quite clear that the cult aspect spirituality is the gift of Tantra and the Vedas is a religio-philosophical system. Śākta, Vaiṣṇava and Śaiva Tantras are spiritual cults and not denominational, religions. They are the pathways to salvation.

In our opinion Rāmānuja was not against Tantra but against the degenerate forms of Tantra practices. It seems he had great regard and admiration for Tāntric Vaiṣṇavism, but he was against absolutistic Tāntric Śaivism and Avidyā Tantra which were probably very popular in the then Hindu society.

Otto Shrader has given an illuminating account of Tāntric Vaiṣṇavism in his monograph, *Introduction to the Pāñcarātra and the Ahirbudhnya Saṁhitā*.[39]

Śaiva Tantra

Śaiva Tantra is an ideo-realistic monism. It believes in three categories (*padārtha*) — God, Soul and the fetters and thirty six principles (*tattvas*). Recognition of more principles is regarded as a new discovery which other systems fail to achieve. According to this system of thought the whole universe has been evolved from one singular reality, Śiva. He is omnipotent, omniscient, gracious and transcendental existence. He carries on the five-fold function of creation, preservation, destruction, concealment and bestowing of grace. Soul is Śiva, but its true being remains concealed by *malas* (impurities).

Āṇava (bondage of individuation), Karma (bondage of *Karma*), and Māyīka (bondage of Māyā) are the three *malas* which are the causes of suffering and bondage. Āṇavamala is responsible for the non-intuition, *akhyāti,* of the true nature of Self. Māyīkamala represents the whole series of categories. Kārmamala is responsible for continuing the fetters of bondage and it is due to this impurity or *mala* that the Self becomes subject to the law of causation and entangles itself in a series of births and deaths. Self becomes subject to good and bad acts.[40] Due to the *mala* (impurity) Śiva becomes self limited, which leads to the false sense of self in non-self.[41] Māyā, Kāla, Niyati, Rāga, Akhyāti and Kalā are the six Kañcukas which have sheathed the Self. Śiva is shrouded by these Kañcukas. Māyā is a Vedyaprathā, the knowledge of difference, the creation of difference between the subject and the object.

A man cannot be liberated from the trammels of *mala* and the bondage of Kañcukas through his effort. The bondage of individuation or *aṇutva* is due to the Self limitation (*ātmasaṅkoca*) of Śiva himself, which can be removed only by His grace (*anugraha*). Limitation (*tirodhāna*), Creation (*sṛṣṭi*), Preservation (*sthiti*), Dissolution (*saṁhāra*) and Grace (*anugraha*) are the five eternal functions of Śiva. With the grace of Siva, the soul is delivered from the false sense of dualism of subject and object. *Idaṁ* (That) is absorbed into *ahaṁ* (I) and *ahaṁ* into *Śivahood,* the *pūrṇāhantā* without which there is no spiritual bliss.

Mṛgendra Āgama which is the knowledge section of *Kāmika Āgama* outlines the quintessence of Śaivism in its very first verse. According to the monograph, 'Śiva is beginningless, free from defects. He is the all knowing entity. He removes from the infinitesimal soul the web of bonds that obscures its nature. According to *Śaiva Tantra* Śiva is the Supreme Reality. He is Cosmic Consciousness. He is the Transcendental Self. He is the soul of the soul and the being of the being. He is Consciousness Bliss personified. As he is the soul of the soul, every soul is consciousness. 'Self is consciousness.'[42] Śaivistic Tāntrism maintains the omniscience and omnipotence of Śiva. The complete immersion of the duality in the unitive consciousness is its central theme. Jīva becomes one with Śiva, *i.e.* the adorer becomes the adored himself. His body is the temple and his soul the idol in it. He is the chief priest not of god above, around, or below but of his own Transcendental Self.

Many schools of Śaivism have been mentioned by different scholars. Vācaspati Miśra (A.D. 840), in his commentary on the *bhāṣya* of Śaṅkara, says that the Maheśvaras consist of the Śaivas, Paśupatas, Kāruṇika-Siddhāntins and Kāpālikas. Mādhava (fourteenth century) mentions Śaivas as being Nakuliśa-pāśupatas in his monograph, *Sarva-Darśana-Saṁgraha.* In this Śaiva-Darśana is the Seventh System. It recognizes three categories of Śiva: Lord (Pati), the Soul (Paśu) and the Fetter (Pāśa), and four feet: Knowledge (Jñāna), Esoteric Practice (Kriyā), Mystic Sādhanā (Yoga) and Moral Code (Caryā). Mādhava says: 'The Guru of the world, having first condensed in one Sūtra the great Tantra, possessed of three categories and four feet, has again declared the same at full length.'[43] He formulates the philosophical doctrines found in the Śaivāgamas and their cognate literature. He also deals with Pratyabhijñā-Darśana separately. Pratyabhijñā is commonly known as Kashmir Śaivism.

Rāmānuja in his *bhāṣya* on the *Brahma Sūtra* (11.2.37) mentions the name of Kāpālikas and Kālamukhas as being the Śaiva sects of anti-Vedic character. Patañjali also gives reference of the Śaiva sect. The followers of it were known as Śivabhāgavatas or devotees of Śiva, the Bhagavat. Śiva is called Bhagavat in *Atharvaśiras-Upaniṣad.* We find some defiled references to the Kāpālikas in the drama of *Mālatī-Mādhava* of Bhavabhūti (A.D. 700-800). According to Bhavabhūti, Śrīśaila was the principal seat of Kāpālikas. The chief preceptor, Aghoraghaṇṭa, and his nun-disciple, Kapālakuṇḍalā, had acquired great occult powers through the esoteric practice of yoga. Kapālakuṇḍalā wears a garland of human skulls. She takes away Mālatī, the heroine of the play, when she was asleep in her father's palace in the dead of night to be sacrificed to propitiate the goddess Karāla-Cāmuṇḍā by her preceptor Aghoraghaṇṭa. However, Mālatī is rescued by her lover Mādhava.

We do not agree with the demoniacal treatment of this subject. In our opinion it reflects the prejudices and sinister scheming of the Āryans to discredit the non-Āryan Tantra. One thing is very clear from Bhavabhūti's accounts of the Kāpālikas, that they were in possession of great occult powers and were in the know of the inner science of Tāntric esotericism.

Frazer also paints a horrible picture of Śaivites in the *Encyclopaedia of Religion and Ethics.* According to him in some of the well-known temples in South India the primitive blood rites and drunken orgies are permitted to be revived yearly as a compromise with the aboriginal worshippers, whose real shrines have been captured by Brahmin priests acting under the protection of local kṣatriya chieftains. Frazer also mentions the name of Śrī-śaila, the Kāpālika centre referred to by Bhavabhūti. According to him non-Brahmins and outcastes were followers of the Śiva cult.

Tantra does not believe in caste and creed. Tāntric social system runs counter to the rigid Vedic system of caste and creed. There is no place for a Brahmin priest in Tantra Sādhanā. That is why Brahmins started a tirade against Śaiva Tantra. The followers of Tantra were declared outcastes. Tantra is a secret Sādhanā. Only an initiate can understand the real and mystic significance of Tantra esotericism. We have already discussed the real meaning of Five Makāras. Mādhava does not mention the demoniac practices of Śaiva sects in his works. *Sarva-Darśana-Saṁgraha* which gives a more authentic account of Śaivism does not mention anything about demoniac Tāntric practices. In our view Frazer's study and exposition of Śaivism is lopsided. Most probably he has identified the whole system with Avidyā Tantra which we shall deal with later in this very chapter. The non-initiates do not understand the deeper and different Tāntric Sādhanās. According to the Śaiva system when a person is established in Yama and Niyama Sādhanā and meekly suffers the indignities and abuses showered on him by other people, he is well established on the path of asceticism. None of the Śaivāgamas mentions the demoniac practices as enjoined upon their followers as stated by Frazer and others. On the contrary *Paśupata Sūtras* speak about detachment and control of senses. Senses should be directed towards righteousness, and they should not be allowed to stray away unto the commission of evil acts.[44] The entire fourth chapter of *Paśupata Sūtra* deals with Paśupata Vrata (the code of conduct of an ascetic). According to *vrata* an ascetic should behave *like* a lunatic, an epileptic, an ignorant dull man, a bad character and the like, so that abuses may be cast on him by the people. This will create a sense of unbelongingness and disinclination to worldly fame and honour and would elevate him. Strict adherence to such a course of conduct and the practice of Yoga will lead him unto the mystic union with the Lord and he will never come to this world again.

The fifth chapter deals with Paśupata-Yoga. This means communion with Maheśvara and complete detachment from all the objects of present, past and future.[45] 1t means complete withdrawal of mind from the physical objects and continuous ideation of Śiva. This ideation results in the mystic unification of soul with Lord Maheśvara.

Kauṇḍinya (fourth century) in his bhāṣya on *Paśupata Sūtra* describes the five subjects of the system as Effect (Kārya), Cause (Kāraṇa), Mystic Sādhanā (Yoga), Moral Code (Vidhi) and Cessation of Suffering (Duḥkhānta).

Vrata, the vow of Śaivites, has been misunderstood by many scholar, Surendranath Dasgupta says: 'The Mahāvrata, meaning the great vow, consists in eating food placed in a human skull and smearing the body with the ashes of human carcasses and others, which are attributed to the Kālamukhas by Rāmānuja.'[46] R.G. Bhandarkar is of the same opinion. His view is based on Jagaddhara's commentary on Mālatī Mādhava who explains Kāpālikavrata by Mahāvrata.[47] The real Mahāvrata does not mean indulgence in obscenity. It is an esoteric determination to scale the steepness of spiritual heights and brave all dangers.

Mṛgendrāgama has been quoted in *Sarva-Darśana-Saṁgraha.* This work is the *jñāna khaṇḍa* (knowledge part) of *Kāmikāgama* which is one of the oldest and authoritative works of Tantra Śāstra, and has been referred to in *Sūta-Saṁhitā,* which is dated to be the work of the sixth century. *Sūta-Saṁhitā* refers to *Kāmikāgama* with reverence which is due to its mystic value. The reverence towards *Kāmikāgama* is the proof of its spiritual importance.

Mṛgendrāgama initiates discussions about the old Vedic forms of worship which have become obsolete and have been superseded by the Śaiva cult. In the second chapter of the work, Śiva is described as being free from all impurities and finitude. He is omniscient. He knows how individual souls are going to behave.

Śiva stands supreme; all the deities of later Brahmanism are merely of the nature of the highest soul, dependent on Śiva to carry out his disposition. He alone is the source from which the cosmos is vitalized throughout the course of creation, preservation and involution. He is the supreme subjectivity and hence he cannot be the object of thought.

Śvetāśvatara Upaniṣad is supposed to be the basis of Śaivism. In tracing the history of Śaivism to it, Barnett writes, 'the elements of Tamil Śaiva Siddhānta, the Sanskrit Āgama and the Śaiva theology of Kashmir are all contained in *Śvetāśvatara Upaniṣad* which was canonical long before the days of Śaṅkara'.[48] According to Frazer these ideas of *Śvetāśvatara Upaniṣad* were formulated into the Spanda and Pratyabhijñā schools of Kashmir Śaivism.[49]

Mādhava has quoted *Tattva-Prakāśa* in explaining Śaiva-Darśana in his work *Sarva-Darśana-Saṁgraha. Tattva-Prakāśa* is ascribed to Bhoja (eleventh century) who wrote *Sarasvatī-Kaṇṭhābharaṇa* and a commentary on *Yoga-Sūtra.* The purpose of the monograph is to cxplain the Śaiva philosophy as has been enunciated by the Śaivāgamas. Śiva is regarded as Jñāna-Śakti. Śiva is the Ultimate Being. He is all by himself, He does not depend on anything. He does not have any body. He is one and unique. He is all pervading and eternal. The soul who attains liberation becomes like Him. But Śiva is unchangeable. He is also devoid of all impurities and passions.

The Absolute in the aspect of pure knowledge is called Śiva and, as pure activity, is called Śakti. When the two are balanced, we have the category of Absolute Sadā Śiva. The eternal coexistence (Samarasatā) of Śiva and Śakti is known as Brahman. Śiva and Śakti constitute one reality. They are like Dīpa and Prabhā. Śiva is Prakāśa and Śakti is the *vimarśa* aspect of the Absolute.[50] When there is predominance of action it is called Maheśvara.

Śiva is the only ultimate category; without Śiva nothing could happen. The category of Śiva is called Bindu. Bindu represents Pure Knowledge and Action beyond all change. It is said that this pure Śiva or Bindu or Mahāmāyā is surcharged with various powers and it is through these that Śakti-Tattva and its offshoots are activated into the creation of the universe. It is the basis of the bondage of *jīva.* The creation is not directly due to Śiva but due to his Śakti.

Śaivism is rightly interpreted as pure monism. When Śiva becomes associated with Māyā, He is called parigraha-Śakti. The presence of Śiva is enough for the various transformations in Māyā. This results in involution and evolution of the cosmos. The relation of Śiva and Śakti can be symbolically stated as the relationship between the sun and the lotus. The lotus blooms by itself in the presence of the sun; the sun remains unchanged. This led to the interpretation of theism. On the other hand, Śiva stands supreme. Śiva is the only reality. On the basis of monistic outlook, *Sūta-Saṁhitā* has termed the whole system as Śivādvaita.

Śaiva Tantra is the oldest religion of India. In the *Mahābhārata* Kṛṣṇa figures as the chief devotee of Śiva. He is initiated into Śiva-Yoga by Upamanya. Equipped with a staff, shaved, clothed in rags, anointed with ghee, and provided with a girdle, living for one month on fruit, for four months on water, standing on one foot, with his arms aloft, he, at length, obtained a glorious vision of Mahādeva and his wife, whom all the gods were worshipping, among them Indra, Viṣṇu (the delight of his mother, Aditi), and Brahmā, all uttering the *rathantara sāman.*[51]

The school of Southern Śaivism is not different from the original Tāntric Śaivism. Tirumular is believed to be the earliest exponent of Śaivism in South India. His work *Tirumandiram*, assigned various dates, from the first century to the ninth century, is highly abstruse and full of symbolism. It declares that to find a Śiva-jñānin once is more righteous than the gift of a thousand temples, or the feeding of a crore of Brahmans versed in the Vedas.[52] *Śiva-jñāna-bodham* of Meykandar is a philosophical attempt to systematize the tenets of Southern Śaivism. It states that Śivam is one; *jñānam* is the mystic realization of Śivam. *Śiva-jñāna-bodham* is a small treatise of twelve aphorisms (Sūtras). The first three Sūtras deal with the three categories of Pati (God), Pāśa (Bondage) and Paśu (Soul). Thus, the nature and content of literature of Southern Śaivism are the same as those of outer Śaivisms.

Śaivism flourished from the pre-Vedic time to the end of the eleventh century and its exponents hailed both from North and South.[53] The twelfth century witnessed the ascendancy of Vaiṣṇavism and the decadence of Śaivism. At this critical hour, Bāsava appeared on the religious horizon of South (Karnataka) and arrested the decline of Śaivism, freed it from the shackles of Varṇāśrama and infused a new life into it.[54] It is this revived, regenerated and revolutionary Śaivism that goes by the name of Vīraśaivism or Liṅgāyata religion.

Mālinīvijayottara Tantram explains Śaiva Yoga as set forth in the Trika system of Kashmir. Abhinavagupta has held Tantra in high esteem and writes in Tantrāloka that Mālinivījaya is the essence of Tāntric Śaivism. It is the quintessence of the complete teachings of Śiva as enunciated by the different schools of Tantra.

According to Tāntric Śaivism, a Sādhaka enters into mystic Sādhanā after taking a purificatory bath and offers worship to the deities. He considers himself an indivisible part of Śiva. The Sādhaka divinizes himself with the mystic power of consciousness consisting in *I am He.* He identifies his body with mātṛkā assigning each part of his body to the corresponding letters of the alphabet according to the arrangement of *mātṛkānyāsa.*

For the layman the esoteric instruction does not carry any sense. The incantation of *mantras* like *I am He* inculcates a cosmic ideation and transforms the individual consciousness into Cosmic Consciousness. The *mātṛkā* letters represent the different stages of evolution. Different letters are the symbols of different acoustic roots of different vibrations. The different parts of the body are represented by different letters. Mātṛkānyās leads to the ascent of human consciousness. The mystic Sādhanā leads to the falling of the cloaks of *mala* which conceal his kinship with Śiva. In this state of mystic identification one has an intuitive realization and one feels that 'I alone am the supreme reality, this whole universe is in me; I am the stay and support of this all'. The spiritual identity of *jīva* with Being, Bliss and Consciousness is established.

Śaivism is a school of Tāntric monism. Mysticism rather than rationalism or ritualism has been recognized as the true guide to the Ultimate Truth. Its aim is mystic realization of the Reality. Śaivites are concerned with the spiritual elevation and intuitive vision of Śiva. Therein the mystic urge for communion with God is achieved.

In our view Tantra is an integral yoga and is an intuitive science. The Śākta, Vaiṣṇava and Śaiva Tantra constitute an organic whole. They are complementary to each other. There is no hostility between them. They cannot be isolated from each other. Each represents a phase of the ascent of human consciousness. Each represents a phase of spiritual life. One cannot be divorced from the other. The Śākta, Vaiṣṇava and Śaiva Sādhanā should be regarded as following one another in spiritual progress and perfection.

One who is Parama Śākta can alone be a Parama Vaiṣṇava and a Parama Vaiṣṇava alone can be Parama Śiva. The stage of Śākta Sādhanā is represented by aggressive spiritualism. It is a state of intense esoteric activities. A Tāntric Sādhaka is subject to all sorts of esoteric allurements and it is with the grace of the Guru alone that he holds his own and does not drift. The Guru acts as an spiritual anchor. The greatest impediments are the temptation of acquisition and display of occult power, the misuse of which leads to spiritual decadence. A Parama Śākta means a successful Sādhaka who does not allow his mind to drift and distract from the path and continues his spiritual march in the midst of adversities.

The stage of Vaiṣṇavism is a state of spiritual enjoyment. It is the state of God-intoxication. From the theistic unitive consciousness emerges divine love. It offers the numinous and moral force, embracing all living creatures as varied forms of God. Man becomes totally unimpeded in his impulses, thought and behaviour. One is beyond the ethical and social norms. Yet, one can do no wrong as all the while one is merged in the loving devotion to God. When one is engaged in action, he is really inactive. One sees God in oneself and oneself in other beings. One becomes a Parama Vaiṣṇava.

The stage of Śaivism is a state of mystic silence. It is a state of spiritual illumination and perfection. It is a state of Tāntric monism. The non-duality of Śiva and Śakti has been stoutly defended. Śakti is separated from Śiva only in a theoretical and conventional analysis, but in mystic realization, She is identical with Śiva. If Śiva is Brahman, She is Brahmamayī. If Śiva is *cit* (consciousness), She is *citi-śakti* (consciousness-form). Tantra is beyond the philosophical measures of *advaita, dvaita* and *dvaitādvaita. Mahānirvāṇa Tantra* says: 'Some say it is *dvaita,* others *advaita,* but in reality it is *dvaitādvaita-vivarjita,* neither the one nor the other.'[55]

The Śākta, Vaiṣṇava and Śaiva schools comprise the mystic and metaphysical culture of Tantra. The different schools and approaches are harnessed and synthesized into one spiritual cult. The different schools are varying steps and stages of one's competence and temperament. The *prima facie* differences in the techniques and practices are in keeping with the basic principles necessary for working out a complete realization. Śākta, Vaiṣṇava and Śaiva Sādhanā, when practised with faith and determination, devotion and vision, will surely lead to the classification of the mystic and scientific principles and their harmonic integration. The different schools are not divergent paths but different phases of the ascent of consciousness. The Śakta, Vaiṣṇava and Śaiva Sādhanās are formed into one spiritual cult.

PSYCHOLOGICAL SCHOOLS OF TANTRA

Dakṣiṇācāra, Madhyamācāra and Vāmācāra

Brahma Yāmala[56] deals with the mystic modes of worship by means of *mantras* in various dispositions. It dwells upon the different Tāntric traditions and other sources. There are three methods for the realization of mystic oneness. They are: Dakṣiṇācāra, Vāmācāra and Madhyamācāra. Dr. P.C. Bagchi states, 'they represent the three Śaktis of Śiva and are characterized respectively by the predominance of each of the three *guṇas — sattva, rajas* and *tamas.* The Tantras of each class follow a particular line of Sādhanā. Hence, there are three classes of Tantras: Dakṣiṇa, which is characterized by *sattva,* is pure (*śuddha*); Vāma, which is characterized by *rajas,* is mixed (*vimiśra*); and Madhyama, characterized by *tamas,* is impure (*aśuddha*)'.[57]

It is commonly said that Dakṣiṇācāra has evolved from the right mouth of Śiva. Vidyā, Mantra, Mudrā and Maṇḍalas are the four *pīṭhas,* modes of Sādhanā of Dakṣīṇācāra. Rudra, Skandas, Brahmā, Yama, Vāyu, Kubera and Indra Yāmalas belong to the Vidyāpīṭha of the Dakṣiṇācāra school. Tantras belonging to this *pīṭha* are Yoginījāla, Yoginīhṛdaya, Mantramālinī, Aghoreśī, Aghoreśvarī, Kṛḍāghoreśvarī, Lākinīkalpa, Mārici, Mahāmārici and Ugravidyāgaṇa. This school also holds that the Bhairavas belong to the Mantra-pīṭha. According to it, Mantra and Mudrā are closely connected with each other.

According to this system, Madhyamācāra has issued from the upper mouth of Lord Śiva. Vijaya, Niśvāsa, Svayaṁbhuva, Vatula, Vīrabhadra, Raurava, Mākaṇṭa and Vīreśa Tantras belong to Madhyamācāra. However, no clear mention has been made regarding the Vāmācāra school. It belongs to 'the Tantras of a higher class'.

Kulārṇava Tantra[58] describes seven ways for the liberation of man. The first is the path of *Karma* or Vedic rituals. This is meant for the man of ordinary mettle. Vaiṣṇava Sādhanā is higher than Vedic rituals and is meant for men of higher comptence. Devotion (*bhakti*) is of greater value than Action (*karma*). Third is the path of Meditation and Knowledge (*jñāna*). Here knowledge means Spiritual Knowledge (parā-jñāna). Action (karma), Knowledge (*jñāna*) and Devotion (*bhakti*) are the successive stages of spiritual evolution and are prescribed for ordinary men and women who are engrossed in mundane existence (*pāśa*). They come within the category of ordinary seekers.

According to *Kulārṇava Tantra*, higher than *Karma*, *Jñāna* and *Bhakti* is Dakṣiṇācāra. Dakṣiṇācāra is a sublime form of spiritual worship. It is superior to the Vaiṣṇava and Śaiva Sādhanā.[59] Here Vaiṣṇava and Śaiva Sādhanā means the path of *bhakti* and *jñāna*. *Karma*, *Jñāna* and *Bhakti* are all synthesized and conserved into the Dakṣiṇācāra school.

Vāmācāra is higher than Dakṣiṇācāra.[60] It is the path of *nivṛtti*, a process of spiritual ascendance. John Woodroffe says in his commentary on *Kulārṇava Tantra* that 'the Vāma is the reverse path where the natural turn outwards, *pravṛtti*, is turned inward, *nivṛtti*, to the source of all and everything in creation is looked upon and used as the means for the return to the one consciousness that bases all and governs all.'[61] The process is one of mystic identification of individual consciousness with the Cosmic Consciousness. Dakṣiṇācāra and Vāmācāra are meant for men of some spiritual attainment, who can fight with the forces of nescience.

Kulārṇava Tantra further says that Siddhānta and Kaula are superior to all other forms of Sādhanā. There is nothing beyond Kaula Dharma.[62] Dakṣiṇācāra and Vāmācāra are the most scientific processes of spiritual enlightenment. Vāmācāra Sādhanā has been wrongly associated with a repulsive connotation. It has been identified with gross fornication.

Agehananda Bharati a monk of the Dasanami Order of Hindu Sāṁyāsins, has identified Tantra with eroticism. He is one of the ardent supporters of free sex in the name of Tantrism and Dasanami Order. He has quoted *Rudra-Yāmala* in his support and describes Vāmācāra as less philistine. Ritualistic intercourse is held with a woman who is not one's wife (the literal translation "and other's wife", though lexicographically correct, may be a distortion of anti-Tāntric writers and interpreters), and women of all castes are equally eligible. Thus is a Left handed practice described which 'bestows all Siddhis, O Benign Goddess.'[63] In support of his thesis, A. Bharati further quotes *Kāmākhyā Tantra* according to which a great ascetic should worship Śakti, the mother of the universe, with wine, meats, fish, *mudrā* and copulation with women.[64]

Tantra Sādhanā is based on mysticism. The real significance of the different words and symbols of Tantra can be known only by the 'initiates'. The symbolism that Tantra, if not correctly understood, is misleading. Tāntric Texts have been written in Sandhyābhāṣā,[65] which is capable of double meaning, the apparent always misleading. The deeper and mystic significance can be understood only by those who are adept in esotericism. The esoteric meaning of *maithuna*[66] is the unification of Śakti and Śiva, the individual and the Cosmos.

In our opinion, Dakṣīṇācāra, Madhyamācāra and Vāmācāra is the psychological classification of Tantra. To bring about liberation from the bondage of *mala* and *kañcukas* is the objective behind Tantra Sādhanā. The mantric incantation and ideation of Śiva (Consciousness) are the chief constituents of Tantra Sādhanā. Māyā stands as an impediment in the path of spiritual realization. To overcome the bondage of Māyā is an essentiality. Dakṣīṇācāra (Right-handed school) offers oblations to Śakti so that she might grant blessings to the Sādhaka. Māyā is the operative principle. Māyā is Śakti. According to Dakṣīṇācāra without the grace of Śakti one cannot attain Salvation. A Sādhaka offers prayers to Śakti to please her.[67] This school is also known as Samayā. Now, the question is whether or not a man can attain salvation with the help of Śakti alone. Śakti is the binding principle. She can help a Sādhaka only to a point. She is the immanent principle of Śiva. Śiva alone can liberate a man from the bondage of Māyā.

Vāmācāra (Left-handed school) is an aggressive spiritualism. It does not make any compromise with the different attributes of Śakti. Kāma (sex), Krodha (anger), Lobha (temptation), Moha (attachment), Mada (egoism), Mātsarya (jealousy), Ghṛṇā (hatred), Lajjā (shame), Bhaya (fear) are the dominant instincts in man which keep him veiled from his real self. The Vamācāra Sādhaka goes to Śmaśāna (cremation ground) in the dead of night and performs Sādhanā with human skulls, etc. After seeing the end of the mortal frame in the form of ashes and skeleton, a sense of renunciation develops in him and he gradually becomes detached from the mundane existence. A man who visits Śmaśāna in the dead of night will certainly overcome the instinct of fear. In the *Upaniṣad* it has been said that Self is not attainable by the weakling.[68] Vāmācāra is a non-compromising spiritual cult. It declares war against Māyā. It is a scientific approach to overcome the influence of Māyā. Kapālika and other forms of Vāmācāra Sādhanā are a positive, mystic and scientific method to sublimate the baser human instincts into higher spirituality. Tantra does not believe in suppression and repression of human instincts. It is a method of sublimation and transformation. What seems to be an obscene and repulsive esoteric practice to a layman is a healthy and positive science of sublimation. With the help of mantric incantative rhythm, a Sādhaka tries to establish a mystic communion with his own individual existence (incantative rhythm) to Cosmic Consciousness. In other words it is a mystic process of unification of Kuṇḍalinī Śakti with Śiva Absolute. Śiva is represented by the red *bindu* (sperm) and Śakti by the white *bindu* (ovum). Śiva and Śakti constitute the Miśra Bindu. Tantra does not allow free sex; rather it is imperative for every Tantra Sādhaka to lead a restrained life. However, Vāmācāra is a very difficult and risky process. Only a man of higher spiritual attainment can practise this Sādhanā. Without proper moral discipline and a Guru of a high order, one should not dare practise it. Otherwise there is every possibility of a fall and degeneration. Sometimes, a Sādhaka gets enamoured of the occult power and forgets his destination. Vāmācāra is only for those who have dedicated their whole lives for spiritual salvation and for the upliftment of mankind.

Madhyamācāra (the central path) is for all. In common parlance, Madhyamācāra is known as Yoga Sādhanā. No risk is involved in it. However, without a proper Guru, one cannot practise this Sādhanā also. But it is a sure though slow process. It is a scientific, easy and universal method to attain salvation. It differs from both Dakṣiṇācāra and Vāmācāra. Like Vāmācāra, it is not an aggressive form of spiritual cult and hence, it does not involve any risk. It is not a compromising and pestering process, it is a positive method to mitigate the influence of *mala* and *kañcukas.* It is a method of constant ideation and incantation. With gradual ideation and incantation a man becomes spiritually evolved and the bondage of Māyā becomes automatically loosened. Yama and Niyama, Āsana, Prāṇāyāma, Pratyāhāra Dhāraṇā, Dhyāna and Samādhi are the constituents of Madhyamācāra Sādhanā.

ESOTERIC SCHOOLS OF TANTRA

Tantra penetrates into the darkest chamber of mind and a Sādhaka becomes conscious of his own unlimited psychic power. A man is a sleeping cosmic being. The awakening of the Kuṇḍalinī leads to the opening of the latent magazine of power (Śakti) and makes it available for use. Kuṇḍalinī Yoga is an esoteric process to make kinetic the dormant divinity. With the arousal of the Kuṇḍalinī a Sādhaka becomes aware of his own occult power. From the esoteric point of view, Tantra can be divided into Avidyā, Upavidyā and Vidyā Sādhanā.

AVIDYĀ TANTRA

Like the material science, Tantra is revelatory in nature. It reveals the mystery of mind and consciousness. The material science lays bare the mysteries of Nature. Nobody could have ever thought of an 'atom' possessing such a tremendous power had Fermi and Bohr not split it and created a revolution in the world of objective science. But some pursue science to serve the humanity while others engage in discovering deadly weapons for the annihilation of human culture.

Like objective science, Tantra can be used for both moral and immoral purposes. The Sādhanā which is done with a material and selfish motive is known as Avidyā Tantra.

Due to the rampant practice of Avidyā Sādhanā, Tantra was looked upon as black magic and obscenity. Māraṇa, Mohana and Uccāṭana are the esoteric processes of doing positive harm to the enemy. It is not a myth but a living reality. Ḍākinī and Yoginī Sādhanās are perfect esoteric sciences. Any man can acquire occult powers if he is properly initiated by a Guru. Most of the Avidyā cults have been imported from China. Vaśiṣṭha went to China to make some sort of a research into Avidyā Tantra and brought Cīnācāra to India. This Cīnācāra is nothing but the Avidyā aspect of

Tantra Sādhanā. *Mālatī Mādhava* describes the Avidyā aspect of Tantra Sādhanā. Kapālakuṇḍalā and Aghoraghaṇṭa were Avidyā Sādhaka and Avidyā Guru respectively. It seems that Avidyā Tantra was more prevalent in those days than Vidyā Tantra (Divine Science) which created a wrong notion about Tantra amongst thc elite, and the intelligentsia. We do admit that Avidyā Sādhanā is part of the Tantra cult. Arthur Avalon also agrees that, 'In this connection I cannot avoid interposing the observation that certain practices are described in Tantra which, though they are alleged to have the results described therein, yet exist 'for delusion.'[69] Weddell has completely identified the Avidyā aspect of Buddhist Tantra with the whole of Buddhist Tantra Sādhanā. It might be that Avidyā Tantra was more prevalent in Tibet, and he could come in contact only with the demoniacal aspect of Tantra.

Secondly, Avidyā Sādhanā is easier than Vidyā Sādhanā. It yields the esoteric result in a very short time. A man becomes conscious of his occult power. He starts its exhibition immediately. It requires superhuman power to resist such a temptation. However, Tantra warns everyone against the wanton misuse of occult power. Mental vigilance and physical alertness are essential for a Sādhaka. Tantra does not sanction misuse and exhibition of those powers. Those who indulge in any such exhibition and misuse are eternally debarred from entering into the kingdom of Divinity. They are spiritual dropouts. Occult powers are the dust of the feet. Where is time for a true spiritual aspirant to stop and appreciate the dust and be doomed?

The Avidyā Sādhaka exhibits supernatural skill with the help of different vibrations. Mind has the para-psychological power. The *Siddhis* are nothing but having control over different vibrations. The vibrations are existential, attributional and actional in nature. The *Siddhis* are attained through the esoteric process which constitutes Mantra and Yantra Sādhanā. With the help of this Sādhanā, the Avidyā Sādhaka attains different *Siddhis.* With the help of occult powers one can change the nature of existential, attributional and actional vibrations. As the whole cosmos is a play of different vibrations, with a change in their nature, the very being of a thing is changed.

UPAVIDYĀ TANTRA

Upavidyā Sādhanā is an amoral process. The *Siddhis* of Upavidyā Sādhanā neither bring any spiritual elevation nor do they cause degeneration. However, purely from a spiritual point of view, it is a wastage of time and energy as it distracts the mind from the mystic oneness of Śiva and Śakti.

The Karṇa Piśāca Sādhanā belongs to Upavidyā Tantra. It gives telepathic power to a Sadhaka. A true Tāntric Sādhaka will not pay any attention to these petty gains and will not allow his mind to falter. Tantra stands for the mystic unification of *jīva* and Śiva. The *Siddhis* and occult powers are called the sword (*khaḍga*) of Cāmuṇḍā (deity).

VIDYĀ TANTRA

Vidyā Tantra is a divine science. It is a real Tantra. According to it the whole universe is Śiva-Śakti incarnate. Macrocosmically and microcosmically everything is Śiva-Śakti. The body is not just flesh and, therefore, sinful and alien. It is an epiphany of Śiva-Śakti. It should be treated as the media for realizing identity with the Divinity. Vidyā Tantra is a process of mystic transformation of all the functions, and every fibre of the mundane existence with cosmic ideation and incantation.

The objective scientists have found a tremendous power in an atom of matter. But they have touched only the outer rings. Matter is a bottled energy. But energy is not the ultimate constituent. Consciousness is the ultimate category and constituent. It is the fundamental stuff and the reality.

The material mass and energy are the different manifestations of Consciousness. Consciousness has descended to the material level. Every unit of the material mass possesses an intrinsic Divine energy. With the help of Vidyā Sādhanā a Sādhaka touches the core of it where resides Mahāmaya or Kuṇḍalinī Śakti. The uncoiling of the coiled Serpent Power essays to lead the mystic flow deeper and deeper to the inmost source of the divine power of Śiva. The toil involved in esoteric Sādhanā results in divine ecstasy, the mystic transformation of *two* into *one.* The mystic unification of Śakti with Śiva connects and consummates *this* with *that.* This mystic unification of Śakti with Śiva is the chief objective of Vidyā Sādhanā. The mystic goes beyond the law of causation. He rises above the idea of death and decay. Death has significance for those who are subject to morality and not for those who have gone beyond this idea and are established in the belief of immortality of the Self.[70]

REFERENCES

1. *Śaktisaṅgamatantra,* ver. 12.
2. *Kubjikā Tantra,* ch. I; *Tantrik Texts,* vol. IX, p. 44. Luzac & Co., 46, Great Russell Street, London, 1922.
3. *Saundaryalaharī,* p. 6.
4. *Ibid.,* p. 85.
5. *Ibid.,* ver. 35
6. *Ibid.,* vv. 9, 34.
7. *Tripurā-Rahasya,* p, 135. Chowkhamba Sanskrit Series, Varanasi, 1965.
8. *Ibid.,* p. 136.
9. अज्ञान तिमिरध्वंसि संसारर्णवतारकम्।
   आनन्दबीजमवतादर्च्यं त्रैपुरं महः ।। 1 ।। *Śāradā Tilaka,* p. 229.
10. अथ वक्ष्ये परां विद्यां त्रिपुरामतिगोपिताम्।
   यां ज्ञात्वा सिद्धिसङ्घानामधिपो जायते नरः ।। 2 ।। *Ibid.*
11. पञ्चभूतमयं विश्वं तन्मयी सा सदानघे।
   तन्मयी मूलविद्या च तदथ कथयामिते ।। 28 ।।

Yoginīhṛdaya (2nd ed.), p. 115, Saraswati Bhavan Granthmālā, vol. 7, Varanasi, 1965.

12. *Ibid.*, p. 15.
13. *Ibid.*, p. 34.
14. *Puraścaryārṇava*, Sundari Stava, p. 20.
15. कदाचिदाद्या ललिता पुंरूपा कृष्णविग्रहा। *Śakti Saṅgama Tantra.*
16. *Muṇḍamāla Tantra*, Paṭala 1.
17. *Toḍala Tantra*, Patala 1.
18. *Puraścaryārṇava*, pp. 13-14.
19. Ghṛṇā (hatred), Lajjā (shame), Bhaya (fear), Kula (sense of ancestry), Śila (superiority complex), Dambha (pride), Māna (sense of prestige) and Jugupsā (backbiting).
    Kāma (sex), Krodha (anger), Lobha (greed), Moha (attachment), Mada (egoism) and Mātsarya (jealousy).
20. त्रिपुरानन्त शक्त्यैक्यरूपिणी सर्वसाक्षिणी।
    सा चितिः सर्वतः पूर्णा परिच्छेदविवर्जनात्॥
    Tripurārahasyam, p. 6. Saraswati Bhavan Granthmālā, vol. 15, Varanasi, 1965.
21. रात्रञ्च ज्ञानवचनं ज्ञानं पञ्चविधं स्मृतम्।
    तेनेदं पञ्चरात्रञ्च प्रवदन्ति मनीषिणः॥ *Nāradapañcarātra*, 1.1.44.
22. शिवपञ्चरात्र, देवीपञ्चरात्र, गणेशपञ्चरात्र, ब्रह्मपञ्चरात्र।
    Kavīndrācārya List (Gaekwad Oriental Series), p. 23. *Mahākālapañcarātra* (A.S.I.V. 4199 A) pertaining to Śakti.
23. *Vaiṣṇavism, Śaivism and Minor Religious Systems*, pp. 38-39.
24. *Ibid.*, p. 39.
25. D.S. Sharma, *Hinduism Through the Ages* (1st ed.), p. 131. Bharatiya Vidya Bhavan, Bombay, 1956.
26. संहिता सेयमाख्याता नानामन्त्रार्थगोचरा॥68॥
    पञ्चरात्रमयी दिव्या नाम्नाहिर्बुध्न्यपूर्विका।
    अर्थैः परकृतिप्रायैः पुराकल्पैश्च संयुता॥69॥
    नानासिद्धान्तसंभेदा नानाविद्योपशोभिता।
    Ahirbudhnya Saṁhitā of the *Pāñcarātrāgama* (2nd ed.), vol. I, p. 10. Adyar Library and Research Centre, Madras, 1966.
27. *Ibid.*
28. *Ibid.*, ver. 24, p. 24.
29. *Ibid.*
30, *Ibid.*, ver. 26, p. 24,
31. *Ahirbudhnya Saṁhitā* of the *Pāñcaratrāgama*, vol. I, p. 259.
32. *Ibid.*, vol. II, p. 618.
33. The *Vedānta Sūtras* (with commentary by Rāmānuja) translated by George Thibaut, *Sacred Books of the East*, vol. XLVIII, p. 526. Motilal Banarsidass, Delhi, 1962.
34. *Ibid.*, p. 529.
35. *Ibid.*, p. 531.
36. *Ibid.*
37. *Ibid.*, p. 524.
38. त्रयी सांख्यं योगः पशुपतिमतं वैष्णवमिति।
    Mahimnastava (4th ed.), ver. 7, p. 33. Ganesh & Co., Madras, 1963.
39. Adyar, 1916.

40. *Īśvara-Pratyabhijñā*, III, 2.4-6.
41. ज्ञानबन्धः (Knowledge is Bondage), *Śiva Sūtra*, I. 2.
42. चैतन्यमात्मा ।। 1 ।। *Śiva Sūtra-Vārttikam*, p. 2.
43. *Sarva-Darśana-Saṁgraha* (3rd ed.), pp. 113-14. Kegan Paul Trench, Trubner & Co. Ltd., Dr. Dryden House, Gerrard Street, W., London, 1908.
44. तस्माद् अकुशलेभ्यो व्यावर्तयित्वा कामतः कुशले योजितानि
    तदा जितानि भवन्ति ।
    Pāśupata Sūtra, ver. 7 (commentary). Trivendrurn Oriental Manuscripts Library, University of Travancore, 1940.
45. एवं महेश्वरे भावस्थस्तदसंगित्वम् इति अर्थः । *Ibid.*, ver. 1.
46, *A History of Indian Philosophy*, vol. V, p. 2.
47. *Vaiṣṇavism, Śaivism and other Minor Religious Systems*, p. 128.
48. *Journal of Royal Asiatic Society*, July, 1910.
49. *Encyclopaedia of Religion and Ethics*, p. 25.
50. तस्य शिवस्य प्रकाशमयस्य प्रथा विमर्शशक्तिः । *Yoginīhṛdayam*, p. 105.
51. Muir, *Original Sanskrit Texts*, vol. IV, p. 194.
52. *Tirumandiram*, 1860-61.
53. *The Cultural Heritage of India*, Viraśaivism, p. 98.
54. Sakhare, *History and Philosophy of Liṅgāyata Religion*, pp. 415-16.
55. *The Cultural Heritage of India*, vol. III, p. 447.
56. Preserved in Nepal in manuscript of A.D. 1052.
57. *The Cultural Heritage of India*, vol. IV, p. 217.
58. *Kulārṇava Tantra*, p. 144.
59. वैष्णवादुत्तमं शैवं शैवाद्दक्षिणमुत्तमम् । *Kulārṇava Tantra*, p. 144.
60. *Ibid.*, p. 145.
61. *Ibid.*, p. 30.
62. सिद्धान्तादुत्तमं कौलं कौलात् परतरं न हि ।। 8 ।। *Ibid.*, p. 145.
63. *Tāntric Tradition*, p. 230.
64. *Ibid.*, p. 267.
65. P.C. Bagchi, *Tantra*, Ch. Sandhyābhāṣā and Sandhavachana Studies
66. *Kulārṇava Tantra*, Ch. V.
67. *Durgā Saptaśatī.*
68. नायं आत्मा बलहीनेन लभ्यः ।
69. *Mahānirvāṇa Tantra*, Preface, p. viii.
70. *Tantrāloka*, vol. I, p. 192.

9 Tantra Sādhanā

Mind cannot maintain its existence without objectivity. Mind is a state in the process of evolution. It is a stage in the process of motion. Every motion is an alternated phase of *pause* and *speed*. Every movement is pulsative. In the stage of pause it gains momentum which it has to express. Mind resorts to certain inter- and intra-ectoplasmic occupations to express itself. These occupations and conations of mind are known as tendencies or *vṛttis*. These tendencies or *vṛttis* are the ways of expression of mind. In psychology, they are called *expressed sentiments* and *emotions*. Sentiments affecting the subsidiary glands are called instincts. Pineal and pituitary glands are two important and most vital glands, the rest are all called subsidiary glands. *Vṛttis* are the psychic objectivities of mind. They are the colours and contours of the mental process.

Vṛttis vary according to the development of the physical body. The developed and higher beings will have an increased number of *vṛttis*. The higher animals will have a greater number of *vṛttis* than the lower ones. There are fifty *vṛttis* in the human structure. They are: Dharma, Artha, Kāma, Mokṣa, Avajñā, Prasraya, Mūrcchā, Aviśvāsa, Sarvanāśa, Krūrata, Lajjā, Piśunatā, Īrṣyā, Suṣupti, Viṣāda, Kaṣāya, Tṛṣṇā, Moha, Ghṛṇā, Bhaya, Āśā, Cintā, Ceṣṭā, Mamatā, Dambha, Viveka, Vikalatā, Ahaṅkāra, Lolatā, Kapaṭatā, Vitarka, Anutāpa, Ṣaḍaja, Ṛṣabha, Gāndhāra, Madhyama, Pañcama, Dhaivata, Niṣāda, Oṁ, Hūṁ, Phaṭ, Voṣat, Vaṣat, Svāhā, Namaḥ, Viṣa, Amṛta, Aparā and Parā.

Vṛttis are represented by different letters of the Saṁskṛta alphabet (Varṇamālā). The fifty letters of Saṁskṛta Varṇamālā are the seed-syllable (*bījākṣara*) of these fifty *vṛttis*. Tantra Sādhanā is an esoteric process to control these fifty *vṛttis*. The sublimation of mental activities (*vṛttis*) is the chief purpose of Sādhanā. With the sublimation of mind's activities, the sense of *I*-ness disappears. Man becomes free from the fetters of Māyā. Sādhanā is a mystic process of psychic sublimation. It is an art of restraining the mind stuff (*citta*) from taking various forms and modifications. Yoga is a mystic process of controlling the mind and restraining it from taking various shapes (*vṛttis*).[1]

The pituitary gland controls two *vṛttis*, *i.e.* Parā and Aparā. It is the controlling station of the conscious mind. It is Saṁkalpātmaka (Parā) and Vikalpātmaka (Aparā). Parā-Vidyā leads to the knowledge of the Supreme Self (Parama Śiva) and Aparā Vidyā stands for the knowledge of the manifest universe. The pineal gland is known as the mystery gland in psychology. It is the controller of all the three mental spheres, *i.e.* Conscious, Subconscious and Unconscious. The pineal controls all the fifty *vṛttis*. These fifty *vṛttis* have one thousand expressions. These fifty *vṛttis* can find expression both internally and externally through all the ten agencies of the mind—five sensory organs and five motor organs. The five sensory organs, (*Jñānendriyas*) are: (1) *Cakṣu* (eye), (2) *Karṇa* (ear), (3) *Nāsikā* (nose), (4) *Jihvā* (tongue), and (5) *Tvak* (skin), and their functions respectively are: Darśana (to see), *Śravaṇa* (to hear), *Āgharāṇa* (to smell), *Āṣvādana* (to taste) and *Sparśana* (to touch). The five motor organs (*Karmendriyas*) are: *Vāk* (vocal cord), *Pāṇi* (hand), *Pāda* (legs), *Pāyu* (anus) and Upastha (genital organs), and their functions respectively are: Kathana (to speak), Śilpana (to work), Caraṇa (to move), Varjana (to let out the waste) and Janana (to give birth). The sensory organs are the receivers of vibrations and the motor organs the creators of vibrations according to the inherent Saṁskāra. Each and every action is the play of *vṛttis*. Every psychic or psychophysical action is the satisfaction of different *vṛttis*. The pineal gland, which is known as Sahasrāra Cakra, controls all the fifty *vṛttis* expressed internally and externally by all the ten organs ($50 \times 2 \times 10 = 1000$). The awakening of the Kuṇḍalinī, the main aim of Tantra Sādhanā, alone can bring about a total control over the pineal gland, or Sahasrāra Cakra, the abode of Śiva. Mūlādhāra is the dwelling place of Kuṇḍalinī Śakti. The esoteric coupling (*maithuna*) of Śiva and Śakti brings liberation from the fetters and trammels of Māyā. With the coupling of Śiva and Śakti the secretion of the pineal nectar starts flowing. *Gandharvamālikā Tantra* says: 'Oh beloved one, the Queen of the Devas unites with Parama Śiva and in a moment, Oh Devī Parameśvarī, nectar is produced. This nectar is issued on the enjoyment of the union of Kulakuṇḍalinī and Parama Śiva.'[2] A man is lost in the world of spiritual beatitude and consciousness. It is the state where he is beyond the approach of all *vṛttis*. Within the scope of *vṛttis* lies the seed of Saṁskāra or a sense of *I*-ness. The attainment of spiritual beatitude means the exhaustion of all the reactive momentum accumulated by *jīva* in the course of his previous journeys in the cosmic circle (Brahma-Cakra).

According to Tantra the Absolute Reality is neutral by nature. It has two aspects: Prakāśa and Vimarśa; Nivṛtti and Pravṛtti, which may be rendered as Transcendental and Immanent, Static and Dynamic, or Positive and Negative. Śiva and Śakti are two aspects of the Absolute Reality. Śiva is pure consciousness and as such a static principle. Śakti is the cosmic energy, the world force. She is the dynamic aspect of the Reality. But neither Śiva nor Śakti is the ultimate Reality; they are inseparable. Absolute Reality or Parama Śiva (Brahman) is the state of neutrality produced through the unification of Śiva and Śakti. The mystic unification of Śiva and Śakti, under one condition, produces the highest state of spiritual bliss and beatitude, and under another, the manifest world or phenomenal process as a whole. When Śakti gets the scope of her manifestation, Śiva undergoes transformation and the world of manifestation is produced. Association of Śiva with his consort Śakti in the realm of *pravṛtti* is responsible for the creation of the visible world but when Śakti, in the form of Kulakuṇḍalinī rises to Śiva in a process of introversion, their union results in a state of Infinite Bliss and Divinity. The metaphysical union, of Śiva and Śakti binds and the mystic unification liberates.

According to Tantra Sādhanā this *tattva* of Śiva and Śakti lies within the body of man. Śiva resides in the highest plexus (Sahasrāra) in the cerebral region and Śakti dwells in the lowest plexus (Mūlādhāra, the sacrococcygeal plexus). Tantra Sādhanā is aimed at the awakening of the Kuṇḍalinī from the lowest plexus and making her proceed in an upward movement till she becomes united with Śiva in Sahasrāra Cakra. In Tāntric esotericism man represents Śiva and woman represents Śakti The mystic commingling of the two is the giver of Perfect Bliss. It results from strict discipline and yogic control. It leads to the spiritual oneness, which is the state of the Absolute. Tantra accepts and leads to the equipollence of Śiva and Śakti. Kaula Mārga is the highest form of spirituality. Bhaskara Ray says that the harmonious relation of Śiva and Śakti is Kaula Marga. Kula is Śakti and Akula is Śiva.[3]

Tantra Sādhanā is a physico-psycho-spiritual process. It seeks to weave yoga into every detail of life. It is an inner yoga of progression from the human into the divine. It is an esoteric process of mystic transformation and spiritual sublimation.

In other forms of spiritual discipline, a man is not allowed to enjoy his mundane existence. He is required to lead an ascetic life. But a man who is in the midst of the world cannot be a yogin. Tantra is a meeting ground of *bhoga* and *Yoga.* A Tantra Sādhaka takes the world as the manifestation of the Divine Principle. With the help of gradual superimposition of cosmic ideation and constant application of the Guru Mantra the mundane activities become the means for release. Bhoga turns into yoga. Tantra Sādhanā is suited to men of all equipments. It promises to award to the Sādhaka not merely liberation but also enjoyment, not merely beatitude (*niśreyasa*) but also progress (*abhyudaya*).[4] Tantra Sādhanā is a synthesis. It is the shortest route to the *summum bonum.* It combines in it Yoga and Bhoga (enjoyment).[5]

Tantra recognizes three distinct stages of Sādhanā. They are: Paśvācāra, Vīrācāra and Divyācāra. Tantra prescribes different methods and rules of conduct of life for men of different volitions. The methods and rules differ according to the physico-psycho-spiritual condition of an individual.

There are three classes of Sādhanās in order of merit, *viz.* Divya, Vīra, and Paśu.

Kālivilāsa Tantra says: 'Listen to three stages, O Devī, they are classified as the Divya (divine), Vīra (aggressive form of spirituality) and Paśu Sādhanā. The first is divine, the second is intensely exciting, the third is always pure and shining white.'[6]

Paśvācāra Sādhanā

In the beginning every man is *paśu.* He is predominantly under the influence of animal instincts. He evolves and rises from this stage. His immediate past life is that of an animal. The experience of animal life is known and fresh. Man does not have any idea of future evolution. The higher life of evolution is unknown. It is general psychology that nobody wants to take the risk of going on an untrodden path. That is why every man is attracted towards physical enjoyment. Paśu (beginner) is a person who does not have self control and yet has the desire to have mastery over his passions and impulses. Such-persons are initiated into Paśvācāra Sādhanā. Paśvācāra is a physico-psychic process. It is meant for the purification of body and mind.

According to *Kulārṇava Tantra* 'there are seven pathways to liberation.'[7] The first is Karma Mārga, the Vedic rituals; the second is Vaiṣṇava path or Bhakti Mārga; and the third is Jñāna Mārga (Śaiva Mārga). Karma Mārga (Vedic rituals), Bhakti Mārga (Vedic Vaiṣṇavism) and Jñāna Mārga (Vedantic way) are meant for the ordinary category of seekers, *paśu*, the creatures who are bound by the bonds of physical existence (*pāśa*).[8] These three disciplines are meant for the ordinary category of Sādhakas. The term *paśu* (animal) is not derogatorily used in Tantra Sādhanā. *Paśu* connotes persons who are under the bondage of fetters (*pāśa*). Śiva, is called Lord of *Paśu* (Paśupati) because he is ever free from the bondage of *pāśa.* He is ever free, omniscient and divine. Haṭha-Yoga and Rāja-Yoga constitute Paśvācāra Sādhanā. It is the beginning of spiritual ascent.

Haṭha-Yoga

The mystic interpretation of Haṭha-Yoga is quite different from the traditional explanation. *Ṭha* (ठ) is the *bīja mantra* of Ājñā Cakra. Ājñā Cakra is the controlling station of mind. Thus *ṭha* (ठ) is the controlling point (*bindu*) of mind also. *Ha* (ह) is the *bīja-mantra* of Svādhiṣṭhāna Cakra, the controlling station of five fundamental principles (Pañca-Bhūta). Sādhanā which gives control over *ṭha* (ठ) by force is known as Haṭha-Yoga. Haṭha means application of force also. *Ha* stands for Sūrya Nāḍī. Sūrya Nāḍī is known as Piṅgalā. *Ṭha* stands for Candra Nāḍī. Candra Nāḍī is called Īḍā in Tantra Sādhanā.

Haṭha-Yoga is confined to the physical culture alone. It does not lead the Sādhaka unto the spiritual unification of Śiva and Śakti. *Gheraṇḍa Saṁhitā* deals with the different processes of Haṭha Yoga. Haṭha Yogis are engaged in the physical culture. They can demonstrate immense physical powers by stopping the breath and the heart beat but these physical feats do not lead one to the realization of the Supreme Self. Haṭha-Yoga puts emphasis on Prāṇāyāma and Āsanas. In the state of Samādhi the process of breathing is nearly suspended due to mental concentration. If anybody can stop the breath with the help of physical culture, it can help one in Sādhanā. However, if the object of Sādhanā is to stop breathing alone, it will not lead one to the attainment of Conscious (चैतन्य) Samādhi. The type of Samādhi which is attained through Haṭha-Yoga is known as Material (जड़) Samādhi. It is not real Samādhi. It is not the state of Divine Bliss. It is a state of senselessness of human mind. However, with the help of Haṭha-Yoga a man can remain in the state of Jaḍa Samādhi for years together without any physical decay and death.

Rāja-Yoga

Rāja-Yoga is a mental process of attaining salvation. With the help of mental concentration and meditation, the different tendencies of mind are controlled and sublimated. Mental concentration expands the objectivity of mind. Oneness in objectivity leads to oneness in subjectivity. The subjective counterpart of the Sādhaka is transformed into the subjective counterpart of the Cosmic Mind. It brings the mystic unification of Jīvātman with Parmātman. Concentration of mind accelerates the process of evolution. In this march towards the Supreme, a Sādhaka feels the nearness of Śiva. The psychic gap between Śiva and Jīva goes on diminishing and a stage comes in the life of the Sādhaka when he becomes one with Supreme Consciousness. The mystic merger of *jīva* with Śiva is known as Yoga.[9]

Incantation of *iṣṭa mantra* results in mental dilation. Mantric incantation associates *jīva* with Śiva. Jīva is like a mirror and the reflected consciousness is like the reflection of the rays of the sun. The association of Śiva Consciousness inculcates divinc feeling. It awakens the divinity. Microcosm is transformed into macrocosm. The esoteric merger of microcosm with macrocosm is known as qualified liberation.

The constant ideation of Śiva results in the gradual expansion of mental objectivity. The enlargement of mind leads to the merger with Śiva. Śiva pervades the whole cosmos with the help of his Citti-Śakti as the sun pervades the whole solar system with the help of its radiation. With the help of Rāja-Yoga, a Sādhaka ideates on the divine nature of Śiva. The ideation of Śiva brings mental dilation. Mental dilation increases the volume and mass of mind. It leads to Divine Effulgence. The Sādhaka starts realizing the divinity within himself. The Sādhaka attains oneness with his true being.[10] He becomes one with Śiva.

Mind cannot remain objectless. It goes on changing its objectivity. It remains in the state of change and fluctuation. Mental concentration means sublimation of different instincts and tendencies. Every action, psychic or psycho-physical, is the externalization of consciousness. The psychic and psycho-physical actions create ripples and vibrations in the spiritual existence of a being. Mental concentration creates the psychic climate for the Self to manifest and shine. It lights up the dark chambers of mind. Mind becomes calm and composed. Man sees, feels and realizes the divine nature of God and he becomes God. This realization is called अहम् ब्रह्मास्मि (I am Brahman).

Tāntric Sādhanā is based on the cardinal principle that the Absolute is to be realized in and through the human body. Man is an epitome of the Cosmos. There is no real distinction between man and God. Every man is a dormant divinity. Human body is the abode of Parama Śiva. The universe is Its manifestation in space and time. The Sādhaka considers his pyhsical body as the abode of Śiva. He awakens his own dormant divinity (Kuṇḍalinī) with the clear conviction that the truth that is realized within is the Truth that pervades the whole universe. Tantra does not believe in useless physical penance and suffering. Haṭha-Yoga is incorporated in Tantra Sādhanā to maintain the physical strength and purity of human body. According to Tantra, human body is not only the abode of the Supreme, but it is the best and the only medium to realize Parama Śiva.

According to Tantra the absolute Reality is the state of neutrality produced through the union of Śiva and Śakti. However, neither Śiva by himself nor Śakti by herself is the absolute principle. They are inseparable, eternally one and indivisible. The union of Śiva and Śakti produces divine bliss and liberation in the state of neutrality and, under different conditions, the same becomes the noumenal cause of the physical existence. When Śakti gets the scope of her manifestation, she associates herself with the principles of nescience, illusion and defilement, transforms Cosmic Consciousness into the world process. But when Śakti rises to Śiva in the process of mystic introversion, their esoteric unification brings infinite bliss and absolute peace.

Spiritual discipline (*abhyāsa*) and renunciation (*vairāgya*) are the mystic processes of sublimating the different instincts (*vṛttis*).[11] In Tantra renunciation does not mean taking *saṁyāsa* and leading an ascetic life in caves and jungles. It means proper utilization of an object. Repulsion is negative attraction. When mind neither gets attracted towards any object nor becomes distracted from the world, it is the state of renunciation. To get involved in the worldly enjoyment is as bad and harmful as to become disgusted, and renounce the world. The world is the manifestation of Śiva. While performing any action one should superimpose the ideation of Śiva. One should live up to the ideals of mysticism. Son is not dear because he is son but he is dear because the Ātman is dear. To treat the different objects as the manifestation of the Supreme in the proper perspective to act and live in the world. Otherwise the constant association of mind with the physical objects will lead to the crudification of mind. Such a man goes back in the process of evolution. Thus, while doing any action man should take the ideation of Śiva. The mystic art of superimposition of cosmic ideation is called Brahmacarya Sādhanā.[12]

Brahmacarya does not mean observation of celibacy. It goes against the biological principle of human organism. Tantra does not encourage such an abnormal life wherein lies the seed of degradation.

Vairāgya and Brahmacarya Sādhanā are the necessary principles of Rāja-Yoga. Tantra believes in the inner renunciation and spiritualization of thoughts and actions. A man who observes these spiritual disciplines lives like a lotus leaf in water. Their disobedience is sure to expose one to the tortures of lower life.

Every action has its reaction. Saṁskāra is the cause of birth and death, enjoyment and suffering. Vairāgya and Brahmacarya Sādhanā are the spiritual techniques to rid oneself of the bondage of Saṁskāra. They do not allow the mind to become associated with the crude waves of physical existence. The mind of a Sādhaka always remains merged in divinity. Siddhi in Brahmacarya Sādhanā leads to Dharmamegha

Samādhi. In this the Sādhaka feels the presence of Śiva in every animate and inanimate object. The whole cosmos is filled with divine effulgence. Acquisition of the true insight into Śiva is the mark of spiritual discipline (*abhyāsa*). True mystic insight one can have only through Sādhanā. Sādhanā widens the range of feeling and leads to the freedom of consciousness. Spiritual attainment consists in inner renunciation and sublimation of all tendencies. The sublimation (*nirodha*) of tendencies (*vṛttis*) comes through spiritual discipline.[13] It is self-transcendence, not annihilation. It is life eternal.

The bondage of Self is due to Saṁskāra. It manifests itself through five miseries: Avidyā (ignorance), Asmitā (egoism), Rāga (attraction), Dveṣa (repulsion) and Abhiniveśa (willingness to live). All actions result from Saṁskāra. It is the root-cause of all modifications of citta. Mental modification ceases with the cessation of Saṁskāra. Self becomes liberated and remains ever in its divine purity and eternal freedom. Paśvācāra Sādhanā begins with the regulation of moral conduct (Yama and Niyama Sādhanā) and mental concentration. Reason cannot establish its supremacy over will and volition. According to Tantra conscious life of reason and volition is only the surface level of a wider and more expansive psychic life of man. The subconscious and the causal mind are not infra-conscious at all but are rather an expansion of Cosmic Consciousness and rooted to whole Consciousness. Human Consciousness is undivided, unlimited and whole. The real life of reason and will is rooted to whole Consciousness. Cosmic Consciousness is the source, substratum and goal of all mental processes.

Śiva is the supreme deity and godhead of Paśvācāra Sādhanā. The Paśvācara Sādhaka addresses Śiva as Paśupati. Paśupati here does not mean Lord of Animals, He stands for the Supreme Godhead which liberates man from the bondage of animality.

VĪRĀCĀRA SĀDHANĀ

Vīrācāra Sādhanā is a psycho spiritual process. Kāpālika Sādhanā and Śava Sādhanā (Sādhanā performed with a dead human body) belong to the Vīrācāra cult. Vīrācāra is an aggressive form of spirituality. This cult has been so named because the Tāntric Sādhaka of this school performs Sādhanā with a dead human body in the posture of Vīrāsana to overcome the Eight Fetters (Pāśas) and Six Enemies (Ripus). The Vīrācāra Sādhaka addresses Śiva as Vīreśvara. Śiva is the giver and bestower of all *Siddhis* and liberation.

KĀPĀLIKA SĀDHANĀ

This Sādhanā is so called because it is performed with a human skull (*kapāla*). It is performed in the dead of night in a cremation ground (*śmaśāna*) to conquer hatred (*ghṛṇā*), shame (*lajjā*) and fear (*bhaya*) along with other *vṛttis* (tendencies). It is called Kāpālika Sādhanā also because it brings absolute victory over letter *ka*, the *bīja-mantra* of expressed universe. *Ka* stands for manifest Brahman (Kārya Brahman). Kāpālika Sādhanā is based on the principles of mysticism and esotericism. It is an intuitional process to awaken the Kuṇḍalinī and rid oneself of the bondage of fetters of Māyā. The Sādhaka acquires occult powers in the course of Sādhanā.

In Kāpālika Sādhanā mind gets immediately concentrated partly due to the esoteric conditions created by the circumstances and partly because of the Mantra and use of Yantra (Mystic Diagram). The Sādhaka attains victory over the five fundamental factors (Bhūtas) by getting control over the Crude (Sthūla), Subtle (Sūkṣma), Purport (Anvaya), Real Nature (Svarūpa) and Real Significance (Arthatattva) of the Created Beings (Bhūta).[14] It leads to the acquisition of occult powers (the eight *Siddhis*) and Kāya Siddhis.[15]

Kāya Siddhi is of great spiritual significance. The physical body of the Sādhaka becomes divinized. Each and every cell of the body becomes supramentalized. It starts secreting subtler and divine waves. The physical appearance becomes lustrous (*lāvaṇya*) and glorious. The body of such a yogi becomes pure, powerful and supramental.[16]

Occult powers are not supernatural powers. They are the mystic realization of the cosmic nature of self. However, one should not run after the acquisition of occult powers. The aim of Kāpālika Sādhanā is the same as of other forms of spiritual practices, *i.e.* unification of *jīva* with Śiva.

Occult powers are detrimental to salvation.[17] One should not indulge in the pursuit of occult powers. The objective of spiritual Sādhanā is the realization of Parama Śiva, the Supreme Reality. In this state of divine realization the physical existence of man is transformed into divine being. In comparison with Samādhi (spiritual trance), occult powers are insipid, valueless and insignificant achievements. The supernatural powers of seeing, touching, hearing, tasting and smelling and the Pratīka Jñāna (divine knowledge) are Siddhis. A true yogi clings to Pratīka Jñāna and parts with the other *Siddhis*. With the acquisition of these *Siddhis*, a yogi can see the unseen, and hear the unheard sound. He can hear a person talking in the farthest corner of the world, and nothing remains hidden from him. A yogi can visualize anything and everything. He possesses the power of telepathy and clairvoyance. These powers and *Siddhis* are an aftermath of Kāpālika Sādhanā.

Tantra has been greatly scandalized due to the use of Pañcamakāra. But Tantra is based on scientific principles. It is a positive method of overcoming the strong desires for sensuous enjoyment. For a person having strong desires for physical enjoyment, Tantra prescribes the crude Pañcamakāra Sādhanā as it does not encourage suppression and repression of unfulfilled desires. Normally, man is dominated by animal desires of hunger, sleep, fear and sex (*Āhāra*, Nidrā, Bhaya and Maithuna). The dominance of such crude desires differs from man to man.

When these desires are dominant in a man he struggles for their fulfilment. Resistance on the part of such a person is an uphill task. Spiritual Sādhanā and higher values do not attract a parched up soul. Only persons who are elevated can abstain from material enjoyment and lead a spiritual life. But Tantra does not abhor material enjoyment. Suppression and repression of instincts lead to immorality. A man may suppress or repress his instincts for a short duration in the beginning but with the passage of time, a volcanic eruption is bound to occur. This was the cause of degeneration in the Buddhist monastery. Immorality and sin in the garb of yellow robe is not a sign of healthy society.

Pañcamakāra Sādhanā comprises Madya (wine), Māṁsa (meat), Matsya (fish), Mudrā (grain) and Maithuna (copulation).[18] This Sādhanā is enumerated in all Tantras of both Hindu and Buddhist provenance. 'Wine, meat, fish and parched rice as well as sexual union, this pentad of Pañcamakāra applies in the union of Śiva and Śakti.'[19]

Pañcamakāra Sādhanā is directed to gain control over the material desires. The use of the crude Pañcamakāra, according to prescribed esoteric disciplines, leads to detachment and inner purification. A man who is addicted to drinking will reduce the quantity of liquor as part of spiritual discipline. This will give him inner strength for moral control over his baser instincts. Wine is used for the release of the senses from their engrossment in their outer objects. The surface consciousness of the mind which is exposed to the shocks and attachment is temporarily suspended and the deeper, expansive, and subliminal spheres of consciousness are opened up. It enables the Sādhaka to gain control over the inner recesses, and work for the sublimation and purification of being. In Tantra Sādhanā, wine is used for the purification of mind (*citta*).[20] But it is not to be drunk in the manner suggestive of animal drinking. It leads to degradation.[21] The Supreme Lord is invoked worshipped and the dedication is sanctified by the prescribed esoteric *mantra*. The use of *mantra* includes incantation and repetition, and invocation of the presiding Deity. The Sādhaka identifies his whole being and consciousness with the Deities and *mantra* in the course of Śava Sādhanā before the use of wine. One who does not know the science of Tantra Sādhanā has no right to perform this Sādhanā. To hell he goes who dares to infringe these conditions and seeks to enjoy wine and women.[22] He is a sinner and libertine. Drinking of wine that is not sanctified is as reprehensible as rape.

One who is addicted to drinking has no sense of proportion. For him there is no meditation, no *tapas*, no worship, no *dharma*, no sense of moral activity, no prudence, no Guru, no thought of his self; he cannot be a votary of Tantra Sādhanā.[23] Such a person drinks liquor, eats meat, and indulges in sex not for true worship and dedication but for his own animal enjoyment. He may be learned in the Śāstras but indeed he is condemnable.

The subtler meaning of wine is not liquor. The mystic interpretation of the word *madya* (wine) means the hormones secreted from the pineal gland. Hormones are secreted from every endocrine gland. The hormone secreted from the pineal gland is partly controlled by the moon (*soma*), and the nectar (hormone) secreted from this gland is known as *Somadhārā* or *Somarasa.* It revitalises the different glands and gives divine bliss. Man does not have any experience of this bliss till the Kuṇḍalinī, awakened and made conscious, rises upward and drinks the pineal nectar.

"From the Mūlādhāra Cakra, the Kuṇḍalinī Śakti goes up again and again to the Brahmarandhra (pineal gland); the divine bliss issues out of this mystic unification of the Kuṇḍalinī and the Moon of Pure Consciousness. The nectar which flows from the lotus in the supreme ether above is the real wine. What is drunk otherwise is only liquor."[24] According to the Āgama Śāstra, 'wine is the *Somadhārā* or lunar ambrosia which drops from the Sahasrāra'.[25]

Māṁsa (meat) Sādhanā does not mean the eating of meat. The animal that is killed involves a moral problem, of good and bad. The real meaning of Māṁsa Sādhanā is to overcome the dualism by yoga. It means to free Consciousness from the bondage of fetters with the sword of Divine Knowledge. The Consciousness so freed is merged with the Supreme Godhead. This is the esoteric meaning of Māṁsa Sādhanā.[26] The other meaning of Māṁsa is tongue or speech. The word *Ma* means tongue. Māṁsa Sādhanā means control over speech.[27] It also means dedication of all action to the Lord *Mam.*[28]

Matsya (fish) Sādhanā means control of breath through a psycho-physical discipline like Prāṇāyāma. It symbolizes the fishes moving in the Gaṅgā and the Yamunā, *i.e.* the two currents of breath, expiration and inspiration, constantly moving in Īḍā and Piṅgalā. Eating of fish means the controlling of breath.[29] The outer meaning of Matsya Sādhanā is the controlling of the senses. The senses are brought under the control of mind and yoked to Self. This is the true eating of fish.[30] The other eating is merely hurting the creatures.

Mudrā does not mean parched rice in the mystic sense of the term. It means detachment from the evil that keeps the soul in bondage. Association with the immoral leads to bondage, with the divine to liberation. To cut off all connection with evil is Mudrā Sādhanā.[31]

The last of Pañcamakāra Sādhanā (Maithuna) has been greatly scandalized and grossly misunderstood. Tantra is based on scientific principles. It does not ignore the biological and psychological aspects of human personality. Maithuna Sādhanā (copulation with woman) is allowed in Tantra. The idea behind this is to enable the Sādhaka to control and sublimate the sex instinct. A man can do this only gradually, by practising restraint. However, the subtler esoteric meaning of Maithuna Sādhanā is the copulation of Śiva and Śakti. The woman to be waited upon is none other than the inner divine power which is lying asleep in the ordinary animal-man and is awake in the Kaula. This Kuṇḍalinī Śakti is to be awakened, served and attended to. 'The divine nectar of Spiritual Bliss that ensues on the meeting of this Divine Pair, the Supreme Śakti (Kuṇḍalinī) and the Supreme Self (Śiva), the Lord that waits above, that is real Maithuna, the final *Ma.* Anything else is only copulation.'[32] According to Tantrasāra and Yāmala the union of Śiva and Śakti is the true yoga and the joy which arises out of it is known as Supreme Bliss.[33]

A Tantra Sādhaka commonly calls his wife his Śakti or Bhairavī. Woman is called Śakti. She is also called Latā (creeper) because she clings to and depends on man as the creeper to a tree. Hence, the ritual in which woman is enjoyed is called Latā Sādhanā. Wine is called Kāraṇavāri (the causal water). Arthur Avalon writes: 'When, therefore, the Vīra eats, drinks or has sexual intercourse he does so not with the thought of himself as a separate individual satisfying his own peculiar limited wants; an animal filching as it were from nature the enjoyment he has, but thinking of himself in such enjoyment as Śiva, saying "*Śivo'ham*", "*Bhairavo'ham*". Right sexual union may, if associated with meditation and ritual, be the means of spiritual advance, though persons who take a vulgar and animal view of this function will not readily understand it.'[34]

Vīrācāra Sādhanā is a mystic process of becoming one with the Supreme Godhead. Vīrācāra Sādhaka calls himself Bhairava. The woman Sādhikā of Vīrācāra is known as Bhairavī. There are three kinds of Vīrācāra Sādhakas: Svabhāva Vīra, Vibhāva Vīra and Mantra-Siddha Vīra. The hymn to Chinnamastā from the Devīrahasya-khaṇḍa of Rudra Yāmala gives a description of the Vīra. Here Vīrācāra Sādhaka says: 'I follow the cult wherein there is enjoyment of wine, flesh and wife as also other different forms of Kula worship. In Bhairavī (the Goddess) I seek my refuge I seek my refuge. To the feet of Guru I am devoted. Bhairava am I. Śiva am I."[35]

Desire is an enemy but it can be made an ally. Tantra does not believe in the suffering and torture of the body and mind. The physical body of man is the only media through which one can attain salvation. The physical body is an expression of the Supreme Self. The manifest universe has been created by Bliss. In the copulation of man and woman the same Bliss is experienced in a lesser intensity. If it is done with a spiritual motivation and under strict esoteric discipline, the physical function is ennobled and divinized. This is called Vīrabhāva. It has been described as 'the profound pagan instinct to glorify the generative impulse with religious ritual.'[36]

Pañcamakāra Sādhanā is a psycho-spiritual process to transform the mental being into a divine being. It is scientific, positive, esoteric and mystic Sādhanā of inner progression. It makes a man pure and powerful. It gives vision and strength. The whole principle of the Pañcamakāra depends upon the ideation and intention. 'A wife is kissed with one feeling, a daughter's face with another.'[37] According to Sarvollāsa Tantra, if a man goes to a woman in the belief that by the commission of such an act he will go to hell, he is sure to go there. Also, even if the act is lawful but is done in the belief that it is unlawful, there is subjective sin. Tantra does not sanction immoral and unlawful satisfaction of carnal desires in the way it does normal eating and drinking and so forth; it demands that man should unite with Śiva-Śakti in worldly enjoyment as a step towards the supreme enjoyment (Parmānanda or Liberation). In so doing he must follow the Dharma prescribed by Śiva.[38]

Kāpālika Sādhanā is scientific but very risky. The man of *paśu-bhāva* is not initiated into this Sādhanā. If a man goes to perform Kāpālika Sādhanā with impure thoughts in his mind, he is thrown out from the *pīṭha* (the place where Sādhanā is performed in the cremation ground) with the force of Yantra (mystic diagram). Inner purification is imperative for a Kāpālika Sādhaka. Adherence to the principles of Yama and Niyama Sādhanā (Supreme Moralism) is necessary. It creates the psychological and esoteric climate in which it is like to walk on the razor's edge.

ŚAVA SĀDHANĀ

This Sādhanā is done for the unification of the Kuṇḍalinī with Parama Śiva. Performed with a dead human body at the dead of night on the New Moon day in a cremation ground, it is the most difficult form of spiritual practice. Detailed rituals have been laid down for this Sādhanā. The Sādhaka has to observe the esoteric principles very strictly. Violation of any rule or ritual results in disastrous consequences. A Mahākaula alone initiates one into Śava Sādhanā. An ordinary Guru cannot. The Guru's grace is most essential, and blessed are those who have got a Guru. This is the most secret part of Tāntric mysticism, but has been greatly misunderstood due to its non-Āryan character.

The dead body should be fresh, complete and uninjured. It should not be mutilated or deformed. No part of the body should be distorted. Even if a finger is missing, or the dead is one eyed, it is unfit for Tantra Sādhanā. It is against the principle of Tantra Śāstra.

In Śava Sādhanā, the Sādhaka sits himself on the dead body in Vīrāsana posture and starts the incantation of *mantra.* This infuses life into the dead body which starts moving. It tries to wake up. The Sādhaka also makes use of Yantra. This protects him from all sorts of allurements he is subject to. An unknown voice, Ākāśavāṇī, promises him everything. It even asks him to take anything from the world. Here the Guru protects him, and does not allow his disciple to run after the allurements. It happened with Lord Buddha also. He was given all sorts of allurements during Sādhanā, but he did not pay any attention to them and remained engrossed in meditation. Arthur Avalon says: 'By the union of Vīra and Śakti, who is a form (*ākāra*) of the Devī, direct union can be had with the latter who being pleased grants all that is desired of Her. There is thus what is technically called Pratayakṣa of Devatā whereas in Kumārīpūjā and in Śava Sādhanā the Devī speaks through, mouth of virgin or the corpse respectively. Vīras communicate with Śiva and Śakti in Avadhūtaloka.'[39]

The life-force which the incantation of *mantra* infuses into the dead body as a result of which it seemingly becomes alive is actually the life-force of the Sādhaka himself. On seeing this if the Sādhaka becomes nervous and falls within the *cakra*, meets his own death, and if he falls outside the *cakra* he becomes permanently mad. But if he holds his own and succeeds in this Sādhanā he attains Salvation. He gets all the occult powers.

In Avidyā Tantra also there is provision for Śava Sādhanā. But an Avidyā Tāntric performs Sādhanā with lower, ulterior motives. He does not attain salvation. He does get some *siddhis* but these become the cause of his degeneration.

Śava Sādhanā is mostly performed in the Mahā-Siddha-pīṭha or Siddha-pīṭha. The Mahā-Siddha-pīṭha is prevalent in Tibet, Nepal, Bengal, Assam and Bihar.

Divyācāra

Divyācāra is a purely spiritual process. It is subtle, sublime and the highest form of mysticism. Pañcamakāra Sādhanā does not mean the crude Pañcatattva. Nilmani Mukhopadhyaya has dealt with the subtle meaning of the Pañcatattva. According to him wine does not mean liquor but that intoxicating knowledge acquired by yoga of the Parabrahman which renders the worshipper senseless as regards the external world.[40] Mudrā ordinarily means gestures and postures. The world process is rhythmic. The rhythm (*chanda*) controls the different manifestations. Tantra is predominant with Mudrā. The Veda is rhythmic. Mudrā. Sādhanā means the attainment of divine knowledge. In the pericarp of the great Sahasrāra lotus Śiva, resplendent as ten million suns and comfortably cool as ten million moons, is united with the Kuṇḍalinī after her ascent from Mūlādhāra Cakra in Divyācāra Yoga. The mystic unification of Śiva and Śakti is the true yoga.[41] This is the esoteric meaning of coition (*Maithuna*) in Tantra. Arthur Avalon writes: 'This is the union on the purely Sāttvika plane which corresponds in the Rājasika plane to the union of Śiva and Śakti in the person of their worshippers. It will have been observed that here in this Divya or Sāttvika Sādhanā "wine", "woman" and so forth are really names for operations.'[42]

The realization of the identity of Self and God which is known as Śivādvaita is the purpose behind Divyācāra. 'The body is the temple of God. Jīva is Sadāsiva. Let him give up his ignorance as the offering which is thrown away and meditate with the ideation "I am He".'[43] The ideation of *I am He* is not a mental contemplation or discursive reasoning. The incantation of the *mantra* is associated with other disciplines. When this *mantra* or any other *mantra* is meditated along with full esoteric disciplines it yields the desired result.

An insect becomes a bee by the force of meditation so becomes man God by dint of spiritual trance (Samādhi).[44] The whole system of Tantra Sādhanā is based on this principle. The unification of Self with God is the central theme of Tantra Sādhanā. The esoteric unification of *jīva* and Śiva cuts asunder the key-knot (Hṛdaya-granthi) that rivets all involvements in the many strands of nature. All doubts are shorn and all actions dwindle away.[45] When a man attains this state of spiritual blessedness, all spiritual disciplines are no more incumbent. For him there is no Yama and Niyama Sādhanā. He does not need any mental concentration and Prāṇāyāma.

There are several states of being. There are many gradations of consciousness in the life of a yogi. Divyācāra is the highest form of spirituality. Divyabhāva is the supreme state of consciousness. It is called Sahajāvasthā, in which mystic oneness with Parama Śiva is attained spontaneously. The Sādhaka becomes Siddha. He bacomes God. He always remains in the state of Eternal Bliss. He is beyond body-mind consciousness. He lives in the Cosmic. He becomes totally unimpeded in his impulses, thoughts and behaviour. Such a soul is beyond moral and social imperatives. He does no wrong. He is always merged in Śiva consciousness; when engaged in action he is really inactive.

Everybody is not entitled to the highest form of Tantra Sādhanā. *Gandharva Tantra* lays down the conditions for a Sādhaka. According to it a person who is prudent (*dakṣa*), theist (*āstika*), pure (*śuci*), non-dualist (*dvaitahīna*), always engaged in doing good to all (*sarvaprāṇihiterata*), abstaining from injury to all beings (*sarva-hiṁsā-vinirmukta*), with senses controlled (*jitendriya*) and who takes refuge in God (Brahma-parāyaṇa) is competent for Tantra Sādhanā. Otherwise, he is no Sādhaka.[46] *Kulārṇava Tantra* presents a long list of qualifications necessary for a Tantra Sādhaka.[47] The person who is heretic, boastful, impotent, wicked, dry, untrue, cruel, foolish, unreliable, plagiarist, passionate, garrulous, libidinous, egoist, coward, crooked, dull, weak, afflicted, ugly, inactive, thief, rough is not entitled to Tantra Sādhanā.[48] The person chosen for Tāntric Sādhanā shall be one who is endowed with auspicious features; given to Sādhanā that leads to Samādhi; of good qualities and culture, wise, devoted to Dharma, gifted with faith and devotion.[49]

Divyācāra is a Rājādhirāja-Yoga. There is a detailed Sādhanā for the sublimation of mind and consciousness. It purifies the different cells and nerve plexuses. All the cells start emanating divine waves and vibrations. It imparts a subtle form of meditation. It leads to the realization of Parama Śiva. A Divyācāra Sādhaka addresses Śiva as Mahādeva (Lord of Lords). He is the greatest yogi. One should follow in the footprints of such a yogi. 'What the masters of yoga tread that is the supreme path; where the sun rises there is the east.'[50]

Tantra Sādhanā is a very difficult process. It is a very risky form of spiritual discipline. A Sādhaka has always to be very careful and vigilant. Success in Tantra Sādhanā brings salvation; a mistake misfortune. Madhusudan Kaul says: 'But no rose is without a thorn. Good and evil run side by side. There is nothing which has unmixed good or unmixed evil in it. The rosy path of the Tāntric is set with thorns here and there. It is, therefore, the foremost duty of the Sādhaka to avoid the thorns and adhere to the rosy path, lest he fall into the trap of the low spirits of nature, who, trying to cause mischief, puts obstacles in his way and thereby retards his progress in the attainment of his desired object. It is only the potency of the *mantras* that brings about tile subjugation of these supersensuous beings.'[51]

The path to salvation is as sharp as the edge of a razor. The *Kaṭha Upaniṣad* says: 'Arise, awake, and learn by approaching the excellent ones. The wise ones describe that path to be as impassable as a razor's edge, which, when sharpened, is difficult in tread on.'[52] The Infinite in man is like the oil in the river bed, or fire in the two pieces of wood.[53] To get oil from sesamum seeds we have to crush them, churn the curds before we can have butter, dig the ground for water, and rub the sticks hard for fire. This is Sādhanā. Till man becomes one with Parama Śiva, he has risks and dangers on the path.

Tantra Sādhanā goes into every detail of life. It weaves yoga into the day-to-day life. It gives meaning and mystic interpretation to a man's activities by making them all means for the effectuation and transformation of inner consciousness of progression from the human into the divine.

SAMĀDHI

The mystic unification of Śiva and Śakti is called Samādhi in Tantra.[54] Śiva is the transcendental reality. Śakti is the eternal principle. According to Tantra, human body is the epitome of the whole universe. Śiva resides in the pericarp of Sahasrāra Cakra. Śiva is known as Mahā-Bindu. Śakti is called Kuṇḍalinī Śakti. Her dwelling place is Mūlādhāra Cakra. When the Kuṇḍalinī rises up piercing the different Cakras, bites Amākalā and drinks the nectar contained in it, a joy issues from this esoteric coition (of Śiva and Śakti) and is called Samādhi. The Kuṇḍalinī goes up again and again and drinks the pineal nectar. Such a soul goes beyond the cycle of rebirth.[55]

Mahā-Bindu is called Parama Pada. The attainment of this divine state of transcendence is called Samādhi. The Veda says: 'The divine beings are always engaged in visualizing the Parama Pada of Viṣṇu.'[56] In Tantra this Parama Pada represents the Consciousness Force (Jñāna Śakti). It is called Śiva-Bindu. Self becomes one with this Śiva-Bindu in Sādhanā with the help of *So'haṃ* (I am He) *mantra*.[57]

Cit, Ānanda, Icchā, Jñāna and Kriyā constitute the fivefold Śakti of the Supreme Being. Salvation means the unfoldment of powers brought about by self-realization. It is not the giving up of the mortal coil. Birth and death are modes and manifestation of the creation. A yogi finds gratification in both.

A Tantra Sādhaka is called Bhairava. He is fearless, heroic and unattached to the mundane existence. He does not have any hankering for worldly desires. Even the name of such a Tāntric Sādhaka excites terror in the destructive agencies, and at whose sweet will the world lives, moves and has its being.[58] Death creates fear and awe for those who are subject to mortality. But for those who have overcome this idea by a living belief in the immortality of soul, death is insignificant and meaningless.[59]

The subjectivization of external objectivity is called empirical knowledge. Mind cannot subjectivize the Supreme Reality because it is supreme subjectivity. Tantra Sādhanā is the mystic process for transforming mind into consciousness. With the unification of Śiva and Śakti, mind is merged and dissolved into Divine Consciousness. The real knowledge issues from this mystic unification of Śiva and Śakti. It is the cause of liberation.[60]

The state of Samādhi is not death but completeness. It is the perfection of consciousness, where there is no *mala* (impurity) to obscure the vision. It is utter purity and transparency through which *Cit, Ānanda* and *Jñāna Śakti* of Parama Śiva pass and repass without let or hindrance. It is complete harmony, supreme love and divine bliss. In this all embracing consciousness, the Kuṇḍalinī and Śiva, the Finite and the Infinite are enfolded in one. It is Self-transcendence and not extinction of the life force. It is total transformation of individual (*jīva*) into cosmic Śiva. It is not abstraction but comprehension, it is not exclusion but inclusion. It is fullness of life and richness of Self. Life dies into the divine fullness.

'When the identification with the body is gone and the Supreme Self is realized. wherever the mind moves there it is Samādhi.'[61] The Self is liberated from the bondage of the guṇas. Once the Self attains illumination it never comes into bondage just as butter once extracted from milk does not, even when put back into milk, return to its original state.[62] The liberated man becomes pure and perfect. He neither hears nor smells, nor touches nor sees; he neither knows pleasure nor pain nor exercises the mind. He becomes one with Śiva. It is called Samādhi.[63] He alone is Yogi. He knows the real Yoga.

In the state of deep Samādhi the life-breath is arrested. The mind of the yogi is absorbed in the Supreme Self. Deep meditation devoid of any form is called Samādhi. The Sādhaka remains in the state of pure consciousness. There is no awareness of sense perception world. Self shines by itself and not by mental thinking. The Sādhaka remains in the state of divine transcendence. He is asleep both in the state of dream or waking. He goes beyond the dualism of subject and object. It is eternal life of divine consciousness.

Samādhi is of two kinds: (i) Savikalpa, and (ii) Nirvikalpa.

Savikalpa Samādhi

This is a state of determinate absorption. In this individual *I*-ness is transformed into *Cosmic I.*[64] In other words when the Kuṇḍalinī reaches Ājñā Cakra after piercing all the other five Cakras, the Sādhaka attains Savikalpa Samādhi. However, there are gradations of the trance of determinate absorption. They are: Sālokya, Sāmīpya, Sārūpya, Sāyujya, and Sāṣṭhi. 'I am Śiva' (Śivo'ham) is the state of Sāṣṭhi, the final state of Savikalpa Samādhi. Continuity in this state is called Mukti (Liberation).

Nirvikalpa Samādhi

It is non-qualified liberation. There is total transformation of mind into the Supreme Self. This is the unification of the Kuṇḍalinī with Parama Śiva. When the Kuṇḍalinī gets united with Parama Śiva in Sahasrāra Cakra, the mind ceases to exist. The Self is merged into Divine Consciousness. There is no trace of duality. In the state of Savikalpa Samādhi, dualism exists. *I am Śiva* or *I am Brahman*, the feeling of *I* and Śiva is there. This is not the final state of Turīya (Trance). Nirvikalpa Samādhi is the state of objectlessness.[65]

Nirvikalpa Samādhi is of two kinds: (i) Sabīja Nirvikalpa, and (ii) Nirbīja Nirvikalpa. When a Sādhaka goes into Nirvikalpa Samādhi, but due to his Saṁskāra comes back to body-mind consciousness, it is called Sabīja Nirvikalpa because the seed of Saṁskāra remains with the Sādhaka. 'The soul of such a Sādhaka is called sūtrātmā. But when the seed of Saṁskāra is burnt and there is no trace of any reactive moments, the Sādhaka attains Nirbīja Nirvikalpa. This is the final state of non-duality. It is called Mokṣa. This state of spiritual beatitude and bliss is indescribable.[66] It is beyond mental comprehension.

There are four states of human consciousness: Wakeful (*Jāgrata*), Dreamful (*Svapna*), Sleeping (*Suṣupti*) and Trance (*Turīya*).

Jāgrata, the wakeful state, is the crudest state of soul. In this the soul is called Catuṣpāda or four phasic. In Jāgrata the states of dream, sleep and trance remain in a dormant condition The witnessing Puruṣa of the wakeful individual is called Viśva and of the wakeful macrocosm Virāṭa. The dream is the second state of human consciousness. It remains latent. In this state soul does not have any connection with the objective physical world. Taijasa and Hiraṇyagarbha are the subjective counterparts of the dreamful state of microcosm and macrocosm. In the state of sleep, human consciousness enjoys a special kind of bliss. It is a state of absolute cognition. Neither the conscious nor the subconscious gets the scope of manifestation. There is absence of crude and subtle, conscious and unconscious functioning of mind. This state of dreamless mind is called *deep sleep*. However, this state is not the real state of self-sublimity or absolute identity with the Cosmic Consciousness. This state of human consciousness is called Prajñā because the seed of Supreme Knowledge lies in it.

The witnessing entity of macrocosm is called Īśvara. The last state of human consciousness is called Turīya (Trance). It is the non-dual state of mind. It is called the divine and eternal (Śīvam and Śāntam) state of human consciousness.[67] Turīya is the witnessing consciousness. It is a state of non-dual and Supreme Bliss. It is the supreme unification of Śiva and Śakti. It is called Absolute Identity (Avikalpa-Yoga) It is beyond all attributes, Language fails to describe it. In this state of Turīya subjectivity does not exist. Only through Tantra Sādhanā can this state of non-dual and Supreme Bliss be attained.

REFERENCES

1. योगश्चितवृत्ति निरोधः। *Patañjali Yoga Sūtra.*
2. *Tāntric Texts,* vol. IX, p. 60, Luzac & Co., Great Russell Street, London, 1922.
3. कुलं शक्तिः इति प्रोक्तम् अकुलम् शिव उच्यते।
कुले अकुलस्य सम्बन्धः कौलमित्यभिधीयते। *Kulārṇava Tantra,* p. 17.
4. *Hindu Sādhanā,* p. 275.
5. *Kulārṇava Tantra,* p. 147.
6. शृणु भावत्रयं देवि दिव्य-वीर-पशुक्रमात्।
दिव्यश्च देववत्प्रायो वीरश्चोद्धत-मानसः।
पशुभावः सदादेविशुद्धश्च शुचिवान् सदा। *Kālivilāsa Tantra,* 6.IV/X.
7. *Kulārṇava Tantra,* p. 30.
8. *Ibid.,* p. 30.
9. यथा जले जलं क्षिप्तं क्षीरे क्षीरं घृते घृतम्।
अविशेषो भवेत्तद्वज्जीवात्मपरमात्मनोः।।15।। *Ibid.,* p. 238.
10. तदा द्रष्टुः स्वरूपेऽवस्थानम्।।1।। *Patañjali Yoga-Sūtra.*
11. अभ्यासवैराग्याभ्यां तन्निरोधः।।1।। *Ibid.*
12. ब्रह्मैव विचरणं ब्रह्मचर्यम्।
13. *Patañjali Yoga-Sūtra,* I. XIII.
14. स्थूलस्वरूपसूक्ष्मान्वयार्थतत्त्वसंयमाद्भूतजयः। *Ibid.,* v.iii.45.
15. ततोऽणिमादिप्रादुर्भावः कायसम्पत्तद्धर्माभिघातश्च। *Ibid.,* v.iii.46.
Following are the eight Siddhis
(1) *Aṇimā* — the esoteric power to become small in size, or to become microscopic objects in full detail. (2) *Mahimā* — to expand in size or in space the intuitive power of viewing the far reaches of the universe. (3) *Laghimā* — to offset the force of gravity or make one's body lighter than air. (4) *Garimā* — the mystic power to increase one's weight, apparently increasing gravitation. (5) *Prāpti* — the power of transporting oneself anywhere, instantly, or of gaining anything by the mere act of reaching out and having it appear. (6) *Prākāmya* — the mystic power which fulfils all desires including that of becoming visible or invisible. (7) *Īśatva* — the divine power to create or nullify by thought, making things and beings appear or disappear. (8) *Vaśitva* — the power to control the different manifestations of the world, so they will act as the Yogi desires.
16. रूपलावण्यबलवज्र संहननत्वानि कायसम्पत्। *Ibid,* v.iii.47.
17. तेसमाधावुपसर्गा व्युत्थाने सिद्धये। *Ibid.,* iii. 38.
18. *Mahānirvāṇa Tantra,* p. 89.
19. मद्यं मांसं तथा मीनं मुद्रा मैथुनमेव च।
मकार-पञ्चकं सेव्यं शिव-शक्ति समागमे। *Meru Tantra.*
20. मदिरा ब्रह्मणः प्रोक्ताः चित्तशोधनसाधनाः।
तासामेकां समाहृत्य पूवाकर्म समाचरेत्।।41।। *Kulārṇava Tantra,* p. 191.
21. पशुपानं विधौ पीत्वा वीरोऽपि नरकं व्रजेत्।।93।। *Ibid.,* p. 196,
22. असंस्कृतं पिबेद्द्रव्यं बलात्कारेण मैथुनम्।
स्वप्रियेण हतं मांसं रौरवनरकं व्रजेत्।।99।। *Ibid.,* p. 197.
23. मदप्रच्छादितात्मा च न किञ्चिदपि वेत्ति च।
न ध्यानं न तपो नार्चां न धर्मं न च सत्क्रियाम्।।102।।

न देवं न गुरुनात्मविचारो न स कौलिकः।
केवलं विषयासक्तः पतत्येव न संशयः।। 103 ।। *Ibid.*

24. आमूलाधारमाब्रह्मरन्ध्रं गत्वा पुनः पुनः।
चिच्चन्द्रकुण्डलीशक्तिसामरस्यः सुखोदयः।। 106 ।।
व्योमपङ्कजनिस्यन्दसुधापानरतो नरः।
सुधापानमिदं प्रोक्तमितरे मदपायिनः।। 108 ।। *Ibid.*, p 198.
25. *Śakti and Śākta*, p. 606.
26. पुण्यापुण्यपशुं हत्वा ज्ञानखड्गेन योगवित्।
परे लयं नयेच्चित्तं पलाशी स निगद्यते।। 109 ।। *Ibid.*
27. *Cosmic Society — An Anthology*, p. 142.
28. *Ibid.*; *Kulārṇava Tantra*, p. 53.
29. *Kulārṇava Tantra.*
30. मनसा चेन्द्रियगणं संयम्यात्मनि योजयेत्।
मत्स्याशी स भवेद्देवि शेषाः स्युः प्राणिहिंसकाः।। 110 ।।
Kulārṇava Tantra, p. 53; *Cosmic Society — An Anthology*, p. 142.
31. सत्संगेन भवेन्मुक्तिः सत्संगेषु च बन्धनम्।
असत्संगमुद्रणं यत् तन्मुद्रा परिकीर्तिता।।
Tantra and Sādhanā; Cosmic Society — An Anthology, p. 143.
32. पराशक्त्यात्ममिथुनसंयोगानन्दनिर्भरः।
य आस्ते मैथुनं तत् स्यादपरेस्त्रीनिषेवकाः।। 112 ।। *Kulārṇava Tantra*, p. 198.
33. *Śakti and Śākta*, p. 607.
34. *Ibid.*, p. 628-29.
35. अलिपिशितपुरन्ध्री-भोग पूजापरोऽहम्।
बहुविधिकुलमार्गारम्भ-सम्भावितोऽहम्।
पशुजनविमुखोऽहम् भैरवीम् आश्रितोऽहम्।
गुरुचरणरतोऽहम् भैरवोऽहम् शिवोऽहम्। *Śakti and Śākta*, Rudra Yāmala, p. 598.
36. *Times Literary Supplement*, June 11, 1922.
37. भावेन चुम्बिता कान्ता, भावेन दुहिताननम्। *Śakti and Śākta*, p. 643.
38. *Ibid.*, p. 644.
39. *Śakti and Śākta*, p. 623.
40. Nilmani Mukhopadhyaya, *Pañcatattva-Vicāra*, p. 85.
41. शिवशक्तिसमायोगो योग एव न संशयः। *Śakti and Śākta*, p. 607.
42. *Ibid.*, p. 607.
43. देहो देवालयोदेवि जीवो देवः सदाशिवः।
तेनज्ञाननिर्माल्यं सोऽहम्भावेन पूजयेत्।। 41 ।। *Kulārṇava Tantra*, p. 241.
44. यथा ध्यानस्थ सामर्थ्यात् कीटोऽपि भ्रमरायते।
तथा समाधिसामर्थ्याद्ब्रह्मभूतो भवेन्नरः।। 16 ।। *Ibid.*, p. 238.
45. भिद्यतेहृदयग्रन्थिश्छिद्यन्ते सर्वसंशयाः।
क्षीयन्ते चास्य कर्माणि तस्मिन् दृष्टौ परात्मनि।। 24 ।। *Ibid.*, p. 239.
46. सोऽस्मिन् शास्त्रेऽधिकारी तद् अन्यत्र न साधकः। *Gandharva Tantra*, Ch. II.
47. *Kulārṇava Tantra*, Ch. XIII.
48. *Ibid.*, pp. 293-94.
49. सच्छिष्यन्तु कुलेनिष्ठं शुभलक्षणसंयुतम्।

समाधिसाधनोपेतं गुणशीलसमन्वितम्।। 23।। *Ibid.*, p. 295.

50. यस्मिंश्चरन्ति योगीशाः स मार्गः परमो मतः।
यस्यामुदेति सूर्यो हि पूर्वाशा सा निगद्यते।। 80।। *Ibid.*, p. 245

51. *Śrī Mālinvijayottara Tantram*, pp. xii-xiii.

52. उत्तिष्ठत जाग्रत प्राप्य वरान्निबोधत।
क्षुरस्य धारा निशिता दुरत्यया दुर्गं पथस्तत्कवयो वदन्ति।। 14।। — I. iii.14.

53. *Śvetāśvatara Upaniṣad*, i. 15.

54. शिवशक्तिसमायोगो यस्मिन् काले प्रजायते।
सा सन्ध्या कुलनिष्ठानां समाधिः स विधीयते। *Kulārṇava Tantra*, p. 236.

55. पीत्वा पीत्वा पुनः पीत्वा यावत् पतति भूतले।
उत्थाय च पुनः पीत्वा पुनर्जन्म न विद्यते। *Ibid.*, p. 222.

56. तद् विष्णोः परमं पदं सदा पश्यन्ति सूरयः दिवीव चक्षुराततम्। *Śruti.*

57. शिवबिन्दुसमाकारमात्मानमनुचिन्तयेत्।
ततोऽस्य योजयेच्छक्तिं सोऽहमित्यपरातित।। 20।। *Śri Mālinīvijayottara Tantram*, p. 42.

58. *Ibid.*, p. x.

59. मोक्षो हि नाम नैवान्यः स्वरूपप्रथने हि सः।
स्वरूपंचात्मनः संविन्नान्यत्र तु या पुनः।। 156।। *Tantrāloka.* vol. I, p. 192.

60. ज्ञानं मोक्षककारणम्। *Ibid.*

61. देहाभिमाने गलिते विज्ञाते परमात्मनि
यत्र यत्र मनो भाति तत्र तत्र समाधय।। 23।। *Kulārṇava Tantra*, p. 239

62. *Ibid.*

63. न शृणोति न चाघ्राति न स्पृशति न पश्यति
न जानाति सुखं-दुखं न सङ्कल्पयते मनः।। 13।।
न चापि किञ्चिज्जानाति न च बुध्यति काष्ठवत्।
एवं शिवे विलीनात्मा समाधिस्थ इहोच्यते।। 14।। *Ibid.*, p. 238.

64. भूमाव्याप्ते महति अहंचित्तयोः प्रणाशे
सगुणा स्थितिः सविकल्पसमाधिः वा। *Ānandā Sūtram*, vv. 1, 21, p. 17.

65. आत्मनि महत् प्रणाशे निर्गुणास्थितिः निर्विकल्पसमाधिः वा। *Ibid.*, vv. 1, 22, p. 18.

66. तस्यस्थिति रमानसिकेषु। *Ibid.*, vv. 1, 23.

67. एष सर्वेश्वर एष सर्वज्ञ एषोऽन्तर्याम्येषः। *Śruti.*

JĀGRATA
(Wakefulness)

- Microcosm
  - Individuality Witnessing Entity
    - Sthūlāvasthā (Crude State)
    - Viśva (The subjective counterpart of unit Casual Mind)
- Macrocosm
  - Collectivity Witnessing Entity
    - Kṣīrābdhi (The Sea of Milk)
    - Virāṭa or Vaiśvānara (The subjective counterpart of causal Cosmic Mind)

SVAPNA
(Dream)

- Microcosm
  - Individuality Witnessing Entity
    - Sūkṣmāvasthā (Subtle State)
    - Taijasa (The subjective counterpart of subtle Unit Mind)
- Macrocosm
  - Collectivity Witnessing Entity
    - Garbhodaka (The Fluid of Creation)
    - Hiraṇyagarbha (The subjective counterpart of subtle Cosmic Mind)

SUṢUPTI
(Sleep)

- Microcosm
  - Individuality Witnessing Entity
    - Kāraṇāvasthā (Causal State)
    - Prajñā (The subjective counterpart of crude Unit Mind)
- Macrocosm
  - Collectivity Witnessing Entity
    - Kāraṇārṇava (The Sea of Causes)
    - Īśvara or Sūtreśvara (The subjective counterpart of Crude Cosmic Mind)

TURĪYA
(Trance)

Īśvaragrāsa
(Cosmic Doom)

(Taken from *Subhāṣita Saṁgraha*)

10 Tantra and Science

Tantra is an intuitional science. Far from being a subjective fancy, it is a science which unveils the mystery of mind and nature, and takes man to the realization of Reality. Parama Śiva is the Absolute. According to Tantra, Parama Śiva is the Supreme Reality and the manifest world is the relative truth. 'Brahma is truth, *i.e.*, Unchangeable. But we cannot say that the changes that are perceived apparently on the Body of Brahma under the influence of Prakṛti and the three fundamental relative factors like time, space and person are false; nor can we say that they are the eternal truths. All that we can say is that they are relative truths, for the apparent changes are dependent on the relativity of these three factors, *viz.* time, space and person.'[1]

There are two extreme views regarding Reality. According to the Parmenedian view the Reality is altogether unchanging and if there is any visible change, it is illusory. On the other hand Heraclitus treats change as the essence of Reality. For him, permanence is illusory. Zeno, a Greek philosopher of Elea (early fifth century B.C.), proves the unreality of change. He gives an example of an arrow in its flight. The arrow is either where it is or it is where it is not. If it is where it is, it cannot be moving. The same argument applies to any other point or moment in the flight of the arrow. At no point or moment does the arrow move and, therefore, its apparent movement is an illusion. Such arguments are advanced to demonstrate the irrationality and untenability of our ordinary conceptions of change, time and space.

Recently Einstein and others have radically changed the Space and Time concept. According to them Space and Time are not absolute and independent but relative and inter- dependent. Time cannot be measured without space and the observation, or measurement of Space, involves Time. They are thus inseparable, and taken together they give rise to the conception of a four dimensional Space and Time. Minkowski says: 'The views of time and space, which I have set forth, have their foundation in experimental physics. Therein is their strength. Their tendency is revolutionary. From henceforth space in itself and time in itself sink to mere shadows, and only a kind of union of the two preserves an independent existence.'[2]

In the relativist's conception the distance between two points must be measured in four dimensions of which one is Time. They prefer to use the four dimensional cone in which we are living. The axis of the cone is Time and the generatrix is the path traced by a beam of light. This statement is subjective fancy for the layman but when it is analysed with the help of mathematics, it solves many empirical problems.

The four dimensional theory needs certain changes and modifications. In the present form it is insufficient and untenable. The relativists overemphasize the material aspects of Space and Time. They do not give due place to *Mind* without which *Time* and *Space* together sink to mere illusion. *Time, Space* and *Person* constitute the relative world. When taken collectively, they preserve an independent existence. In our view *Time* cannot be the axis of the four dimensional cone. The relativists suffer from the faulty Kantian notion of Time and Space as *a priori* categories. The acceptance of the Kantian view of *a priori* will lead to the naive realist's world of make-believe.

The Tāntric conception of the Absolute, Bindu, Nada and Kāla is most scientific. According to Euclid's definition, 'That which has position but no magnitude is called a point'. The Tāntric exposition of *point* is not only a discovery of nature but of truth. Bindu is a colourless (*āvarṇa*) and formless (*arūpa*) entity. Euclid has defined a line as 'that which has position and length but neither breadth nor thickness'. A line which lies evenly between points on it is called a straight line. Euclid's definition was further modified by Leonhard Enter and J. L.Lagrange. According to the new definition, 'a straight line becomes the shortest distance between two points'. But this new definition poses a serious problem as it does not conform to the *flat space* of Euclid. According to this view every straight line becomes an arc of a great circle. Einstein tries to solve this problem by his historical definition, 'A straight line is the path of a beam of light'. This definition needs certain modifications. Light is an energy. It requires certain medium to manifest. Energy is always material. The medium stands as an obstruction in the path of a beam of light to travel in a straight line. There cannot be any straight line in the world of relativity. The Tāntric concept of Bindu and Nāda solves this problem. According to Tantra a straight line is that which has an infinite or zero wavelength. There is no spiritual difference between zero and infinite. The wave of Pure Consciousness, *i.e.* Parama Śiva, alone travels in a straight line. Parama Śiva is one without a second. The wavelength of Pure Consciousness is zero or infinite. It is not the beam of light but the Divine effulgence which travels in a straight line. We can have the genuine conception or realization of a straight line, zero and infinite in the realm of intuition. We cannot draw any straight line in the world of relativity. Einstein had to be satisfied with the beam of light because in the world of objectivity light has the highest velocity. But it does not have the absolute velocity. Parama Śiva is the only entity which has absolute speed and absolute pause. This apparent contradiction does not pose any problem as there is no difference between absolute speed and absolute pause which is the nature of Pure Consciousness. Parama Śiva is the ultimate source of energy and life. Parama Śiva alone possesses luminosity. It is intrinsic to Him. No other objects have the light of their own. For the luminosity that does not exist naturally cannot impart it to others. A pot does not illumine others, whereas the luminous things like the sun, etc., are seen to do so. The Absolute alone is the ultimate source of light, life and base of existence. Everything has emerged from it. 'That the same Brahman is known from His external signs from whom the whole universe has sprung, in Whom when so sprung it exists, and into Whom all things return.'[3] The Absolute does not come within the scope of our perception and conception because It has either no dimension or infinite dimensions.

The relativistic concept of Matter, Space and Time is the foundation-stone of modern science. However, there is a missing link in the theory of relativistic conception of the world and reality. The relativist thinkers have not given due importance to a 'thinking man' or 'Person'. The existence of the whole relativistic world is thwarted in the absence of the thinking mind. 'Time is neither the ultimate category of existence nor the axis of the four-dimensional cone. It is a mental measurement of any action.'[4] One cannot think of Space and Time without a thinking mind. No observation of Space and Time is possible without 'Person'. A.C. Wellington says: 'We decide that time is relative to an observer; that is to say, we admit that an observer on another star, who carries out all the rest of the operations and calculations as specified in our definition, is also measuring time — not our time, but a time relative to himself.'[5]

Let us take the case of Person. Suppose there is a table before us. An engineer will describe it in terms of square feet and usefulness. And one of us, who is interested in aesthetics, will describe it as 'beautiful' or 'ugly'. In this way, one of us will add the dimension of 'usefulness' and another of 'thickness', etc. All our perceptions are coloured according to our Saṁskāra. In our day-to-day life what appears to be 'green' to Mr. *X* may not originally be green. It may be 'red'. That is why the knowledge of the Real is not possible unless one gets rid of his Saṁskāra. Only after the exhaustion of Saṁskāra the knowledge of the Real is possible. Tantra provides the spiritual Sādhanā which burns the very seed of Saṁskāra and leads to the mystic realization of the Truth.

The relativistic concept has further thrown new light on the problem of perception. We know that Lord Buddha was born in India two thousand five hundred years ago. For us it is an event of remote past. But suppose the light-wave takes four thousand years to travel to planet *X* from earth. Let us suppose that planet *X* has human habitation. In that case, for the people of planet *X* Lord Buddha is yet to be born on earth. On the other hand if the light-wave takes two thousand five hundred years to reach some other planet *Y*, the people of that planet will be seeing Lord Buddha preaching his sermons among his disciples at Sarnath!

The visible world is nothing but a pattern of waves, which collectively impress upon the sensory-cum-mental plate. We discover these sensible and ultra-sensible subtle elements (*tanmātra*) by the vibrations emanating from human actions or from objects. Actually, these vibrations are the characteristic essence of an act or body. We perceive the form which our mental plate has. Kant also contends that things-in-themselves are an indisputed source of sensations. The things-in-themselves are the thought-projection of the Cosmic Mind.

What is the ultimate Reality? Is the Reality atoms and molecules, or something else of which these atoms are the different manifestations? The difference between a spiritualist and an objective thinker is based on the nature of Reality. The objective thinker holds the belief that Reality is crude matter of which mind is a chemical reaction. Due to the clash and cohesion in the material structure, consciousness has emerged. Hence, it is an epiphenomenon. We do agree with the materialist that mind is a by-product of matter but how it is possible for this mother-matter to beget the child mind without the conception of Spirit? We know nothing can come out of nothing. Hence, the matter is not devoid of consciousness. Indeed matter is nothing but a crude manifestation of Spirit. Einstein made a radical change in the concept of matter. His $E=mc^2$ made a historical departure from the traditional definition of matter. Matter is not a dead, inert substance which occupies some space. It is bottled up energy. To the spiritualist, energy is the crude manifestation of Consciousness. Consciousness is the Supreme Reality. All other objects and beings are metamorphosed forms of Consciousness. Parama Śiva is the Supreme Reality. He is the Supreme Subjectivity. All other subjectivities or objectivities are mere blendings of the Supreme Consciousness.

Tantra binds individual ends and values. The highest end is the realization of the Eternal, Unchanging and Universal Principle. Values change with human evolution. They are embedded in the relative and finite things, ideas and values. They change with the change in time, space and person. Values and moral norms are not eternal principles. They are subordinate to the spiritual end. The unification of Śiva and Śakti is the goal of life. The realization of Parama Śiva is the spiritual end of moral life. The principles of Tantra Sādhanā are based on para-science and mysticism. According to Tantra man and universe are the modes and manifestation of Parama Śiva. There is a spiritual nisus in man to realize the Transcendence in his own being by awakening the dormant Divinity. The evolution and elevation of human consciousness is the manifestation of the divine in man and nature. Tantra Sādhanā accelerates the process of evolution. It awakens the dormant Divinity and brings to the individual the realization of Total Consciousness.

Further, Tantra does not ignore the social and biological ends of man, namely, Wealth (*Artha*), Desire (*Kāma*) and Virtue (*Dharma*). The attitude of Tantra is scientific. It approaches the different problems with a settled resolve to experiment with the spiritual truth. Verification is essential. The truth and the validity of Tantra Sādhanā are to be verified in the course of intuitional experience. Mantra is efficacious, Yantra is potent and the Kuṇḍalinī is a Divine Force. Mantra, Yantra and Kuṇḍalinī Sādhanā lead to higher and higher levels of perfection, till one becomes perfect Being-Consciousness-Bliss. Sādhanā establishes one's rapport with the divine ideation from which the universe originates and in which it subsists. The Sādhaka becomes one with the Cosmic Consciousness by meditation, devotion and self purification.

Tantra is a science of psychic power. It is a process of transformation and sublimation of the vital force into consciousness. The vital energy can be transformed into so many energies. When we talk we convert the vital energy into sound energy. We transform the vital energy into mechanical energy. Similarly, the vital energy can be transformed into heat energy, electrical energy or some other energy. Suppose a man wants to see from here (India) what his friend in New York is doing at such and such time. In that case he will have to transform his vital energy into psychic energy, and after expanding the projection of his psychic power, he will *see.* We call this occultism. Every man has this power. It is only a question of development. However, it is not general, but it is not supernatural. Tantra provide a spiritual process to study and acquire those occult powers with the help of yogic practices. This aspect of human life and consciousness does not come within the purview of material science. The English word 'science' is used as a short term for natural science, though the nearest German equivalent, Wissenschaft, still includes all systematic study, not only of what we call science, but also of history, psychology and philosophy. The word 'science' derived from Latin *scientia* (scire, to learn, to know) means learning or knowledge. Science means an ordered knowledge of natural phenomena and the rational study of the relations between the concepts in which these phenomena are expressed. According to the Theory of Relativity we observe 'relations', and these relations are the causal connections between the physical concepts.[6] The world of naive realists has been destroyed. The physicists belonging to the old school assumed that they perceived objects directly. The Quantum Theory says substance vanishes. According to this school man experiences probabilities. Future probabilities can be determined though the knowledge about the future observation is indeterminate. The whole fate of future events and observation is beyond the ken of determinism. However, betting in favour of a particular event may be so high that it comes to a mathematical certainty. Science will have to depend on the laws of chance for making any prediction about the future.

Our world consists of 'waves' of Quantum and 'curvatures' of Relativity. The 'waves' and 'curvatures' have become the laws of nature. These laws of nature are subjective laws which have been developed out of the subjective aspect of physical knowledge.[7]

Ultimate Cause Beyond Science

Logic, Mathematics and Physics are the discoveries of human ingenuity to formulate in compact and manageable form what we already know. But we cannot achieve complete success because science is essentially mechanical and deterministic. It deals with the 'parts' and does not encompass the 'whole'. With its analytical method it discloses certain aspects of the Reality, draws plans, diagrams and sketches for a model of nature. With axioms, assumptions and definitions, science gives a differential view of the Cosmos. The greatest beauty of the scientific world is that the more advancement it makes, the larger becomes the surface of contact with the unknown. Physicists, who deal with the ultimate concepts, are conscious of this outer darkness and their limitations. Science derives and formulates conclusions from effect to cause. But what is the Ultimate Cause is beyond the domain of science. Newton says: 'The business of Natural Philosophy is to argue from Phenomena . . . and to deduce causes from effects, till we come to the very first cause, which certainly is not mechanical.'[8] The mechanical and deterministic approach of science cannot lead us to the realization of Reality. Dampier says: 'In electron wave groups and quanta of action we reach ideas which certainly are not mechanical. We are to give up the familiar conceptual mechanism which, for two hundred and fifty years, has interpreted the structure of the natural world with such marvellous success..... But now or later, intelligible mechanism will fail and we shall be left face to face with the awful mystery which is reality.'[9]

In spite of the limitation, ignorance and folly, science is becoming increasingly important and the measuring rod of standard and certitude. However, it is shifting its field of operation and interest. It is passing from mechanics to physics, from physics to biology and from biology to psychology and is slowly but surely adapting itself to the unfamiliar world. None but scientists themselves are aware of the power and limitations of science. The concepts of science are mere symbols and not Reality itself. Eddington says: 'The symbolic nature of the entities of physics is generally recognized, and the scheme of physics is now formulated in such a way as to make it almost self evident that it is a partial aspect of something wider . . . . The problem of the scientific world is part of a broader problem—the problem of all experience. We all know that there are regions of the human spirit untrammelled by the world of physics. In the expression of art, in a yearning towards God, the soul grows upward and finds the fulfilment of something implanted in its nature. Whether in the intellectual pursuits of science or in the mystic pursuits of spirit, the light beckons ahead and the purpose surging in our nature responds.'[10] The symbolism of science offers a model of nature. With the astounding success of science we are led to believe that Reality is something like the model; but the fact remains that it is a model, which can be seen and utilized in part. Man is not a material being. We judge his whole being from the materialistic point of view. Judging purely from the mechanical point of view, he is a machine, dead and inert. If he is seen and examined spiritually, he is a rational mind and a living soul. Science cannot bound the spirit of man with the trammels of axioms, laws and formulas. He is free to approach the Divine. Tantra leads man from Relativity to the Absolute. It rids man of the Time and Space bondage and takes him to the world of Pure Being and Consciousness which he *is* in essence and reality. Tantra keeps divinity in organic contact with the whole of life. 'The mystics find the basis of their method not in logic but in life: in the existence of a discoverable "real" a spark of true being, within the seeking subject, which can, in that ineffable experience which they call the "act of union", fuse itself with and thus apprehend the reality of the sought object.'[11] Mysticism is the science of ultimate realities. It is the science of self-evident Reality, which cannot be reasoned about because it is the object of pure reason or perception.[12] The mysticism of Tantra is founded on the impregnable rock of intuitive experience. In the mystic exultation, the Sādhaka lives and moves and has his being in Parama Śiva. Religion needs rituals, dogmas, theology and mythology to clothe its vision and experience. But religion based on theology and mythology is bound to fall and fail. Spirituality, mysticism and intuition do not fall with the fall of any set of theories and denominal doctrines. Doctrinal theology is badly exposed to historical, anthropological, philosophic and scientific criticism, and religion has fared badly in such an encounter. Tantra is not an institutionalized religion. It is a way of life. The intuitive experience of the Divine is normal, real and perpetual as the breath of life. It is 'ineffable' and of 'noetic quality'.[13] For those who attain the mystic unification of their selves with Śiva, it is not necessary to define this state of Bliss and Consciousness. The arousal of the Kuṇḍalinī means the awakening within the self of a new and embryonic consciousness. It is opposed and different from the awareness of the illusory sense-perception, the world in which mind is immersed. Evelyn Underhill says: 'All man's dreams and diagrams concerning a transcendent Perfection near Him yet intangible, a transcendent vitality to which he can attain —whether he calls these objects of desire God, grace, being, spirit, beauty, "pure idea"— are but translation of his deeper self's intuition of its destiny. This supernal thing, the adorable substance of all that is the synthesis of Wisdom, Power, and Love, and man's apprehension of it, his slow remaking in its interest, his union with it at last; this is the theme of mysticism . . . . It is also the crown of human evolution, the fulfilment of life, the liberation of personality from the world of appearance, its entrance into the free creative life of the Real.'[14] Science must admit the psychological validity of mystic experience. The intuitive apprehension of Parama Śiva is as real as the perception of the external world.

Śiva (Pure Consciousness) is not different from an individual Self. The contact of Pure Intelligence with ignorance (*mala*) gives rise to Avidyā. Man forgets his identity with Self. This lost unity cannot be regained by any objective method. One will have to subjectivize oneself to see that the Divine Self is already within us. The subjective method of Tantra Sādhanā is a psychological approach to cut one's false attachments, involvements and infatuations. The psychological presentation of the opposite takes away the strong attachment to the objects of sense pleasure, and one's libido, in the Jungian sense, is turned inward to seek the permanent and eternal source of unmixed happiness.

Ego is the cause of split. It knows the things as objects. It sees the eternal source — the Self—as an object or as a state of consciousness. The Self is the supreme Subjectivity. It is not the object of mind. It cannot be seen and realized unless the *I*-ness is dissolved. With the dissolution of *I*-ness man attains his lost unity. In ceasing to see, he really sees. With the advancement of scientific researches, psychology and physics are coming closer to each other. The traditional concepts of both are being replaced by new concepts capable of greater accuracy. Matter and motion of physics have failed to explain the intricate problems of life and existence. So have 'perception' and 'consciousness' with which psychology was content, until very recently.

For a common man 'perception' does not create any problem. It is a perfectly straightforward mental process. However, much an analytical study of the perceptual process may lead us to a conclusion, the object of perception remains a mystery to be solved. When we perceive the sun, there are many factors to be reckoned. There are ninety three million miles of intervening space, the sympathetic vibrations created in the optical nerves, the retina, the brain, etc. The image or the forms created in the mind have no resemblance to the sun itself. The object of perception is like Kant's things-in-themselves. It remains outside our experience. To have an idea of the object of perception, we must have the necessary knowledge of physics and the physiology of the sense organs. We must know what is in the intervening space — between the sense organ and the object. Having all this exhaustive information, and assuming the objective existence of the Reality, we can form some highly abstract concept about the object perceived. The certitude and immediacy of the perception is vanished in this mathematical formulation of the inference.

The word 'consciousness' is very difficult to define in psychological terms. We say we are conscious beings and that is why we are different from sticks and stones. According to psychology we are conscious when we are awake but not when we are asleep. Russell says: 'When we say we are "conscious", we mean two things: on the one hand, that we react in a certain way to our environment; on the other, that we seem to find, on looking within, some quality in our thoughts and feelings which we do not find in inanimate objects.'[15] The notion of consciousness is linked with introspection. The seeing is closely connected with memory. To see does not mean to know unless the process of perception is coordinated. The coordinated perception is concept. But the coordination is possible only in the state of introspection. What the modern psychology meant by consciousness is very difficult to define.

The world of physicists and psychologists has assumed some new dimensions, The unbridgeable gap between the body and the mind no longer exists. The matter has lost its medieval solidity and the mind is divested of its spiritual character. The data of physics are no longer hundred per cent objective and of psychology are personal and subjective. 'This difference, however, is only one of degree. No two people can perceive exactly the same object at the same time, because the difference in their points of view makes some difference to what they see. The data of physics, when closely examined, are seen to have the same kind of privacy as those of psychology . . . . The facts which form the starting point of the two sciences are, at least in part, identical. The patch of colour that we see is a datum for physics and psychology equally.'[16]

Of all the branches of science, psychology is still backward. The problems of perception and consciousness are becoming more complex and enigmatic with the advancement of knowledge. There is a growing awareness amongst the scientists about the limitation of intellect and reason. Sir J. Arthur Thomson says: 'Science as science never asks the question why? That is to say, it never inquires into the meaning, or significance, or purpose of this manifold Being, Becoming, and Having Been . . .. Thus science does not pretend to be a bedrock of truth.'[17] Sir Arthur Eddington and Sir James Jeans have aroused scientists and objective thinkers from their dogmatic slumber. The two scientists agree that the theories and concepts of contemporary physics are tending in the direction of idealism. According to Eddington 'the idealistic tinge' in his conception of the physical world 'arose out of mathematical researches on the relativity theory'.[18] The Mysterious Universe of Sir James Jeans has provoked scientists and philosophers equally. According to him the greatest achievement of the twentieth century physics consists in the general recognition that man is not yet in contact with the ultimate Reality. He writes: 'We are still imprisoned in our cave, with our backs to the light, and can only watch the shadows on the wall.' This leads us to believe that the Reality is exposed to 'intuition' alone. Scientific methods are not applicable to the mystical and spiritual realms. In the words of Malinowski, 'religious revelation is an experience which, as a matter of principle, lies beyond the domain of science'.[19] Sir James Jeans has used Plato's famous simile of the cave. His contention is that man is imprisoned in an alien world. From the above proposition it follows that what he knows is appearance and not the reality. According to him we may assume the 'objective realities exist' on the ground that 'certain things affect your consciousness and mind in the same way'.[20] But such assumptions are not correct. When we say these 'things' are 'real' or 'ideal' it is going too far in our assertion. The proper word is 'mathematical' which connotes the whole of pure thought. According to him there is a 'mysterious world outside ourselves which our minds can never penetrate'.

Intuitional Sādhanā the Answer

We agree with Sir James Jeans' view that there is a 'mysterious world outside ourselves' but we differ from him that it is unknowable. The Reality is unknown but it is knowable. And Tantra provides the intuitional Sādhanā which leads one to the experience of the Reality. It is Truth which makes man free. Ignorance is bondage. Man is profoundly ignorant about his real nature and being. The mystic process of Tantra awakens the dormant Divinity in him. Man attains emancipation. But the mystic illumination cannot be achieved artificially. The scientific study of Tantra throws some new light on the mystic illumination. Tantra Sādhanā is a mystical process of arriving at Truth. What we know about the outer world is vague and incomplete. The knowledge (of the outer world) reaches the sense organs through the framework of space and time which are not the realities but the mental framework of our own creation. The knowledge which comes through the gateway of retina is appearance and not reality. Mysticism alone can integrate man with Reality. The mystic builds on the intuitional experience the superstructure of Divine Life.

Bertrand Russell admits the emotional and spiritual validity of mystic experiences. He writes: 'The mystic emotion, if it is freed from unwarranted beliefs, and is not so overwhelming as to remove a man wholly from the ordinary business of life, may give something of very great value — the same kind of thing, though in a heightened form, that is given by contemplation. Breath and calm and profundity may all have their source in this evolution, in which, for the moment, all self centred desire is dead, and the mind becomes a mirror for the vastness of the universe.'[21]

Physicists have explained the world of atoms and molecules and the biologists have given explanations of the evolution of life. However, with all the spectacular advancement of science and technology, man remains an enigma to man. Science has utterly failed to explain the *total man* through whom we can resolve the mysteries of universe. But Tantra has made this *total man* the object of its study. 'Man has got both an outward exterior which is comprised of his physical body, his brain, his mind and an inward self which functions intuitionally rather than emotionally and which may be termed as Supreme Consciousness. Science has studied the first part of it but it has done very little to study scientifically the latter part, that is, the inner self and the Supreme Consciousness or Soul with which one is supposed to obtain the key to the universe. A state like this is claimed to be produced in a Yogi when he enters into Samādhi, that is, in deep meditation.'[22]

Physics does not give a complete picture of the Reality. It does not represent the real truth about the familiar world. Study of man is the most neglected branch of knowledge. Eddington observes in his famous paper, 'The Domain of Physical Science', that 'physics does in practice give preference to the view of the microbe over that of the man'.[23] Limitations of science must be borne in mind when attempting to evaluate the domain of physical science.

In the ultimate analysis of the subject we come to the conclusion that Tantra and Science are not hostile to each other. They have the same ultimate objectives in view, but the methods are radically different. Science is analytical and objective, Tantra is intuitive and subjective. Tantra is based on mysticism and intuition. A yogi attains the ultimate Truth by the intuitional practice of awakening the Kuṇḍalinī. And when the Kuṇḍalinī is awakened and reaches Sahasrāra Cakra (the pineal gland), the Yogi has the vision of the Absolute. The scientific study of the pineal gland has thrown new light on the psychological and biological functions of human life. It is a coordinating principle in psychological and biological processes in human life and its advancement. Dr. P.K. Kymal says: 'A new compound, melatonin, has been identified from the pineal gland which has a blanching effect on amphibian skin. Biochemically the compound is a methoxylated indole requiring a methyl group attached to an oxygen atom for its biological activity. The pineal contains all the biochemical machinery needed to make this compound from an amino acid precursor, which is obtained from the blood stream. As far as is known, the enzyme system necessary for the formation of the compound is found only in the pineal.'[24] In Tantra the hormones secreted from the pineal gland (Sahasrāra Cakra) is called nectar. The Kuṇḍalinī is awakened by the Tāntric yogi to drink the pineal nectar which ofers eternal blessedness to the mankind. 'The beautiful Kuṇḍalinī drinks the excellent red nectar issuing from Parama Śiva, and returns from there where shines Eternal and Transcendent Bliss in all its glory along the path of Kula and again enters the Mūlādhāra.'[25] All the yogis who have attained this spiritual height have gained similar experience whereas the scientists are discarding the old concepts and ideas and are in search for new truths. We cannot fathom the true nature of man through science, its analytical methods notwithstanding. It has utterly failed to explain the intuitive experience of a yogi, to whom, on attaining Samādhi, everything — present, past and future— becomes clear and for whom the concept of time and space continuum vanishes. In this state of mystic experience, he is raised to an entirely new sphere of consciousness.

REFERENCES

1. ब्रह्म सत्यं जगदपि सत्यमापेक्षिकम्। *Ānanda Sūtram*, vv. 11, 14, p. 27.
2. Raum and Zeit, Physik, Zeitschrift, vol. X, p. 104. Werke vol. 2, p. 43.
3. *Mahānirvāṇa Tantra,* ch. III, ver. 9, p. 32.
4. *Subhāṣita Saṁgraha.*
5. *The Mathematical Theory of Relativity,* pp. 4-5, Cambridge University Press, 1960.
6. Sir William Cecil Dampier, *A History of Science and its Relations with Philosophy and Religion* (4th ed.), p. 491. Cambridge University Press, 1961.
7. *Ibid.*, pp. 491-92.
8. *Ibid.*, pp. 500-1.
9. *op. cit.*, p. 497.
10. Sir William Cecil Dampier, *op. cit.*, p. 497.
11. Evelyn Underhill, *Mysticism*, p. 24. University Paperbacks, Methuen & Co. Ltd., 36, Essex Street, Strand, London, 1960.
12. *Ibid.*, p. 25.
13. William James, *The Varieties of Religious Experience*, p. 367. Fontana Library, London, 1960.
14. *op. cit.*, p. 447-48.
15. Bertrand Russell, *Religion and Science*, p. 131. Oxford University Press, London, 1960.
16. *Ibid.*, p. 133.
17. *Ibid.*, p. 175.
18. L. Susan Stebbing, *Philosophy and the Physicists*, p. 265. Dover Publication Inc., New York.
19. *Religion and Science*, p. 175.
20. Sir James Jeans, *The Mysterious Universe*, p. 137.
21. *op. cit.*, p. 189.
22. Dr. R.M. Kasliwal, *Parapsychology*, vol. IV, no. 4. Jaipur, 1962-63.
23. *Science, Religion and Reality*, p. 195.

24. *The Pineal Gland : Its Function, 'Cosmic Society,'* vol. III, No. 7, New Delhi, July, 1967.
25. लाक्षाभं परमामृतं परशिवात्पीत्वा पुनः कुण्डली
नित्यानन्दमहोदयात्कुलपथान्मूले विशेत्सुन्दरी।
तद्दिव्यामृतधारया स्थिरमतिः संतर्पयेद्दैवतं
योगी योगपरंपराविदितया ब्रह्माण्डभाण्डस्थितम् ।।53।। *Ṣaṭcakra Nirūpaṇa,* p. 93.

11 Conclusion

The foregoing chapters offer a mystical and scientific study of Tantra. We have dealt with the subject from the esoteric and philosophical points of view. We have also tried to give a critical and comparative study of Tantra and the Veda, Hindu Tantra and Buddhist Tantra, and Tantra Sādhanā and other forms of Sādhanā.

Tantra is known as Āgama Śāstra. It is both monotheistic and monistic. Monotheism is the spiritual cult and monism is the metaphysics of Tantra. Śiva is the Supreme Godhead and the Absolute. He is Ādi Guru. He is Cosmic Consciousness. He is the fundamental stuff and the noumenal cause of the phenomenal universe. He is the supracosmic Reality and the Truth of the cosmos. He is Bliss. He is called Parama Śiva, who is beyond the categories of existence and non-existence. As every affirmation is negation and every negation is affirmation, the Absolute of Tantra, *i.e.* Parama Śiva, is rightly beyond mental comprehension.

Śakti is the immanent aspect of the Absolute. She is the creative matrix. She eternally co-exists with Śiva. Monism in Tantra means the eternal co-existence of the two. Śiva is the Jñāna Śakti and Umā is the Kriyā Śakti. Śakti is Nityā (eternal), Satyarūpā (of the nature of truth), Divyā (divine) and Omni active. Śakti is the creative principle. When she gets the scope of her manifestation, she becomes the efficient cause of creation. She becomes the operative principle. She is called Māyā. She remains merged into Cosmic Consciousness, in the non-qualified (*nirguṇa*) existence of Parama Śiva. She exists at all levels of Consciousness.

The unification of Śiva and Śakti manifests in creation. When Śakti gets manifested, Śiva undergoes transformation. He becomes the universe, Śiva is the primary and material cause of the universe. The world is the manifestation (*ābhāsa*) of the supreme Reality. It is neither the ultimate Reality nor an illusion. The world is the relative truth. The theory of evolution known as Ābhāsavāda offers a logical and scientific explanation of the phenomenal world. It is different from the Sāṅkhya's Pariṇāmavāda and the Vedantic Vivartavāda. We observe that both Pariṇāmavāda and Vivartavāda fail to provide a scientific basis of the material world.

Śiva is the male principle and Śakti the female. Śiva is consciousness in stasis and Śakti the dynamic consciousness. Parama Śiva is the composite form of both. They are inseparable. Their relation is known as Avinābhāvin, *i.e.* the existence of one is not possible in the absence of the other. They form dualism in theory but in reality are one inseparable existence. They are symbolically represented by Ardha-nārīśvara. In Buddhist Tantra Śiva and Śakti are called Prajñā and Upāya or Śūnyatā and Karuṇā. Vajrasattva is the Absolute of Buddhist Tantra. Vajrayāna, Kālacakra, Mantrayāna are the major developments of Tāntric Mahāyāna. We observe that there is no difference between Hindu Tantra and Buddhist Tantra. Both are based on the mystic and scientific principles. The objective of both is the identification of the individual self with the Cosmic Self.

Jīva is Śiva. The former remains in bondage, the latter is eternally free. The bondage is due to one's impurities (*malas*). These are of three kinds: Āṇavika, Kārma and Māyīka. Āṇavika is the bondage of individuation.

The feeling of *I*-ness is an impediment in the path of spiritual realization. It has to be removed by the gradual merger of individuality into Śivahood. The Kārma Mālā is the bondage of metempsychosis (*saṁskāra*). Every action has its reaction. Reaction in its potentialities is called *saṁskāra.* The bondage of saṁskāra can be removed by the cosmic ideation and superimposition of Brahmabhāva. But Māyika Mālā is the greatest obstruction. However, with the awakening of the Kuṇḍalinī, the bondage of Māyā is cut asunder. The Self is liberated from bondage. Jīva becomes Śiva.

Tantra believes in thirty six principles (*tattvas*). Tantra Sādhanā is directed to purify them all. This brings liberation from Mālā and Kañcukas (Sheaths). Mālā and Kañcukas cloud the transcendental nature of the Soul and It identifies itself with the lower ego. But with the purification of the *tattvas* and the removal of the bondage, the ego is crucified. All taints and blemishes of Mālā and Kañcukas are removed and It attains Śivahood.

The awakening of the Kuṇḍalinī is the mystic process of purifying the tattvas. The Kuṇḍalinī is a dormant divinity in individuality. She is a divine principle. The whole esoteric science of Tantra pivots round this mystic spiritual force. The awakening of this mystic force is the central theme of Tantra Sādhanā. When the Kuṇḍalinī is made conscious the bondage of Māyā is loosened. It takes man to the realization of Parama Śiva, the Supreme Godhead, which is beyond the dualism of subject and object.

The awakening of the Kuṇḍalinī is known as Puraścaraṇa. Mantrāghāta, Mantra-caitanya and Mantra-dīpinī are the three principles necessary for the awakening of the Kuṇḍalinī which remains in a sleeping state at Mūlādhāra Cakra. It is three and a half times coiled anti-clockwise around the Svayaṁbhū Liṅga. It is made conscious with the incantation of mantra. It then forces its passage through the different cakras and excites them into action. With the awakening and rising of the Kuṇḍalinī mind is opened, mystic visions appear and occult powers come to the Yogi. He goes beyond body mind consciousness, and the Soul becomes free in all respects.

Kuṇḍalinī Yoga is a physico-psycho-spiritual process of transformation. 'With the incantation of mantra and the ideation of Cosmic Consciousness the mind is gradually transformed into Self. The transformation of mind into Self is called Salvation.

Sahasrāra Cakra (the pineal gland) is the abode of Śiva. It is a thousand-petalled lotus. Amā Kalā, Nirmāṇa Kalā and Nirmāṇa Śakti are the three mystic principles or layers of Consciousness. Parama Śiva resides above them. It is known as Mahā Bindu. When the Kuṇḍaliṇī reaches the pineal gland, it bites Amā Kalā and drinks the pineal nectar contained in it. The Yogi becomes God intoxicated. He loses his own individuality. He becomes one with the Divine Principle. It is called the unification of Śiva and Śakti. The mystic oneness of the Kuṇḍalinī and Śiva is necessary for the attainment of liberation.

Mahā-Bindu or Parā-Bindu is Parama Śiva. The whole universe has emanated from this transcendental point. All the waves have originated from it. Parā-Bindu is a force of liberation. The realization of Parā-Bindu is called the attainment of the supreme state of spiritual advancement. It is called the attainment of Parama-Pada. The attainment of this state of transcendental realization is possible only after the esoteric necessity of the piercing of the different *cakras*, the real obstructions, by the Kuṇḍalinī is fulfilled and it is awakened.

Realization of the non-dualistic existence is the main aim of Tantra Sādhanā. Mȧntra is the life force. It is the mystic formula practised by the Sādhaka. The incantation of a mantra creates an acoustic vibration which makes the Kuṇḍalinī conscious. It is awakened and makes an upward journey.

Mantras are the mystic force behind Tantra Sādhanā. They are the first principles of Tāntric mysticism. The *bīja mantras* are the acoustic roots of the different waves and vibrations. The world is a collection of different waves and vibrations. Each vibration has its own colour and sound. There are fifty fundamental vibrations in the world symbolically represented by the fifty letters of Sanskrit Varṇamālā. Each letter from *A* (अ) to *kṣa* (क्ष) is the *bīja-mantra.* Oṁkāra is the collective form of all the fifty main sounds. With the help of Nāda-Bindu-Yoga, one gains control over all the waves and vibrations. One goes beyond the manifest world and attains the supreme state of Parā Saṁvita.

Sanskrit alphabets are of Tāntric origin. The fifty letters of Sanskrit Varṇamālā are the fifty basic vibrations, which constitute the entire universe. They are the *Bījākṣara* of Tāntric mysticism. These *Bījakṣara* control the fifty instincts (*vṛttis*) of man which are expressed in one thousand ways both internally and externally through the ten organs.

There are various kinds of *mantras.* Of them only the Siddha Mantra is effective. *Mantra Caitanya* is a necessary condition of Tantra Sādhanā. Mantra without its consciousness-force is barren. It does not yield any esoteric result. However, the incantation of mantra remains associated with the ideation of Parama Śiva. The constant ideation of Parama Śiva straightens the wavelength of mind. Salvation is possible only when there is perfect harmony between the rhythms of incantations, ideation and pulsation. The ideation of *mantra* is a mystic process of superimposition of the Cosmic Consciousness. It transforms mind into consciousness. The process of transformation is scientific. In the scientific language we can say that the Conscious

(*Ātman*) has the infinite wavelength or zero. There is no difference between zero and infinite here. Mind is a relative and functional organism. It is represented by a curvature. The constant ideation of Parama Śiva establishes psycho-spiritual parallelism which is necessary for the attainment of the mystic oneness of Śiva and Śakti.

Mind cannot maintain its existence without an object. It goes on changing its objectivity. It is involved in certain inter- and intra-ectoplasmic occupations. It is a process of externalization. The process of externalization creates waves and vibrations in the divine world of Self. Mental concentration and meditation are necessary for inner transformation. Mind by its very nature remains in a state of change and fluctuation. Tantra Sādhanā overpowers its nature, and it loses its existence and entity. It is sublimated, becomes calm and composed. It is transformed into Self. The Yogi is divinized. He becomes God. *Cit, Ānanda, Icchā, Jñāna* and *Kriyā* are the five functions of the Supreme Being. The mystic oneness of Śiva and Śakti endows the Yogi with all thc five functions of the Divine. In the state of Bliss, man loses his individuality and becomes Divine.

Tantra is the gift of non-Āryan cultures. The Āryans were ignorant of Tantra Sādhanā. The available sources unmistakably lead us to conclude that India is the original home of Tantra. The discovery of the Indus Valley civilization has revolutionized the concept of Indian culture. The non-Āryans were enjoying a sublime form of cultural life when the Āryans were still in search of one. They came into contact with Tantra when they entered the eastern part of India. Tantra brought the two cultures nearer to each other. This resulted in a blend of culture which was altogether new. Hinduism is the name of this new culture. It is neither the gift of the Āryans nor an achievement of the non-Āryans.

The Veda is the greatest achievement of the Āryan culture. It is a religio-philosophical system. Tantra is the priceless treasure of the non-Āryan culture. It is a cult rooted in mysticism and intuition. The happy blending of Tantra and the Veda gave birth to a healthy, integrated and spiritual way of life. This new cult and culture is known as Hinduism. Tantra and the Veda are the original sources of Hindu culture. The intuitional science of Tantra and the religio-philosophical schools of the Veda are its two aspects. It is wrong to say that the Āryans alone were the builders of Hindu culture. The non-Āryans were partners in this. The excavation of the Harappan civilization has made it abundantly clear that the non-Āryans were the architects of a very highly developed culture known as the Indus Valley civilization.

Śiva is the most remarkable figure among the male gods of the non-Āryan pantheon. He is seated on the throne in a yogic posture. He is the Supreme Godhead as well as founder (Ādi Guru) of the Āryans. The Harappan culture bears the stamp of the non-Āryan civilization. Śiva is the non-Āryan deity. With the cultural metamorphosis of Āryan and non-Āryan ways of life, He also became an important deity of the Āryan pantheon.

Tantra covers the whole gamut of human life. The intuitional science of Tantra combines both mysticism and social codes of life. It is the result of a very long and complex development. The different schools of Tantra represent the different phases of spiritual development and ascents of consciousness. Śākta, Vaiṣṇava and Śaiva Tantra are the metaphysical schools of Tantra. They represent the different phases of spiritual development of human consciousness. In no way are they contradictory to each other. Every man is a Śakta in the beginning. He has to fight with Māyā. When mind becomes pure and impeccant, the Sādhaka enjoys the divine presence of the Supreme. He becomes God intoxicated. This state of spiritual development is known as the highest condition of perfection in the Vaiṣṇava thought. In the mystic oneness of Śiva and Śakti, man becomes one with Parama Śiva and realizes the condition of Śiva.

Vidyā, Upavidyā and Avidyā are the esoteric schools of Tantra. Dakṣiṇācāra, Madhyamācāra and Vamācāra are the psychological schools of Tantra. These schools are like different departments of science, e.g. physics, chemistry and mathematics which reveal and understand the complex problems of scientific truths of different nature and import. Similarly the different schools of Tantra are the varied ways to exploit the psychic powers of man. The different methods are the different approaches to reveal the manifold aspects of Consciousness. They are all synthesized into one, the objective being to bring the realization of unitive consciousness. The occultism of Tantra is an applied form of psychology. Tantra is full of symbolism which is replete with mystic and esoteric significance. Tantra is an integral yoga. The different branches of Tantra, which form the basis of the intuitional science and mysticism of the Tantra Śāstra, are complementary to each other.

There are some misconceptions about Tantra. In spite of its rich literature and profound philosophy, it has remained a neglected branch of study. Many grave charges have been levelled against Tantra Sādhanā. According to some Tantra is full of obscenities and superstitions. Some even relegate it to the class of black magic and morbid practices. This, according to us, only reflects the ignorance about the science and mysticism of Tantra. There are no doubt some works which deal with black magic and apparent obscenities, but they do not form the basis or the main trunk of the Tāntric literature. Tantra Sādhanā and its literature are very important parts of the Hindu culture. The misconception is only due to the fact that the Tāntric literature is full of symbolism, the truth of which is revealed only to the initiates. Tāntric symbolism is of great esoteric significance. A layman cannot comprehend it. His failure to understand and appreciate the deeper spiritual and mystic significance of the different symbols renders his understanding of the intuitional science of Tantra shallow and superficial.

The practice of Pañcamakāra has also created great misunderstanding. According to some critics it involves the religious sanction of wanton use of wine and women. They say that wine and women are freely used for the satisfaction of senses and impulses. According to them, Tantra Sādhanā commits sin religiously. This is a misconception and has risen because Pañcamakāra or Five M's have been taken literally. Madya (wine), Māṃisa (meat), Matsya (fish), Mudrā (parched rice) and Maithuna (copulation), the Five M's, have an esoteric meaning. Wine stands for the pineal nectar contained in Amā Kalā. Madya Sādhanā means the drinking of the pineal nectar in the mystic process of the unification of the Kuṇḍalinī Śakti with Parama Śiva at Sahasrāra Cakra. When the Kuṇḍalinī leaves Mūlādhāra Cakra in divine pilgrimage to Kailāśa (Sahasrāra Cakra) to meet Lord Śiva, she is wedlocked in divine oneness. This spiritual oneness of the male (Śiva) and the female principle (Śakti) is called Maithuna Sādhanā. It is called yoga or union. However, Tantra does not believe in false asceticism. Copulation with wife under a strict spiritual discipline is part of Tāntric Sādhanā. The wife is called Bhairavi and the Sādhaka Bhairava. Use of sex and wine under some esoteric disciplines sublimates the baser instincts. Tantra recognizes that sex and hunger are inherent in man, but they can be sublimated. Pañcamakāra Sādhanā forms an aspect of Tantra teachings and practices. In recognition of the gradual development of human consciousness Tantra takes cognizance of the baser and crude aspects of human nature and introduces a spiritual discipline to sublimate them into higher forms of divine life.

It is this aspect of the Tāntric culture which distinguishes it and provides it with a strong psychological footing. In the recent past, science has made a departure from the physical to the psychical, from facts to concepts. Religions which are divorced from a psychological basis stand rejected today. Tantra presents a contrast to religion. It harmonizes the monism of mysticism with the dualism of science. That is to say, it recognizes the principle of one Absolute as the source and goal of evolution. But it does not ignore the world of relativity. It believes that mystic oneness is achieved through objective adjustment.

The so-called reprehensible practices associated with Tantra Sādhanā are used to tame, control and sublimate the sensual impulses. They elevate human consciousness from the crude to the subtle state. Tantra Sādhanā transforms the physical existence into the beatitude of divine existence.

Pañcamakāra Sādhanā is an esoteric method employed for the transformation of desire. Hunger and sex are innate biological needs. They cannot be ignored. Man's indisciplined satisfaction of them leads to his degeneration. But when these are satisfied under spiritual discipline and guidance they become his allies, helpers and ultimately liberators. The principle behind Pañcamakāra Sādhanā is that man must rise with the aid of that Śakti which if misused will cause his fall. The science behind it is that the poison which kills becomes the elixir of life when suitably treated and tested by the wise physician. Man has to work out his salvation, not by negating his desire and suppressing evil tendencies, but by so canalizing them that they are sublimated into the higher forms of spiritual life.

According to some Western critics, the lofty conceptions of earlier and purer beliefs are obscured by senseless rites. Mantra may appear to the prejudiced Western mind as a nonsense syllable, but for the Tantra Sādhaka it is full of mystic power. The incantation of mantra awakens the dormant Divinity in an individual. The word (*śabda*) is the first manifestation of the Supreme. It is called Śabda Brahman. The subtle comes out of the crude in the process of its unfolding. When the process is reversed the gross disappears into the subtle. The different symbols and images used as gross materials, accessories in Tantra Sādhanā, are the forms of *mantra.* One's Devata is the form of the Absolute evolved out of one's *mantra.* The Īṣṭadevatā (chosen deity) is another name for his image of Parama Śiva. *That* is really in *this.* Mantra Sādhanā is a process of the realization of one's inherent perfection and divinity.

The whole universe is the expression of Śiva-Śakti. Body is not merely flesh, it is the temple of Śiva-Śakti. It is an epiphany of the Divine Consort. Mantra Sādhanā is a process of spiritualization of all actions and emotions. The Yogi feels the divine presence in every fibre of his physical body.

Tantra, downgraded to the class of black magic and condemned as a burial ground of all the dead and obsolete religious rites, is, if properly understood, a scientific system of spiritual discipline based on human psychology. It is an elaborate process of 'auto- and outer-suggestion'. It can be said that the elements of 'magic' and 'auto suggestion' are contained in the body of the Śāstra if the words 'magic' and 'auto suggestion' are understood in a scientific and psychological sense. The scientific study of the magical powers has proved beyond any doubt that the human mind has parapsychological powers. Tantra Sādhanā is aimed at the cessation of different mental states. With the cessation of mental modifications, the Sādhaka attains the powers of clairvoyance and clairaudience. The sense organs and secretions of the body are kept in proper order through mental concentration and other forms of Tantra Sādhanā. It is a science of religion. Its auto-suggestion establishes one's rapport with the Divine Consciousness from which the universe arises and in which it subsists. The Sādhaka achieves rapport with Śiva, the giver of all boons. With the establishment of divine rapport, the Yogi attains occult powers.

The attainment of occult powers is wrongly termed as black magic. A close and rational analysis of such supramental powers has shown they have a scientific basis. Our knowledge of mind and consciousness is very limited and incomplete. The multi-dimensional aspects of human consciousness are yet to be understood. The intuitional science of Tantra alone can help one fathom one's deepest consciousness and become aware of the immense power of occultism. The Sādhaka through Tantra Sādhanā rises to higher and higher levels of perfection till he becomes perfect Being-Consciousness-Bliss.

Vāmācāra Sādhanā is another invective against Tantra. Kāpālika and Śava Sādhanās (performed with a corpse) form part of the practice in the Vāmācāra school. Kāpālika Sādhanā is directed to conquer the instincts of fear, shame and hatred. These three pāśas (bondages) are the greatest obstacles against spiritual development. They obscure the emergence of Pure Experience. The letter *ka* (क)

stands for the Effect Brahman. The Sādhanā which leads to control over the manifest universe is called Kāpālika Sādhanā.

Śava Sādhanā is the highest form of esotericism. One's gravest impediment is one's attachment or addiction to the objects of sense. The purpose of Śava Sādhanā is to draw the mind away from them. The excessive attachment to the world of sensibility obstructs the spirit of inner renunciation from empirical thinking. The Sādhaka must cultivate a healthy habit of thought and action which may lead him to the attainment of maximum spiritual ascent. He must control his feelings as well as thoughts and actions. So long as a man is under the influence of sensuous enjoyment, no amount of intellectual endeavour to fix the mind on higher pursuits would succeed. When a Sādhaka performs Sādhanā with a human corpse he gains the realization of the illusory knowledge of physical existence, and dispassion thrives under such condition. It eradicates the root cause of all distraction. Vāmācāra Sādhanā or the 'Left hand path' is an aggressive form of spiritual discipline based on the profound knowledge of the 'return current' which seeks to reverse the whole current of life from the crude to the subtle state. It is aimed at full control over the six *ripus* (enemies) and eight *pāśas* (bondages). The Sādhanā of Mantra, Yantra and the Kuṇḍalinī, constituents of Vāmācāra, leads to the integrated elevation and evolution of human personality. The use of the Five M's brings no demerit on the Sadhaka. He looks upon wine and meat as Śakti and Śiva. It is to be observed that the Five M's have a different meaning for different classes of worshippers. What is required to be offered is the *tattva* (principle, essence), and not the article itself. Vāmācāra means the path of renunciation. The woman, who is associated with this Sādhanā, helps the Sādhaka in his path of renunciation. A woman is never used in Tantra Sādhanā just for animal gratification. She occupies the highest place of veneration in all the schools of Tantra. She is the embodiment of Śakti. She is revered as the Supreme Goddess. It is a sin to speak disparagingly of any woman.

Tantra Sādhanā is based on mysticism and intuitional science. It recognizes spiritual gradation of human evolution. It takes into active consideration both debasing and divine aspects of human life. It formulates different disciplines to elevate man from animality to divinity. However, Tantra is not confined to Vāmācāra Sādhanā alone. It is only a fractional part of Tantra teaching and practice.

Tantra is a cult. It is a spiritual discipline which leads one to the realization of Supreme Beatitude and Bliss. According to Tantra Śāstra, Parama Śiva is the highest Truth. Consistent with the spirit of Āgama Śāstra, the Yogic school of Tantra holds that the body is the abode of Truth. It is the best medium for the attainment of the mystic unification of Jīva and Śiva. Jīva is represented by the Kuṇḍalinī Śakti. The Kuṇḍalinī is associated with all the gross principles of defilement. She is the principle of phenomenalism. She is to be awakened and dissociated from all the principles of defilement. When the Kuṇḍalinī is made conscious, *jīva* starts losing its finitude. Finally, she reaches Sahasrāra Cakra (the pineal gland) which is the region of Perfect Rest, Purity and Bliss. In Tantra Sādhanā, every man is Śiva and every woman is

Śakti. The 'red ovum' is the symbol of Śakti and 'the white sperm' of Śiva. During Sādhanā, the man and the woman sublimate their corporeal existence and realize that they are the true manifestations of Śiva and Śakti. With such a mystic realization they unite and control the sex act in such a way that their downward motion is arrested and their upward movement is accelerated till they reach the highest region of Sahasrāra. The Sādhaka then realizes the Infinite Bliss, the ultimate nature of the Absolute.

Tantra locates seven plexuses (*cakras*) in the different parts of the body, along the spinal column. The first is Mūlādhāra Cakra situated in the anus region or at the end of the tail bone. It is the abode of the Kuṇḍalinī. The second is Svādhiṣṭhāna Cakra situated at the root of the genital organ. Maṇipūra and Anāhata Cakras are situated in the navel and cardiac regions respectively. (In Buddhist Tantra, Maṇipūra Cakra and Anāhata Cakra are called Nirmāṇa Cakra and Dharma Cakra. They represent Nirmāṇakāya or one's spiritual existence and Dharmakāya or the non-dual cosmic existence.) The fifth, Viśuddha Cakra, is situated in the region of neck. (In Buddhist Tantra it is called Saṁbhoga Cakra and represents Saṁbhogakāya or the body of bliss.) The sixth, Ājñā Cakra, is situated in the region of the pituitary gland. It controls the conscious and the subconscious mind. Beyond it are the non-mental spheres. Sahasrāra Cakra is the highest plexus. In Buddhist Tantra it is called Uṣṇisakamālā. It is the seat of the Absolute. The Kuṇḍalinī remains as the principle of fundamental negativity in Mūlādhāra Cakra and is associated with the gross principle of bondage (Māyā). She gets dissociated from the principle of bondage by Sādhanā and starts moving upward through Suṣumṇā Nāḍī.

Īḍā is an important nerve on the left of Suṣumṇā, and Piṅgalā is on its right. They represent the moon and the sun, the Gaṅgā and the Yamunā respectively. When the Kuṇḍalinī is made conscious, nerves Prajñā and Upāya get unified in the middle path called Suṣumṇā or Avadhūti. When the Kuṇḍalinī reaches Sahasrāra Cakra, the Sādhaka has the realization of Parama Śiva. It results in the mystic unification of Śiva and Śakti, Prajñā and Upāya. Prajñopāya is equivalent to Mahāsukha (Supreme Bliss), Sāmantabhadra (entirely auspicious) and Sadā Śiva (Eternal Bliss).

Tantra is mysticism. According to Tāntric mysticism man is a Cosmic Being. To arise, awake and realize the cosmic nature of Reality is the aim behind Tantra Sādhanā. Reality is open to mysticism alone. The incomprehensible certainty of the Absolute is not to be explained by metaphysics. The mystic experience is characterized by vividness, directness, freshness and bliss. In the intuitive experience, the Yogi feels the impact of Reality. He feels the presence of Parama Śiva (Cosmic Consciousness) and does not indulge in philosophical polemics.

There are two kinds of knowledge, *i.e.* Aparā-Jñāna (empirical knowledge) and Parā-Jñāna (spiritual knowledge). When Ātmabhāva (Consciousness) becomes one with Vastubhāva (objectified) it is called empirical knowledge. An epistemological analysis of the empirical knowledge has proved that mind does not know the object directly. The 'datum' is a phenomena between mind and object. The relation between the object and the 'datum' is still a mystery to be resolved.

The empirical knowledge is incomplete and differential. It lacks directness. But Parā Jñāna (spiritual knowledge) is complete and comprehensive. It comes through mysticism. Tāntric mysticism brings about spiritual identification of the Sādhaka with the blissful Absolute. In Tantra, knowledge means the realization of the Absolute which is immanent in the Self and nature.

Tantra is an intuitional science. It is a science of the psychic power. It has two fundamental divisions: physical and intuitional. The physical science (Jaḍa Vijñāna) deals with relativity. It gives a differential view of the whole. The intuitional science (Brahma Vijñāna) deals with the existence and realization of the Absolute. It gives an integral view of the Cosmos. Reason is the measure of all empirical truths. But it has its own limitations. We cannot comprehend the Absolute with its help. Intuition is self illumination. It gives insight into the Self. It alone leads one to Divine realization. Every man is endowed with the mystical power of intuition. It remains, however, in a dormant condition. But with the awakening of the Kuṇḍalinī and its gradual upward movement progressive development of one's intuitive faculty takes place. Every man is a hibernated God. But because of the association of the principle of defilement and illusion, he is unaware of this. However, with the help of mantric incantation and the awakening of the Kuṇḍalinī the binding current is reversed and an ascent from crude to subtle intuition takes place; the trammels of Māyā are cut asunder and the Soul becomes free from bondage and limitation. *Aham* and *Idam*, the knower and the known, are then equated with each other, and man realizes his Divine Being.

Tantra is spirituality and not religion. The degeneration of humanity in the present age cannot be stopped through the institutionalized religion and speculative philosophy. It can be done only through spiritual discipline and mantric practices. Tantra Sādhanā vibrates the material incrustations of the humanity and shakes Consciousness into activity. It arrests the decline of Dharma and human values. The Tāntric mantras are not mere words, they are a mass of divine energy. They awaken the spiritual power of man.

The present age is not getting and will not get the regenerating insight from the dead religions and hollow philosophies. The philosophy of renaissance is always ahead of the times. Salvation does not lie in the materialization of Consciousness. The general vulgarization of human society in the name of progressive ideology has endangered the very existence of human race and civilization. The whole human society is at a crossroad. And the only sure guide at this juncture is the spiritual humanism of Tantra. It alone can save humanity from its decay and degeneration. Tantra is a science of being and metaphysics of existence. It harmonizes idealism and realism. Its ideo-realistic approach is the need of the hour. Its mysticism and spiritual humanism alone will help humanity in its spiritual realization.

Tantra is a philosophy of renaissance. It advocates an ideology of universal brotherhood. Every man, according to it, is Śiva-incarnate. Everyone is a spiritual being. But to bring about this realization of one's being and consciousness, the awakening of the Kuṇḍalinī is essential. Mere study of the Śāstra may give some theoretical idea about the Absolute but only the intuitional practice of Tantra helps in the realization of the Absolute. Spiritual illumination comes to those who practise Sādhanā in the manner enjoined by the Śāstra. The Yogi knows realization of the Absolute needs no scriptural study beyond a certain stage.

The unified existence of Śiva-Śakti is the greatest contribution of Tantra philosophy. Abhinavagupta, Bhāskararāya, Lakṣmidhara and other eminent writers and commentators strongly defend the identity of the two. If *Śiva* is *Sat* (Being) *Śakti* is *Satī* (Being as Power), if *Śiva* is *Cit* (Consciousness) *Śakti* is *Citi* (Consciousness as Power), and if *Śiva* is *Ānanda* (Bliss) *Śakti* is *Parmānanda-Sandoh-rūpa* (Soul of Bliss). If *Śiva* is *Brahman, Śakti* is *Brāhmamayī.* Tantra gives equal importance to the feminine principle. According to it all quarrels about the duality and non-duality are settled when the Sādhaka starts practising Sādhanā. Some say, according to *Mahānirvaṇa Tantra,* that Truth is Advaita (non-dual) and some others speak of it as Dvaita (dual), but it is Dvaitādvaita-vivarjita—neither the one nor the other. It is beyond dualism and non-dualism.

To conclude, Śakti, according to Tantra, is all pervading. She is immanent in all living creatures and also in the non-living, in the form of energy. But modern science has discovered this only now, that there is universal permeation or energy. This has brought Science and Spirituality nearer. And Tantra provides the most congenial meeting ground for them. It is not hostile to scientific advancement. Only it believes in the integrated development of human personality. It wants spiritual development should be ahead of scientific advancement. If not, the human civilization will be doomed to destruction. Scientific achievements are welcome otherwise it will amount to insult to human intelligence but they should be utilized for the service and happiness of mankind. Spiritual men, therefore, should be at the helm of affairs or at least have a restraining influence so that science is not used for the maiming, mutilation and even annihilation of mankind.

Bibliography

Source Books

Abhinavagupta, *Tantrāloka,* 12 vols., Kashmir Sanskrit Texts and Studies, vols. 27-39, Kashmir Government Publications, Srinagar, 1921-38.

——, *Tantrasāra,* Kashmir Sanskrit Texts and Studies, vol. 17, Srinagar, 1918.

——, *Parmārthasāra,* Kashmir Sanskrit Texts and Studies, Srinagar, 1916.

Avalon, Arthur (Sir John Woodroffe), *Mahānirvāṇa Tantra* (The Great Liberation), 3rd ed., Ganesh & Co., Madras, 1953.

——, *Kulārṇava Tantra,* Ganesh & Co., Madras, 1965.

——, *Hymn* to *Kālī* (Karpuradi-stotra), 3rd ed., Ganesh & Co., Madras, 1965.

Bhaskara, *Shiva Sūtra Vārtika,* Kashmir Sanskrit Texts and Studies, Srinagar, 1916.

Bhattacharya, Benoytosh (ed.), *Guhyasamāja Tantra,* Gaekwad Oriental Series, Baroda, 1931.

——, *Sādhanamālā,* 2 vols., Gaekwad Oriental Series, XXVI & XLI, Baroda, 1925-28.

——, *Niṣpannayogāvalī of Abhayakar Gupta,* Gaekwad Oriental Series, no. 109, Baroda, 1949.

Bhattacharya, Jīvananda Vidyasagar (ed.), *Rudra Yāmalam Uttaratantram,* Vacaspati Press, Calcutta, 1937.

Brown, W. Norman (ed.), *Saundaryalaharī,* Harvard Oriental Series, vol. 43, Cambridge, Massachusetts, 1958.

Kaviraj, Dr. Gopinath (ed.), *Tripurā Rahasyam,* Saraswati Granthamala, vol. 15, Varanasi, 1965.

——, *Yoginihṛdayam,* vo1.7, Saraswati Granthamala, Varanasi.

Kṣemarāja, *Svacchanda Tantram,* 6 vols., Kashmir Sanskrit Texts and Studies, Srinagar, 1921-25.

Lakshmanadesikendra, *Śāradā Tilakam,* Chowkhamba Sanskrit Series Office, Varanasi, 1963.

Leidecker, Kurt, F. (ed.), *Pratyabhijñāhṛdayam* (The Scent of Recognition), Adyar Library, Madras, 1938.

Ramanujacharya, M.D. (ed.), *Ahirbudhnya-Saṁhitā of the Pañcarātrāgama,* 2 vols., Adyar Library and Research Centre, Madras 20, 1966.

Sastri, Haraprasad (Ed.), *Advayavajra Saṁgraha,* Gaekwad Oriental Series, no. XL, Baroda, 1927.

Shastri, Madhusudan Kaul (ed.), *Sri Mṛgendra Tantram,* Kashmir Sanskrit Texts and Studies, no. L, Srinagar, 1930.

——, *Mālinīvijayottara Tantram,* Kashmir Sanskrit Texts and Studies, Srinagar, 1922.

——, *The Śivadṛṣṭi,* Kashmir Sanskrit Texts and Studies, Srinagar 1934.

Snellgrove, D. L., *The Hevajra Tantra,* 2 vols., London Oriental Series, Oxford University Press, London, 1959.

General Books

Abhinavagupta, *Tantrasāra,* Kashmir Sanskrit Texts and Studies, vol. 17, Srinagar, 1918.

——, *Paramārthasāra,* Kashmir Sanskrit Texts and Studies, Srinagar, 1916.

Amratanandanatha, *Yoginīhṛdaya Dīpikā,* Saraswati Bhavan Series, Varanasi.

Anandamurti, *Ānanda Sūtram,* Ananda Marga Pracaraha Samgha, Anandanagar, P.O. Baglata, Purulia (W. Bengal), 1964.

——, *Subhāṣita Saṁgraha,* 4 vols., Anandanagar, P.O. Baglata, Purulia (W. Bengal).

Aurobindo, Sri, *Bases of Yoga,* Arya Publishing House, Calcutta, 1949.

——, *On the Veda,* International University Centre, Pondicherry, 1956.

——, *Synthesis of Yoga,* Sri Aurobindo Ashram, Pondicherry, 1955.

Avalon, Arthur (Sir John Woodroffe), *The Serpent Power,* Ganesh & Co., Madras, 1958.

——, *Tantrik Texts,* 2 vols., Luzac & Co., 46 Great Russell Street, London, 1922.

——, *Shakti and Shakta,* 2nd ed., Ganesh & Co., Madras.

——, *The Garland of Letters* (Varṇāmālā), Ganesh & Co., Madras, 1963.

——, *Kāma-Kalā Vilāsa,* Ganesh & Co., Madras, 1963.

——, *Principles of Tantra,* (Tantratattva), Ganesh & Co., Madras, 1955.

——, *Hymn to Kālī* (Karpūrādi Stotra), Ganesh & Co., Madras, 1965.

——, *Hymn to Goddess,* Ganesh & Co., Madras, 1964.

——, *The Greatness of Śiva,* Ganesh & Co., Madras, 1963.

——, *Introduction to Tantra Śāstra,* Ganesh & Co., Madras, 1963.

——, *Tantrarāja Tantra,* Ganesh & Co., Madras, 1952.

Ayangar, S. Krishnaswami (ed.), *Paramasaṁhitā of the Pañcarātra,* Gaekwad Oriental Series, LXXXVI, Baroda, 1940.

Bagchi, P. C., *Studies in the Tantras,* University Press, Calcutta, 1939.

——, *Kaulajñāna-nirṇaya and Some Minor Texts of the School of Matyendranatha,* Calcutta Sanskrit Series III, Calcutta, 1934.

Banerjee, Akshaya Kumar, *Philosophy of Gorakhnātha,* Mahant Digvijay Nath Trust, Gorakhnath Temple, Gorakhpur.

Basham, A.L., *The Wonder That Was India,* Sidgwick and Jackson, London.

Besant, Annie, *Brahma Vidyā,* Theosophical Publishing House, Adyar, Madras, 1927.

Bhattacharya, Chintamani (ed.), *Matrikabhenda-Tantra*, Sanskrit Series no. VII, Calcutta.

Bhattacharya, Śrī Jīvānanda Vidyāsagar (ed.), *Rudrayāmalam-Uttaratantram*, Vacaspati Press, Calcutta, 1937.

Bhattacharya, B. (ed.), *Śaktisaṅgama-tantra*, Gaekwad Oriental Series, LXI, XCI, XIV, 3 vols., Baroda, 1932, 1941, 1947.

Bhattacharya, Benayatosh, *An Introduction to Buddhist Esotericism*, vol. XLVI, Chowkhamba Sanskrit Series, Varanasi.

——, *Buddhist Iconography*, Oxford University Press, London, 1924.

Bharati, Agehananda, *Tāntric Tradition*, Rider & Company, London, 1965.

Bloomfield, M., *Atharva Veda evaṁ Gopatha Brāhmaṇa*, Chowkhamba Sanskrit Series, Varanasi, 1964.

Bose, D. N. & Haldar, H.L., *Tantras—Their Philosophy and Occult Secrets*, Oriental Publishing House, Calcutta, 1956.

Bose, Manindra Mohan, *The Post Chaitanya Sahajīya Cult of Bengal*, University Press, Calcutta, 1930.

Briggs, G. W., *Gorakhanātha and the Kānphaṭa Yogis*, Oxford University Press, London, 1938.

Carelli, Mario (ed.), *Sekoddeśaṭīkā of Nādapāda (Nāropa)*, Gaekwad Oriental Series, Baroda, 1941.

Chakravarti, Chintaharan, *The Tantras: Studies on their Religion and Literature*, Punthi Pustaka, Calcutta, 1963.

Chakravarti, Chintaharan, *Srinivāsa, Saubhāgyasubhadaya*, Library of the Maharaja of Alwar, Rajasthan, no. 2445.

——, *Śrīvidyākhaḍgamālā*, Chowkhamba Sanskrit Series, Varanasi, 1963.

——, *Śrīvidyā-Nityāracanam*, Chowkhamba Sanskrit Series, Varanasi, 1962.

Chakravorty, P. C., *Doctrine of Śakti in Indian Literature*, General Printers and Publishers, Calcutta, 1940.

Chatterjee, J. C., *Kashmir Shaivāism*, Research & Publication, Government of Jammu & Kashmir, Srinagar, 1962.

Chaudhuri, Pandit B. (ed.), *Śaktisādhanā*, Chowkhamba Sanskrit Series, Varanasi, 1963.

Coomaraswamy, A.K., *Elements of Buddhist Iconography*, Cambridge, Massachusetts, 1935.

——, *The Dance of Śiva*, Noonday Publication, New York, 1957.

Cowell & Mitra, *Principal Upaniṣads*, 3 vols., Theosophical Publishing House, Adyar, Madras, 1932.

Dumpier, Sir William Cecil, *A History of Science and its Relations with Philosophy and Religion*, Cambridge University Press, 1961.

Das, Sudhendu Kumar, *Śakti on Divine Power*, Calcutta University, Calcutta, 1934.

Dasgupta, Surendranath, *Yoga Philosophy and Religion*, Kegan Paul, London, 1924.

——, *History of Indian Philosophy*, 5 vols., Cambridge University Press, 1963.

Dasgupta, Shashi Bhushan, *Obscure Religious Cults*, 6/1A Banchharan St., Akrur Lane, Calcutta, 1946.

Dasgupta, S. B., *An Introduction to Tantrik Buddhism*, University Press, Calcutta, 1950.

——, *Obscure Religious Cults as Background of Bengali Literature*, University Press, Calcutta, 1946.

Dave, Sakratal Y. and Sastri, A. Mahadeva, (eds.), *Paraśurāmakalpasūtra*, Gaekwad Oriental Series, XXII, Baroda, 1950.

Diksit, Pandit Ramanath (ed.), *Samatantra*, Chowkhamba Sanskrit Series, Varanasi, 1963.

Dikshitar, V. R., *The Lalitā Cult*, University of Madras, Madras, 1942.

Eliade, Mircea, *Le Yoga : Immortaliteet*, Paris, 1954. English version (trans.), W.R. Trask. *Yogi : Immortality and Freedom*, Bolligm Series, Pantheon Inc., New York, 1958.

Ernest Mackay, *The Indus Civilization.*

Evans-Wentz, W. (ed.), *Tibetan Yoga and Secret Doctrines — Seven Books of Wisdom of the Great Path*, Oxford University Press, London, 1935.

——, *The Tibetan Book of the Dead* (Bardo Thodol) (trans.), Oxford University Press, London, 1949.

——, *Tibet's Great Yogi Milarepa*, Oxford University Press, London, 1928.

Farquhar, J. N., *Religious Literature of India*, Motilal Banarsidass, Delhi, 1966.

Fitzerald, Edward, *The Religions of Tibet*, Allen & Unwin, London, 1958.

Foucher, Max-Pol, *The Erotic Sculpture of India*, Allen & Unwin, London, 1959.

Gambhirananda, Swami, *Eight Upanisads*, vols. 2, Advaita Ashram, Calcutta-14, 1963.

Geden, A.S., *Tantra's Entry in the Encyclopaedia of Religion and Ethics*, J. Hastings, vol. XII.

Ghose, Atal Behari, *Śiva and Śakti*, Rajashahi, 1935.

Ghoshal, U. N., *Studies in Indian History and Culture*, University Press, Calcutta, 1955.

Glasenapp, H.V., *Buddhistische Mysterien*, Stuttgart, 1940.

Gordon, Antoinette, *Tibetan Religious Art*, New York, 1952.

——, *The Iconography of Tibetan Lamaism*, New York, 1939.

Gordon, D.H., *The Prehistoric Background of Indian Culture*, N. M. Tripathi Pvt. Ltd., 164, Princess Street, Bombay-2.

Govinda, Lama Anagarika, *Foundations of Tibetan Mysticism*, Rider & Co., London, 1959.

Griffith, R.T.H., *Hymns of the Ṛg-Veda*, E.J. Lazarus & Co., London, 1920.

Guenther, H.V., *Yuganaddha— The Tāntric View of Life*, Chowkhamba Sanskrit Series, Varanasi, 1964.

——, *The Life and Teaching of Narapa*, Clarendon Press, Oxford, 1963.

Hoffmann, H., *The Religions of Tibet*, Allen & Unwin, London, 1961.

Jacobs, H., *Western Psychology and Hindu Sādhanā*, Allen & Unwin, London, 1961.

Jaiswal, Suvira, *The Origin and Development of Vaiṣṇavism*, Motilal Banarsidass, Delhi, 1967.

James, William, *The Varieties of Religious Experience*, The Fontana Library, London, 1960.

Jhaveri, M.B., *Comparative and Critical Study of Mantra Śāstra*, Sarabhai Manilal Nawal, Ahmedabad, 1944.

Jñānānanda Paramahamsa, *Kāntāvalinirṇaya Tāntric Texts*, vol. XIV, Agamanusandhana Samiti, Calcutta, 1928.

Kaviraj, Dr. Gopinath, *Bharatiya Saṁskṛti Aur Sādhanā*, Bihar Rastrabhasa Parisad, Patna.

——, *Tantrik Vāṅmaya men Śāktadṛṣṭi*, Bihar Rastrabhasa Parisad, Patna, 1963.

Kṛṣṇapriyācārya (ed.), *Maheśvara-tantram*, Chowkhamba Sanskrit Series, Varanasi, 1963.

Kṛṣṇamācārya, V., *Lakṣmītantram*, Chowkhamba Sanskrit Series, Varanasi, 1966.

——, *Lalitāśaraṇam* (Stotram), Vavillu Rāmasvāmi Sāstralu & Sons, Madras, 1955.

Macdonell, A.A., *Hymns from the Ṛg-Veda*, Oxford University Press, London, 1922.

Mādhavācārya, *The Sarva-Darśana-Saṁgraha*, Kegan Paul Trench, Trubner & Co. Ltd., Dryden House, Gerrard Street, London, 1908.

Maheśvarananda, *Mahārtha-mañjarī*, Kashmir Sanskrit Texts and Studies, no. XI, Srinagar, 1918.

——, *Maheśvarī-tantram*, Chowkhamba Sanskrit Series, Varanasi, 1963.

Majumdar, R.C., *An Advanced History of India*, Macmillan, London, 1958.

——, *Ancient India*, Motilal Banarsidass Delhi.

Mallik, Kalyani, *Nāth-Sāmpradāyer Itihās*, University Press, Calcutta, 1950.

Marshall, Sir John, *Mohenjo-daro and the Indus Valley Civilization*, 41, Great Russell Street, London, 1931.

Max Müller (Ed.), *Atharva Veda*, Sacred Books of the East, Vol. XXIX, Motilal Banarsidass, Delhi.

Minkowski, Raum and Zeit, Physik, Zeitschrift.

Misra, Pandit Kanhaiyalal (ed.), *Yoginī-tantra*, Gangaviṣṇu Śrīkṛṣṇadas, Kalyan, Bombay, 1957.

Mitra, A.K., *Kulacūḍāmaṇi-nigama*, Ganesh & Co., Madras, 1956.

Munshi, K.M. (ed.), *The History and Culture of Indian People*, Bharatiya Vidya Bhavan, Bombay, 1950.

Narayan, *Tantra-sāra-saṁgraha*, Chowkhamba Sanskrit Series, Varanasi, 1963.

Nikhilananda, Swami, *The Gospel of Ramakrishna*, Ramakrishna Math, Madras, 1950.

——, *Hinduism : Its Meaning for Liberation of the Spirit*, Allen & Unwin, 1958.

Oldenberg, Hermann, *Vedic Hymns*, Part II, *Sacred, Books of the East*, Clarendon Press, Oxford, 1897.

Oman, J.C., *The Mystics, Ascetics and Saints of India*, T.F.Unwin, London, 1903.

Pandey, K.C., *Abhinavagupta*, Chowkhamba Sanskrit Series, Varanasi, 1935.

Panigrahi, K.C., *Obscene Sculptures of Orissian Temples* in Proceedings of the Indian History Congress, VIII, 94-7.

Petech, L., *History of Medieval Nepal*, Serie Orientale Roma, Rome, 1960.

Piggot, *Pre-Historic India*, Harmondsworth, 1950.

Poleman, H. (ed.), *Tantra, Śaiva and Spanda, A Census of India Manuscripts in the United States and Canada*, American Oriental Society Monograph, vol. 12, 1938.

Pott, P.H., *Yoga en Yantra*, Leiden, 1946.

——, *Introduction to the Tibetan Collection of the National Museum of Ethnology*, Leiden, 1946.

Prasad, Durga (ed.), *Rājataraṅgiṇī*, Bombay, 1892.

——, *Kālikā-sahasranāma-stotram*, Sri Ram Press, Madras, 1957.

——, *Kālīvilāsa-tantra*, Chowkhamba Sanskrit Series, Varanasi, 1963.

——, *Kāmya-Yantroddhāra*, H.P.S., Calcutta, 1953.

Pratyagātmānanda, Swami, *Japasūtram*, Bharatiya Vidya Prakashan, Varanasi, 1966.

——, *Pāśupata Sūtra*, Trivendrum Oriental Manuscripts Library, University of Travancore, 1940.

Pūrṇānanda, *Śrītattvacintāmaṇi*, Calcutta Sanskrit Series, no. 19.

——, *Śyāmārahasya*, P.C. Paul & Bros., Calcutta, 1948.

Radhakrishnan, S., *Eastern Religion and Western Thought*, Oxford University Press, 1940.

——, *Indian Philosophy*, 2 vols., Macmillan, London, 1930.

Rājānakabhāskara, *Lalleśvarī-vyākhyāna*, Chowkhamba Sanskrit Series, Varanasi, 1963.

Ramanuja, *The Vedānta Sūtra* (Commentary), translated by George Thibaut, *Sacred Books of the East*, vol. XLVIII, Motilal Banarsidass, Delhi, 1962.

Ramcharana, Sri, *Mātṛ-sūpāsna*, Kalyan Mandir, Katra, Allahabad, 1949.

Rao, Gopinath, *Elements of Hindu Iconography*, 4 vols., Madras, 1914-16.

——, *The Naturalistic Tradition in Indian Thoughts*, University of Washington Press, Seattle, 1961.

——, *Rudrayāmala*, Anusandhāna Samiti, Calcutta, 1895.

Rele, Vasant G., *The Mysterious Kuṇḍalinī*, D.B. Taraporevala Sons & Co., Bombay, 1960.

Russell, Bertrand, *Religion and Science*, Oxford University Press, London, 1960.

Samkṛtyayuana, Rahul, *Siddha Sarāhapāda Kṛta Donākaśa*, Bihar Rastrabhāṣā Parisad, Patna, 1957.

Santoshi, Sri, *Kaula-Kīrtana*, Chowkhamba Sanskrit Series, Varanasi, 1963.

Sarmā, Paṇḍit Caturpal, *Anuṣṭhāna-prakāśa-mahānibandha*, Khemraj Srikṛṣṇadass, Bombay, 1951.

Sastry, K.S. Subrahmaṇya, *Descriptive Catalogue of Sanskrit Manuscripts*, vol. XX, Sri Vanivilas Press, Srirangam, 1951.

Sastri, R. Ananthakrishna, *Lalitā Sahasranāman*, Theosophical Publishing House, Adyar, Madras, 1951.

Sastri, Siva Sankar Avasthi, *Mantra Aur Mātrikāon Kā Rahasya*, Chowkhamba Sanskrit Series, Varanasi, 1966.

Sastri, Pandit Raghunath (ed.), *Merutantra*, Lakṣmivenkaṭeśvar Steam Press, Kalyan, Bombay, 1940.

Sastri, Pandit Ganesa and Gokhle, R.R., (ed.), *Jñānāva-tantra*, Anandāśrama Sanskrit Series, no. 69, Bombay, 1952.

Sastri, Pandit T. Ganpati, (ed.), *Mañjūśrīmūlakalpa* (Arya), Trivandrum Sanskrit Series, Trivandrum, 1920.

——, *Mantramahārṇava*, Sri Lakṣmiveṅkaṭeśvar Steam Press, Kalyan, Bombay, 1940.

——, *Mantrasiddhi Kā Upāy*, Chowkhamba Sanskrit Series, Varanasi, 1963.

——, *Mātrikābheda-tantra*, Chowkhamba Sanskrit Series, Varanasi, 1963.

Sastri, Haraprasad (ed.), *Advayavajra Śaṁgraha*, Gaekwad Oriental Series, no. XL, Baroda, 1927.

Sastri, Hirananda, 'Origin and Cult of Tarā', Archaeological Survey of India, *Memoir No.* 20.

Sastri, Pandit Madhusudan Kaul (ed.), *The Siddhitrayī and the Pratyabhijña-kāvṛti*, Kashmir Sanskrit Texts and Studies, XXXIV, Srinagar, 1921.

Sastri, Pandit Mukunda Rana (ed.), *Sitikaṇtha Mahānsyaprakāśa*, Kashmir Sanskrit Texts and Studies, vol. XXI, Srinagar, 1918.

——, *Śrīvidyāstavamañjari*, Chowkhamba Sanskrit Series, Varanasi, 1963.

——, *Śrīvidyāratnasūtra*, Sarasvati Bhavan Series, vol. XI, Banaras.

Satyānveśī, *Kaula Kīrtan*, , Kalyan Mandir, Prayag.

Schietner, F.A., *Tārānātha's Geschichte des Buddismus in India*, Kaisseriche Akademic der Wissenschaften, St. Petersburg, Russia, 1869.

Shah, Priyabala (ed.), *'Mudrā-vicāra-prakaraṇam mudrā-vidhi'*, Chowkhamba Sanskrit Series, Varanasi, 1963.

Shah, V. P., *A Peep into the Early History of Tantra in Jain Literature*, Bharata Kaumudi, vol. II, Allahabad, 1947.

Sharma, Bhadra Śīla, *Todala Tantram*, Kalyan Mandir, Prayag.

Sharma, Bhadra Śila, *Bhairavi Cakra Pūjan,* Kalyan Mandir, Prayag.

——, *Kāmadhenu Tantra,* Kalyan Mandir, Prayag, Samvat, 2021.

——, *Niruttara Tantra,* Kalyan Mandir, Prayag, Samvat, 2017.

Sharma, D.S., *Hinduism Through the Ages,* Bharatiya Vidya Bhavan, Bombay, 1956.

Shastri, Har Prasad, *Bauddhagā Dohā,* Vāṅgiya Sāhityā Pariṣad, Calcutta, 1959.

Shastri, Mukunda Ram, *Parā Triṁshikā,* Kashmir Sanskrit Texts and Studies, Srinagar, 1918.

Shastri Madhusudan Kaul, *Īśvarapratyabhijñā,* 2 vols., Kashmir Sanskrit Texts and Studies, Srinagar, 1921.

——, *Vāmkeśvarmatam,* vol. LXVI, Kashmir Sanskrit Texts and Studies, Srinagar, 1945.

——, *Netra Tantram,* Kashmir Sanskrit Texts and Studies, Srinagar, 1939.

——, *Śrī-Mālinī Vijaya Vārttikam,* Kashmir Sanskrit Texts and Studies, no. XXXl, Srinagar, 1921.

Singh, Mohan, *Gorakhnath and Medieval Hindu Mysticism,* Lahore, 1937.

Śivapadesundaram, S., *The Saiva School of Hinduism,* Madras, 1934.

Stebbing, L. Susan, *Philosophy and the Physicists,* Dover Publication Inc., New York.

Subramanya, Cidānandanātha Brahmaśrī, *Śrīvidyā nityāhnikan,* Chowkhamba Sanskrit Series, Varanasi, 1963.

——, *Śrīvidyā-mantra-bhāṣyam,* Chowkhamba Sanskrit Series, Varanasi, 1963.

Subramanyasastri, K.S. (ed.), *Mantraśāstra-mātṛka-granthām-vivaraṇātmika sūcikā,* Chowkhamba Sanskrit Series, Varanasi, 1963.

Sukla, Ramādatt, *Hindi Tantrasāra,* Kalyan Mandir, Katra, Allahabad, 1958.

——, *Śyāmā-rahasya-tantram,* Chowkhamba Sanskrit Series, Varanasi, 1963.

Suzuki, D.T., *Laṅkāvatāra-Sūtra,* English translation, 1932.

Thakur, Devanath, *Mantrakaumudi,* Chowkhamba Sanskrit Series, Varanasi, 1963.

Thompson, E.J. & Spencer, A.A. (ed.), *Bengali Religious Lyrics: Sākta,* Oxford University Press, 1923.

Tripathi, Lakshminarayan, *Mantra Dīpikā,* Govind Mudranalaya, Varanasi.

Tucci, Giuseppe, *Theory and Practice of Naṇḍala,* Rider & Co., London, 1961.

——, *Tibetan Painted Scrolls,* Rome, 1949.

——, *Some Glosses upon the Guhyasamāja,* vol. III, 339-53, Brussels, 1934-35.

Underhill, Evelyn, *Mysticism,* University Paperbacks, Methuen & Co. Ltd., 36, Essex Street Strand, London, 1960.

Utpaladeva, *The Īśvara Pratabhijña,* 2 vols., Kashmir Sanskrit Texts and Studies, Srinagar, 1921.

Van Manen, John (ed.), *Minor Tibetan Texts,* New Series, no. 1426, Calcutta, 1919.

Vasavada, A.V., *Tripura Rahasya,* Chowkhamba Sanskrit Series, Varanasi, 1965.

Vedāntatirtha, Giriscandra (ed.), Tarātantram, Chowkhamba Sanskrit Series, Varanasi, 1963.

Viresvarānanda, Swami, *Brahma Sūtra,* Advaita Ashram, Entally Road, Calcutta, 1963.

Vivekananda, Swami, *Rāja-Yoga,* Advaita Ashram, Entally Road, Calcutta, 1962.

Waddell, L.A., The Dhāraṇī Cuttin Buddhism Ostasiatische Zeltschrift. I. 155-95, Berlin, 1921.

——, *The Buddhism of Tibet or Lamaism,* London, 1895.

Wellington, A.C., *The Mathematical Theory of Relativity,* University Press, Cambridge, 1960.

Zimmer, H., *The Art of Hindu Asia,* Bollingen Series, New York, 1955.

——, *The Philosophies of India,* Meridan, New York, 1958.

——, *Zur Bedeutungdes Indischen Indeschen Tantra-Yogo,* Eranos Tanrbuch, vol. I, Zürich, 9-94.

Index